CONTENTS

CONTENTS

R. Gupta's®

Madhya Pradesh GENERAL KNOWLEDGE

A Concise Description of History, Geography, Economy, Polity, Flora & Fauna, Culture, and more...

CHAPTERWISE MCQ WITH ANSWERS

Latest Edition

2026 EDITION

RAMESH PUBLISHING HOUSE, NEW DELHI

Published by
O.P. Gupta *for* Ramesh Publishing House
Admin. Office
12-H, New Daryaganj Road, Opp. Officers' Mess
New Delhi-110002 ✆ 23275224, 23245124
E-mail: info@rameshpublishinghouse.com
For Online Shopping: www.rameshpublishinghouse.com
Showroom
- Balaji Market, Nai Sarak, Delhi-6 ✆ 23253720, 23282525
- 4457, Nai Sarak, Delhi-6, ✆ 23918938

Book Code: R-1662

ISBN: 978-93-86845-24-5

Price: ₹ 130

Printed at: Deepak Offest, Delhi

STATE GOVERNMENT

GOVERNOR

Mangubhai Chhaganbhai Patel

CHIEF MINISTER

Dr. Mohan Yadav

General Administration, Home, Jail, Industrial Policy and Investment Promotion, Public Relations, Narmada Valley Development, Aviation, Mineral Resources, Public Service Management, Non-Resident Indian, And other Departments not allotted to any other Minister.

CABINET MINISTERS

- **Jagdish Devda** (Deputy Chief Minister) : Finance, Commercial tax, Planning, Economics & Statistics
- **Rajendra Shukla** (Deputy Chief Minister) : Public Health and Medical Education
- **Kunwar Vijay Shah** : Tribal Affairs Department, Public Assets Management Department, Bhopal Gas Tragedy Relief & Rehabilitation
- **Kailash Vijayvargiya** : Urban Development and Housing, Parliamentary affairs
- **Prahalad Patel** : Panchayat and Rural Development, Labour
- **Rakesh Singh** : Public Works Department
- **Karan Singh Verma** : Revenue
- **Uday Pratap Singh** : Transport, School Education
- **Sampatiya Uike** : Public Health Engineering

- **Tulsiram Silawat** : Water Resources
- **Edal Singh Kanshana** : Farmer Welfare and Agriculture Development
- **Nirmala Bhuria** : Women and Child Development
- **Govind Singh Rajput** : Food, Civil Supplies & Consumer Protection
- **Vishvas Kailash Sarang** : Sports & Youth Welfare, Cooperatives
- **Narayan Singh Kushwaha** : Social Justice and Empowerment of Persons with Disabilities, Horticulture and Food Processing
- **Nagar Singh Chouhan** : Forest, Environment, Scheduled Caste Welfare
- **Pradhuman Singh Tomar** : Energy
- **Rakesh Shukla** : New & Renewable Energy
- **Chetanya Kumar Kashyap** : Micro, Small and Medium Enterprises
- **Indar Singh Parmar** : Higher Education, Ayush, Technical Education

MINISTERS OF STATE (Independent Charge)

- **Krishna Gaur** : Backward Classes and Minorities Welfare, Denotified, Nomadic & Semi-Nomadic Welfare
- **Dharmendra Singh Lodhi** : Culture, Tourism, Religious Trusts & Endowment
- **Dileep Jaiswal** : Cottage and Village Industries
- **Gautam Tetwal** : Skill Development & Employment
- **Lakhan Patel** : Animal Husbandry and Dairy
- **Narayan Singh Panwar** : Fishermens Welfare and Fisheries Development

MINISTERS OF STATE

- **Narendra Shivaji Patel** : Public Health & Medical Education
- **Pratima Bagri** : Urban Development and Housing
- **Dileep Ahirwar** : Forest, Environment
- **Radha Singh** : Panchayat and Rural Development

MEMBERS OF LOK SABHA (2024)

S. No.	Name	Constituency	Party
1.	Balaghat	Bharti Pardhi	BJP
2.	Betul	Durgadas Uikey	BJP
3.	Bhind	Sandhya Ray	BJP
4.	Bhopal	Alok Sharma	BJP
5.	Chhindwara	Bunty Vivek Sahu	BJP
6.	Damoh	Rahul Singh Lodhi	BJP
7.	Dewas	Mahendra Singh Solanki	BJP
8.	Dhar	Savitri Thakur	BJP
9.	Guna	Jyotiraditya M. Scindia	BJP
10.	Gwalior	Bharat Singh Kushwaha	BJP
11.	Hoshangabad	Darshan Singh Chowdhary	BJP
12.	Indore	Shankar Lalwani	BJP
13.	Jabalpur	Ashish Dubey	BJP
14.	Khajuraho	Vishnu Dutt Sharma	BJP
15.	Khandva	Gyaneshwar Patil	BJP
16.	Khargone	Gajendra Singh Patel	BJP
17.	Mandala	Faggan Singh Kulaste	BJP
18.	Mandsaur	Sudhir Gupta	BJP
19.	Morena	Shiv Mangal Singh Tomar	BJP
20.	Rajgarh	Rodmal Nagar	BJP
21.	Ratlam	Anita Nagarsingh Chauhan	BJP
22.	Reva	Janardan mishra	BJP
23.	Sagar	Lata Wankhede	BJP
24.	Satna	Ganesh Singh	BJP
25.	Shahdol	Himadri Singh	BJP
26.	Sidhi	Rajesh Mishra	BJP
27.	Tikamgarh	Virendra Kumar	BJP
28.	Ujjain	Anil Ferozia	BJP
29.	Vidisha	Shivraj Singh Chauhan	BJP

MEMBERS OF RAJYA SABHA

S. No.	Name	Party
1.	Sumitra Balmiki	BJP
2.	Dr. L. Murugan	BJP
3.	George Kurian	BJP
4.	Dr. Sumer Singh Solanki	BJP
5.	Ashok Singh	INC
6.	Maya Vikram Singh Naroliya	BJP
7.	Balyogi Umeshnath	BJP
8.	Digvijaya Singh	INC
9.	Banshilal Gurjar	BJP
10.	Vivek Kumar Tankha	INC
11.	Kavita Patidar	BJP

GOVERNORS OF MADHYA PRADESH

S.No.	Name	Period
1.	Dr. B. Pattabhi Sita Ramaiya	01.11.1956–13.06.1957
2.	Hari Vinayak Patskar	14.06.1957–10.02.1965
3.	K.C. Reddy	11.02.1965–02.02.1966
4.	Justice P.V. Dixit (acting)	03.02.1966–09.02.1966
5.	K.C. Reddy	10.02.1966–07.03.1971
6.	Satya Narain Sinha	08.03.1971–13.10.1977
7.	Niranjan Nath Vanchu	14.10.1977–16.08.1978
8.	Cheppudira Muthna Punaccha	17.08.1978–29.04.1980
9.	Bhagwat Dayal Sharma	30.04.1980–25.05.1981
10.	Justice G.P. Singh (acting)	26.05.1981–09.07.1981
11.	Bhagwat Dayal Sharma	10.07.1981–20.09.1983
12.	Justice G.P. Singh (acting)	21.09.1983–07.10.1983
13.	Bhagwat Dayal Sharma	08.10.1983–14.05.1984
14.	K. M. Chandi	15.05.1984–30.11.1987
15.	Justice N.D. Ojha (acting)	01.12.1987–29.12.1987
16.	K. M. Chandi	30.12.1987–30.03.1989
17.	Sarla Grewal	31.03.1989–05.02.1990
18.	Kunwar Mehmud Ali Khan	06.02.1990–23.06.1993
19.	Mohd. Safi Quareshi	24.06.1993–21.04.1998
20.	Dr. Bhai Mahaveer	22.04.1998–06.05.2003
21.	Ram Prakash Gupta	07.05.2003–01.05.2004
22.	K. M. Seth (Add. Charge)	02.05.2004–29.06.2004
23.	Balram Jhakar	30.06.2004–29.06.2009
24.	Rameshwar Thakur	30.06.2009–07.09.2011
25.	Ramnaresh Yadav	08.09.2011–07.09.2016
26.	Om Prakash Kohli (Add. Charge)	08.09.2016–22.01.2018
27.	Anandiben Patel	23.01.2018–28.07.2019
28.	Lalji Tandon	29.07.2019–30.06.2020
29.	Anandiben Patel (Add. Charge)	01-07-2020–08-07-2021
30.	Mangubhai Chhaganbhai Patel	08-07-2021–

CHIEF MINISTERS OF MADHYA PRADESH

S.No.	Name	Period
1.	Pt. Ravi Shankar Shukla	01.11.1956–31.12.1956
2.	Bhagwant Rao Annabhau Mandloi	01.01.1957–30.01.1957
3.	Dr. Kailash Nath Katju	31.01.1957–14.04.1957
		15.04.1957–11.03.1962
4.	Bhagwant Rao Annabhau Mandloi	12.03.1962–29.09.1963
5.	Pt. Dwarka Pd. Misra	30.09.1963–08.03.1967
		09.03.1967–29.07.1967
6.	Govind Narain Singh	30.07.1967–12.03.1969

7.	Raja Naresh Chand Singh	13.03.1969–25.03.1969
8.	Shyama Charan Shukla	26.03.1969–28.01.1972
9.	Prakash Chand Sethi	29.01.1972–22.03.1972
		23.03.1972–22.12.1975
10.	Shyama Charan Shukla	23.12.1975–29.04.1977
●	**President Rule**	30.04.1977–25.06.1977
11.	Kailash Chand Joshi	26.06.1977–17.01.1978
12.	Virendra Kumar Saklecha	18.01.1978–19.01.1980
13.	Sunder Lal Patwa	20.01.1980–17.02.1980
●	**President Rule**	18.02.1980–08.06.1980
14.	Arjun Singh	09:06.1980–10.03.1985
		11.03.1985–12.03.1985
15.	Motilal Bora	13.03.1985–13.02.1988
16.	Arjun Singh	14.02.1988–24.01.1989
17.	Motilal Bora	25.01.1989–08.12.1989
18.	Shyama Charan Shukla	09.12.1989–04.03.1990
19.	Sunder Lal Patwa	05.03.1990–15.12.1992
●	**President Rule**	16.12.1992–06.12.1993
20.	Digvijai Singh	07.12.1993–30.11.1998
		01.12.1998–07.12.2003
21.	Uma Bharati	08.12.2003–23.08.2004
22.	Babu Lal Gaur	24.08.2004–29.11.2005
23.	Shiv Raj Singh Chouhan	30.11.2005–16.12.2018
24.	Kamal Nath	17.12.2018–22.03.2020
25.	Shiv Raj Singh Chouhan	23.03.2020– 12.12.2023
26.	Dr. Mohan Yadav	13-12-2023– ....

SPEAKERS OF MADHYA PRADESH

S. No.	Name	Tenure
1.	Pt. Kunji Lal Dubey	1956 to 1967
2.	Sri Kashi Pd. Pandey	1967 to 1972
3.	Tej Lal Tembhare	1972 to 1972
4.	Sri Gulsher Ahmad	1972 to 1977
5.	Mukand Newalker	1977 to 1980
6.	Yagdutt Sharma	1980 to 1983
7.	Ram Kishore Shukla	1984 to 1985
8.	Sri Rajendra Pd. Shukl	1985 to 1990
9.	Porf. Brij Mohan Misra	1990 to 1993
10.	Sriyut Sri Niwas Tiwari	1993 to 2003
11.	Sri Ishwar Das Rohani	2003 to 2013
12.	Sitasharan Sharma	2014 to 2019
13.	Narmada Prasad Prajapati	2019 to 2020
14.	Girish Gautam	2021 to 2023
15.	Narendra Singh Tomar	20.12.2023 to ....

MEMBERS OF LEGISLATIVE ASSEMBLY (ELECTION 2023)

Name	Name of Constituency	Name of Party
1. Madhav Singh (Madhu Gehlot)	Agar (SC)	BJP
2. Bhairon Singh "Bapu"	Susner	INC
3. Chouhan Nagar Singh	Alirajpur (ST)	BJP
4. Sena - Mahesh Patel	Jobat (ST)	INC
5. Bisahu Lal Singh	Anuppur (ST)	BJP
6. Dilip Jaiswal	Kotma	BJP
7. Phundelal Singh Marko	Pushprajgarh (ST)	INC
8. Haribaboo Rai	Ashok Nagar (SC)	INC
9. Jagannath Singh Raghuwanshi	Chanderi	BJP
10. Brajendra Singh Yadav	Mungaoli	BJP
11. Bhagat Singh Netam	Baihar (ST)	BJP
12. Anubha Munjare	Balaghat	INC
13. Gaurav Singh Pardhi	Katangi	BJP
14. Rajkumar Karrahe	Lanji	BJP
15. Madhu Bhau Bhagat	Paraswada	INC
16. Vivek Vicky Patel	Waraseoni	INC
17. Rajan Mandloi	Barwani (ST)	INC
18. Shyam Barde	Pansemal (ST)	BJP
19. Bala Bachchan	Rajpur (ST)	INC
20. Montu Solanki	Sendhwa (ST)	INC
21. Dr. Yogesh Pandagre	Amla (SC)	BJP
22. Hemant Vijay Khandelwal	Betul	BJP
23. Mahendra Singh Keshar Singh Chouhan	Bhainsdehi (ST)	BJP
24. Ganga Sajjan Singh Uikey	Ghoradongri (ST)	BJP
25. Chandrashekhar Deshmukh	Multai	BJP
26. Hemant Satyadev Katare	Ater	INC
27. Narendra Singh Kushwah	Bhind	BJP
28. Keshav Desai	Gohad (SC)	INC
29. Ambrish Sharma "Guddu"	Lahar	BJP
30. Rakesh Shukla	Mehgaon	BJP
31. Vishnu Khatri	Berasia (SC)	BJP
32. Bhagwandas Sabnani	Bhopal Dakshin -paschim	BJP
33. Arif Masood	Bhopal Madhya	INC
34. Atif Arif Aqueel	Bhopal Uttar	INC
35. Krishna Gaur	Govindpura	BJP

Name	Name of Constituency	Name of Party
36. Rameshwar Sharma	Huzur	BJP
37. Vishvas Sarang	Narela	BJP
38. Archana Didi	Burhanpur	BJP
39. Manju Rajendra Dadu	Nepanagar (ST)	BJP
40. Bablu Rajesh Shukla	Bijawar	BJP
41. Ahirwar Dileep	Chandla (SC)	BJP
42. Lalita Yadav	Chhatarpur	BJP
43. Kamakhya Pratap Singh (Teeka Raja)	Maharajpur	BJP
44. Bahin Ramsiya Bharti	Malhara	INC
45. Arvind Pateriya	Rajnagar	BJP
46. Kamlesh Pratap Shah	Amarwara (ST)	INC
47. Kamal Nath	Chhindwara	INC
48. Choudhary Sujeet Mersingh	Churai	INC
49. Sunil Uikey	Junnardeo (ST)	INC
50. Neelesh Pusaram Uikey	Pandhurna (ST)	INC
51. Sohanlal Balmik	Parasia (SC)	INC
52. Vijay Revnath Chore	Saunsar	INC
53. Jayant Malaiya	Damoh	BJP
54. Umadevi Lalchand Khatik	Hatta (SC)	BJP
55. Dharmendra Bhav Singh Lodhi	Jabera	BJP
56. Lakhan Patel	Pathariya	BJP
57. Phool Singh Baraiya	Bhander (SC)	INC
58. Bharti Rajendra	Datia	INC
59. Pradeep Agrawal	Sewda	BJP
60. Murli Bhawara	Bagli (ST)	BJP
61. Gayatri Raje Puar	Dewas	BJP
62. Manoj Narayansingh Choudhari	Hatpipliya	BJP
63. Aashish Govind Sharma	Khategaon	BJP
64. Dr. Rajesh Sonkar	Sonkatch (SC)	BJP
65. Bhanwarsingh Shekhawat "Babu Ji"	Badnawar	INC
66. Neena Vikram Verma	Dhar	BJP
67. Kalusingh Thakur	Dharampuri (ST)	BJP
68. Umang Singhar	Gandhwani (ST)	INC
69. Baghel Surendra Singh Honey	Kukshi (ST)	INC
70. Dr. Hiralal Alawa	Manawar (ST)	INC
71. Pratap Grewal	Sardarpur (ST)	INC
72. Omkar Singh Markam	Dindori (ST)	INC
73. Omprakash Dhurwey	Shahpura (ST)	BJP
74. Rishi Agrawal	Bamori	INC

Name	Name of Constituency	Name of Party
75. Priyanka Penchi	Chachoura	BJP
76. Panna Lal Shakya	Guna (SC)	BJP
77. Jaivardhan Singh	Raghogarh	INC
78. Mohan Singh Rathore	Bhitarwar	BJP
79. Suresh Raje	Dabra (SC)	INC
80. Pradhuman Singh Tomar	Gwalior	BJP
81. Dr Satish Sikarwar	Gwalior East	INC
82. Sahab Singh Gurjar	Gwalior Rural	INC
83. Narayan Singh Kushwah	Gwalior South	BJP
84. Dr. Ramkishore Dogne	Harda	INC
85. Abhijeet Shah (Ankit Baba)	Timarni (ST)	INC
86. Dr. Sita Saran Sharma	Hoshangabad	BJP
87. Thakurdas Nagwanshi	Pipariya (SC)	BJP
88. Premshankar Kunjilal Verma	Seoni-malwa	BJP
89. Vijaypal Singh	Sohagpur	BJP
90. Manoj Nirbhay Singh Patel	Depalpur	BJP
91. Usha Babu Singh Thakur	Dr. Ambedkar Nagar (Mhow)	BJP
92. Kailash Vijayvargiya	Indore - 1	BJP
93. Ramesh Mendola	Indore - 2	BJP
94. Golu Shukla Rakesh	Indore - 3	BJP
95. Malini Laxmansingh Gaur	Indore - 4	BJP
96. Mahendra Hardia	Indore - 5	BJP
97. Madhu Verma	Rau	BJP
98. Tulsiram Silawat	Sanwer (SC)	BJP
99. Neeraj Singh Lodhi	Bargi	BJP
100. Ashok Ishwardas Rohani	Jabalpur Cantt	BJP
101. Lakhan Ghanghoria	Jabalpur East (SC)	INC
102. Abhilash Pandey	Jabalpur North	BJP
103. Rakesh Singh	Jabalpur West	BJP
104. Sushil Kumar Tiwari (Indu Bhaiya)	Panagar	BJP
105. Ajay Vishnoi	Patan	BJP
106. Santosh Varkade	Sihora (ST)	BJP
107. Dr. Vikrant Bhuria	Jhabua (ST)	INC
108. Nirmala Dileepsingh Bhuria	Petlawad (ST)	BJP
109. Veersingh Bhuriya	Thandla (ST)	INC
110. Dhirendra Bahadur Singh Dhiru	Barwara (ST)	BJP
111. Pranay Prabhat Pandey (Guddu Bhaiya)	Bahoriband	BJP
112. Sandeep Shriprasad Jaiswal	Murwara	BJP

Name	Name of Constituency	Name of Party
113. Sanjay Satyendra Pathak	Vijayraghavgarh	BJP
114. Kunwar Vijay Shah	Harsud (ST)	BJP
115. Kanchan Mukesh Tanve	Khandwa (SC)	BJP
116. Narayan Patel	Mandhata	BJP
117. Chaya More	Pandhana (ST)	BJP
118. Sachin Birla	Badwaha	BJP
119. Kedar Chidabhai Dawar	Bhagwanpura (ST)	INC
120. Jhuma Dr Dhyansingh Solanki	Bhikangaon (ST)	INC
121. Sachin Subhashchandra Yadav	Kasrawad	INC
122. Balkrishn Patidar	Khargone	BJP
123. Rajkumar Mev	Maheshwar (SC)	BJP
124. Narayan Singh Patta	Bichhiya (ST)	INC
125. Sampatiya Uikey	Mandla (ST)	BJP
126. Chainsingh Warkade	Niwas (ST)	INC
127. Chandar Singh Sisodiya	Garoth	BJP
128. Jagdish Devda	Malhargarh (SC)	BJP
129. Vipin Jain	Mandsour	INC
130. Dung Hardeepsingh	Suwasra	BJP
131. Devendra Ramnarayan Sakhwar	Ambah (SC)	INC
132. Narendra Singh Tomar	Dimani	BJP
133. Pankaj Upadhyay	Jaura	INC
134. Dinesh Gurjar	Morena	INC
135. Sarla Vijendra Rawat	Sabalagadh	BJP
136. Aidal Singh Kansana	Sumawali	BJP
137. Uday Pratap Singh	Gadarwara	BJP
138. Mahendra Nagesh	Gotegaon (SC)	BJP
139. Prahlad Singh Patel	Narsingpur	BJP
140. Vishwanath Singh "Mulam Bhaiya"	Tendukheda	BJP
141. Omprakash Sakhlecha	Jawad	BJP
142. Aniruddha (Madhav) Maroo	Manasa	BJP
143. Dilip Singh Parihar	Neemuch	BJP
144. Rajesh Kumar Verma	Gunnour (SC)	BJP
145. Brijendra Pratap Singh	Panna	BJP
146. Prahlad Lodhi	Pawai	BJP
147. Surendra Patwa	Bhojpur	BJP
148. Dr. Prabhuram Choudhary	Sanchi (SC)	BJP
149. Devendra Patel	Silwani	INC
150. Narendra Shivaji Patel	Udaipura	BJP
151. Narayan Singh Panwar	Biaora	BJP

Name	Name of Constituency	Name of Party
152. Hajarilal Dangi	Khilchipur	BJP
153. Mohan Sharma	Narsinghgarh	BJP
154. Amar Singh Yadav	Rajgarh	BJP
155. Gautam Tetwal	Sarangpur (SC)	BJP
156. Dr. Chintamani Malviya	Alot (SC)	BJP
157. Rajendra Pandey "Raju Bhaiya"	Jaora	BJP
158. Chetanya Kasyap "Bhaiyyaji"	Ratlam City	BJP
159. Mathura Lal Damar	Ratlam Rural (ST)	BJP
160. Kamleshwar Dodiyar	Sailana (ST)	BAP
161. Girish Gautam	Deotalab	BJP
162. Nagendra Singh	Gurh	BJP
163. Engineer Narendra Prajapati	Mangawan (SC)	BJP
164. Pradeep Patel	Mauganj	BJP
165. Rajendra Shukla	Rewa	BJP
166. Abhay Mishra	Semariya	INC
167. Divyaraj Singh	Sirmour	BJP
168. Siddharth Tiwari 'Raj'	Teonthar	BJP
169. Veerendra Singh Lodhi	Banda	BJP
170. Adv. Nirmla Sapre	Bina (SC)	INC
171. Brijbihari Pateriya"Gudda Bhaiya"	Deori	BJP
172. Er. Pradeep Lariya	Naryawali (SC)	BJP
173. Gopal Bhargava	Rehli	BJP
174. Shalendra Kumar Jain	Sagar	BJP
175. Govind Singh Rajput	Surkhi	BJP
176. Dr. Rajendra Kumar Singh	Amarpatan	INC
177. Surendra Singh Gaharwar	Chitrakoot	BJP
178. Shrikant Chaturvedi	Maihar	BJP
179. Nagendra Singh	Nagod	BJP
180. Pratima Bagri	Raigaon (SC)	BJP
181. Vikram Singh (Vicky)	Rampur-Baghelan	BJP
182. Dabbu Siddharth Sukhlal Kushwaha	Satna	INC
183. Gopal Singh Engineer	Ashta (SC)	BJP
184. Ramakant Bhargava	Budhni	BJP
185. Karan Singh Verma	Ichhawar	BJP
186. Sudesh Rai	Sehore	BJP
187. Kamal Marskole	Barghat (ST)	BJP
188. Rajneesh Harvansh Singh	Keolari	INC
189. Yogendra Singh Baba	Lakhnadon (ST)	INC
190. Dinesh Rai Munmun	Seoni	BJP

Name	Name of Constituency	Name of Party
191. Sharad Juglal Kol	Beohari (ST)	BJP
192. Manisha Singh	Jaisinghnagar (ST)	BJP
193. Jaisingh Maravi	Jaitpur (ST)	BJP
194. Ghanshyam Chandravanshi	Kalapipal	BJP
195. Arun Bhimawad	Shajapur	BJP
196. Inder Singh Parmar	Shujalpur	BJP
197. Babu Jandel	Sheopur	INC
198. Mukesh Malhotra	Vijaypur	INC
199. Khatik Ramesh Prasad	Karera (SC)	BJP
200. Mahendra Ramsingh Yadav Khatora	Kolaras	BJP
201. Preetam Lodhi	Pichhore	BJP
202. Kailash Kushwah	Pohari	INC
203. Devendra Kumar Jain 'Patte Wale'	Shivpuri	BJP
204. Ajay Arjun Singh	Churhat	INC
205. Kunwar Singh Tekam	Dhauhani (ST)	BJP
206. Riti Pathak	Sidhi	BJP
207. Vishwamitra Pathak	Sihawal	BJP
208. Radha Ravindra Singh	Chitrangi (ST)	BJP
209. Rajendra Meshram	Devsar (SC)	BJP
210. Ram Niwas Shah	Singrauli	BJP
211. Khatik Harishankar	Jatara (SC)	BJP
212. Chanda-surendra Singh Gour	Khargapur	INC
213. Anil Jain	Niwari	BJP
214. Nitendra Brajendra Singh Rathore	Prithvipur	INC
215. Yadvendra Singh (Jaggu Bhaiya)	Tikamgarh	INC
216. Jitendra Uday Singh Pandya	Badnagar	BJP
217. Satish Malviya	Ghatiya (SC)	BJP
218. Dinesh Jain Boss	Mahidpur	INC
219. Dr. Tejbahadur Singh Chauhan	Nagda-khachrod	BJP
220. Mahesh Parmar	Tarana (SC)	INC
221. Anil Jain Kaluheda	Ujjain North	BJP
222. Dr. Mohan Yadav	Ujjain South	BJP
223. Shivnarayan Gyan Singh (Lallu Bhaiya)	Bandhavgarh (ST)	BJP
224. Meena Singh	Manpur (ST)	BJP
225. Harisingh Raghuwanshi "Badda"	Basoda	BJP
226. Hari Singh Sapre	Kurwai (SC)	BJP
227. Surya Prakash Meena	Shamshabad	BJP
228. Umakant Sharma	Sironj	BJP
229. Mukesh Tandan	Vidisha	BJP
230. Bhoopendra Singh	Khurai	BJP

CURRENT AFFAIRS

BUDGET 2025-26

The Finance Minister of Madhya Pradesh, Mr. Jagdish Devda, presented the Budget for the state For the financial year 2025-26 on March 12, 2025.

Budget Highlights— • The **Gross State Domestic Product** (GSDP) of Madhya Pradesh for 2025-26 (at current prices) is projected to be ₹ 16,94,477 crore, amounting to growth of 13% over 2024-25. • **Expenditure (excluding debt repayment)** in 2025-26 is estimated to be ₹ 3,75,335 crore, an increase of 14% from the revised estimate of 2024-25. In addition, debt of ₹ 29,980 crore will be repaid by the state. • **Receipts (excluding borrowings)** for 2025-26 are estimated to be ₹ 2,96;435 crore, an increase of 11% as compared to the revised estimate of 2024-25. • **Revenue surplus** in 2025-26 is estimated to be 0.04% of GSDP (Rs 618 crore), as compared to a revenue surplus of 0.07% of GSDP (₹ 1,026 crore) at the revised estimate stage in 2024-25. • **Fiscal deficit** for 2025-26 is targeted at 4.7% of GSDP (₹ 78,900 crore). In 2024-25, as per the revised estimates, fiscal deficit is expected to be 4.2% of GSDP, higher than the budgeted 4.1% of GSDP.

Policy Highlights— • **Youth Affairs:** Madhya Pradesh Institute of Technology will be set up in each division of the state in the next five years. A skill development program will be launched in the state. • Families below the poverty line will be provided a package of schemes under the new Mukhya Mantri Samriddha Pariwar Yojana. The scheme has been allocated ₹ 100 crore in 2025-26. • **Agriculture and Farmers Welfare:** ₹ 850 crore has been allocated for the Mukhya Mantri Krishak Unnati Yojana. Under the scheme, farmers will be offered incentives to adopt crop diversification.

INDORE : MP'S FIRST TO GET METRO RAIL SERVICE CITY

The country's cleanest city Indore has become Madhya Pradesh's first city and India's 16th to get an operational metro rail service. Prime Minister Narendra Modi on May 31, 2025 virtually inaugurated the commercial run of Indore's much-awaited metro rail service. Conceptualized to cover a stretch of more than 31 km with 28 stations in multiple phases at a total cost of ₹ 7500 crore, around ₹ 1520 crore has been spent on the 6-km long five stations-strong super priority corridor on which the commercial run started on 31 may.

MADHAV NATIONAL PARK DECLARED INDIA'S 58TH TIGER RESERVE

Madhav National Park in Shivpuri, Madhya Pradesh, has been designated India's 58 Tiger Reserve and the 9th in MP in March 2025. Originally a hunting ground for Scindia Maharajas, it became a national park in 1958, spanning 355 sq. km in the Upper Vindhyan Hills. The park features diverse landscapes, including forests, grasslands, lakes like Sakhya Sagar & Madhav Sagar, supporting rich biodiversity.

MADHYA PRADESH

GENERAL KNOWLEDGE

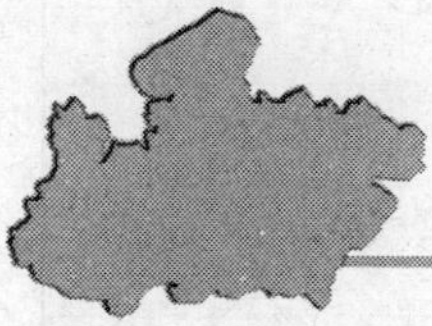

Madhya Pradesh At a Glance

Population (2011)	: 72,626,809
Capital	: Bhopal
Area	: 308,000 km^2
Geographical Location	: 21°-6' North Lat. to 26°-54' North Lat. and 74° East Long. to 82°-47' East Long.
Present Form	: 1st November, 2000
Nomenclature	: Being situated in middle, it is also called Hirdey Pradesh.
Location	: Mid part of the country.
Extent	: Length from East to West 870 km. Breadth from North to South 605 km.
Boundaries	: Uttar Pradesh in the North, Chhattisgarh in the East and North-east, Maharashtra in the South, Rajasthan and Gujarat in the West.
Decadal Growth (2001-2011)	: 20.3%
Rural Population	: 5,25,57,404
Urban Population	: 2,00,69,405
Sex Ratio	: 931 per 1000 male (2011)
Density	: 236 persons per km^2 (2011)
Literacy	: 69.32% (2011)
Male Literacy	: 78.73%
Female Literacy	: 59.2%
Division	: 10

Districts	:	52
Assembly	:	Unicameral
No. of M.L.A.	:	(230 + 1 Anglo-Indian)
No. of M.P.	:	29
No. of Rajya Sabha	:	11
Language	:	Hindi
Other Languages	:	Urdu and other regional languages
Important Cities	:	Indore, Bhopal, Jabalpur, Gwalior and Ujjain
Important Railway Junctions	:	Bhopal, Jabalpur, Indore, Katni, Bina, Itarsi, Ratlam, Hoshangabad, Shahdol and Khandwa
Aerodrom	:	Bhopal, Gwalior, Indore, Jabalpur and Khajuraho
High Court	:	Jabalpur (bench in Indore and Gwalior).
State Day	:	1st November
State Tree	:	Bargad, (Banyan tree)
State Animal	:	Antelope (Swamp Deer))

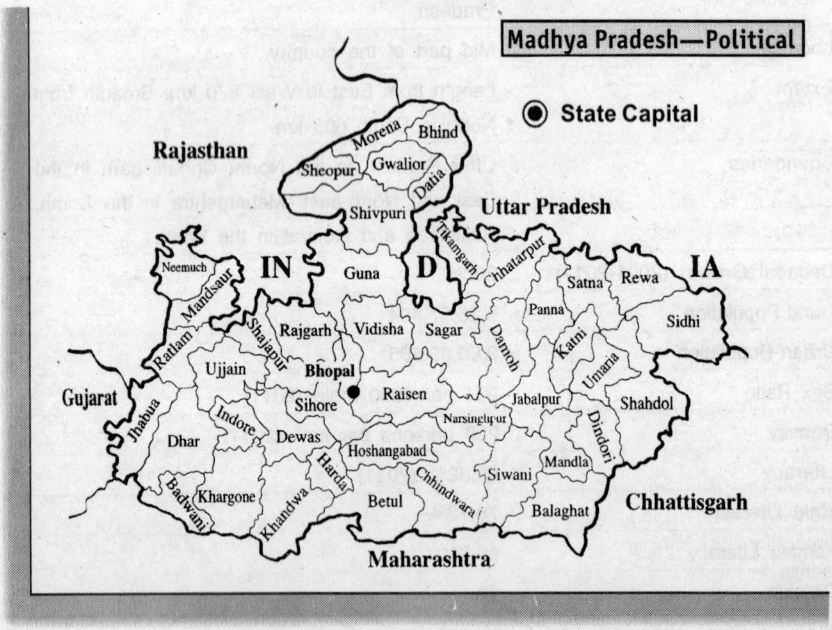

Important Crops of Madhya Pradesh and Producing Area

Crops	Producing Areas
Wheat	Gwalior, Sagar, Ratlam, Mandsaur, Vidisha, Ujjain, Guna, Rewa, Hoshangabad, Dewas, Sehore, Jhabua, Indore, Satna, Jabalpur, Khandwa
Rice	Balaghat, Mandla, Chhindwara, Betul, Rewa, Sidhi, Satna, Shahdol and Gwalior
Jowar	Mandsaur, Neemach, Ratlam, Ujjain, Rajgarh, Shajapur, Dewas, Khandwa, Khargon
Gram	Mandsaur, Neemach, Vidisha, Guna, Sehore, Jhabua, Devas, Bhopal, Indore, Ujjain, Ratlam, Hoshangabad, Narsimhapur, Jabalpur, Raisen, Tikamgarh, Harda, Bhind, Morena
Opium	Mandsaur
Sugar Cane	Ujjain, Sihore, Jawara, Shajapur, Dabra, Shivpuri and Morena
Cotton	Indore, Gwalior, Ujjain, Dhar, Bhind, Morena, Sheopur, Shivpuri, Chhindwara, Bhopal
Arhar (Tuar)	Chhindwara, Bhind, Indore, Ujjain, Dewas, Khandwa, Rewa, Satna, Sagar, Damoh, Chhatarpur, Panna, Tikamgarh, Dhar, Gwalior, Morena, Bhopal
Ground Nut	Mandsaur, Neemach, Khargon, Dhar
Oil Seed	*Sesamum*-Chhatarpur, Hoshangabad, Shivpuri, Sidhi; *Linseed*—Balaghat, Satna, Rewa, Hoshangabad, Jhabua, Sagar, Guna and Panna
Hemp	Tigria, Badgaon, Gugar, Jamli, Linepur and Rushtampur of Khandwa district

Institutions of Madhya Pradesh, Related to Industries

Institutions and Offices	Est. Year	Aims
Madhya Pradesh Industrial Corporation, Bhopal	1969	Management of cooperative industries and help in establishing the industries of joint sector.
Madhya Pradesh Industrial Development Corporation, Bhopal	1965	To provide assistance for development of every type of industries.
Madhya Pradesh Small Scale Corporation, Bhopal	1969	To provide raw material to the private and public sector unit and help in trade of production
Madhya Pradesh Corporation, Indore	—	Above all and financial assistance
Madhya Pradesh Handicraft Corporation, Bhopal	1972	To decide development of handicraft
Madhya Pradesh Textile Corporation, Indore	1970	Management of cotton textile mills
Madhya Pradesh Agro-Industries Corporation, Bhopal	—	To assure the development of agro based industries

Institutions and Offices	Est. Year	Aims
Madhya Pradesh Mining Corporation, Bhopal	—	Investigation of precious minerals and help in mining and trade
Madhya Pradesh Corporation, Bhopal	1977	To assure the management of production and export of small scale industries
Madhya Pradesh Handnalaya Management, Bhopal	1976	Besides handloom industries, to establish the industrial cooperative societies and management of finance and help in their development
Madhya Pradesh Khadi and Gramodyog Board, Bhopal	—	To encourage the production of Khadi Vastra

Industries of Madhya Pradesh and Cities where they are Located

Industries	Cities
Cotton Textile	Indore, Ujjain, Gwalior, Burhanpur, Mandsaur, Ratlam, Dewas, Bhopal and Khandwa
Rayon Silk Industry (Artificial Fibre Industry)	Nagda, Indore, Gwalior
Krempai Yarn	Dewas
Synthetic Yarn	Ujjain
Fire Brick Factory	Jabalpur and Katni
Ordnance	Katni
Gun Koz Factory	Jabalpur
Paper Mills	Amlai Nepanagar (News paper)
Jute Mill	Rajgarh
Cement Factory	Banmore, Satna, Kalmur, Jamol, Silta, Meihar
Leather Industry	Dewas
Dry Battery	Bhopal
Mini-Steel Plant	Indore, Ratlam, Dewas, Jabalpur
Sulphuric Acid	Nagda and Kumhari
Insecticide Medicines	Bhopal
Biscuit Factory	Gwalior
Steel Casting Foundry and Rerolling Mill	Dewas, Kumhar, Bangrod, Gwalior, Indore, Ujjain, Mandsaur, Shajapur
Textile Mechinary	Gwalior
Electric Pump	Dewas
Currency and Bank Note Press	Dewas and Hoshangabad (currency paper)
Asbestos Cement Factory	Kaimur
Coal Factory	Chhindwara, Sahadol Sidhi, Betul
Sugar Industry	Dabra, Sheor, Kailaras, Baloda, Mahidpur
Maida Mill	Indore, Bhopal, Ganj basoda

Places and Causes of their Importance

Places	Causes of Importance
Bhimbetaka and Chaturbhuj Nath	Rock Paintings
Amlai	Paper mill
Nepa Nagar	Newspaper mill
Singrauli	Coal mine
Khajuraho	Artistic temple
Bhera Ghat	Marble rocks
Majhgaon	Diamond mines
Panna	Diamond mines
Alazkhand	Copper mines
Panchmarhi	Hill station
Gondwana	Minerals
Mandsaur	Opium
Bandhavgarh	Tiger Safari

Awards and Honours

Awards and Honours	Area	Amount
Kalidas Samman	Classical music, Rupankar Art, Theatre and Classical dance	₹ 2 Lakh
Shikhar Samman	Literature, Exhibited Art, Rupankar Art	₹ 1 Lakh
Tansen Samman	Classical music	₹ 2 Lakh
Tulsi Samman	Folk and Traditional Art	₹ 2 Lakh
Lata Mangeshkar Award	Light music	₹ 2 Lakh
Jawahar Lal Nehru Award (established in 1982)	Basic science, Technical Development, Engineering Science	₹ 1 Lakh
Maithili Sharan Gupta Samman	Hindi Pootry	₹ 2 Lakh
Kabir Samman	Hindi Poetry	₹ 3 Lakh
Iqbal Samman	Urdu literature	₹ 2 Lakh
Mahatma Gandhi Samman	Social work according to Mahatma Gandhi philosophy	₹ 10 Lakh
Sharad Joshi Samman	Hindi comic writing	₹ 2 Lakh
Kumar Gandharv Samman	Young classical musician	₹ 1 Lakh 25 thousand
Kishor Kumar Samman	Music	₹ 2 Lakh
Devi Ahilliyabai Samman	Special area	₹ 2 Lakh

Other Awards

Awards	Area
Veer Singh Dev Award	Novel
Ghajanan Madhav Mukti Bodh Award	Story
Bhawani Pd. Misra Award	Poetry
Seth Govind Das Award	Drama and Mono-play
Makhan Lal Chaturvedi Award	Poetry
Subhadra Kumari Chauhan Award	Story
Bal Krishan Sharma Navin Award	Song management
Vishwanath Singh Award	Novel
Hari Krishna Premi Award	Drama and Mono-play
Madhav Rao Sapray Award	Renowned persons of state, place and historical manuscript of prose or poetry
Ram-Bilas Sharma Award	First Act of Writing
Sharad Joshi Award	Irony
Rajendra Mathur Award	Picture, remembrance, travel, autobiography, paper or reportage
Ravi Shankar Shukla Award	Children literative (for children aged about 12 years)
Dushyant Kumar Award	First act of writer below 35 years of age
Anil Kumar Award	Small magazine of state
Ishuri Award	Folk language act

Important Newspapers of Madhya Pradesh

Newspapers	Publishing Place
Nai Duniya	Indore and Bhopal
Bhaskar	Ujjain, Bhopal, Jabalpur, Gwalior
Nav Bharat	Jabalpur, Bhopal
Aaj	Gwalior
Jagran	Rewa-Bhopal
Prasaran	Jhabua, Ratlam
Agradoot	Bhopal, Jabalpur
Swadesh	Indore
Indore Samachar	Indore
Sandhya Prakash	Bhopal
Madhya Pradesh Cronicle	Bhopal

Historical and Worthseen Places of Madhya Pradesh

Tourist Places	Worthseen Places
Kalia Deh (Ujjain)	Bhartrihari caves
Bhilsa (Vidisha)	Caves of Udaigiri
Khandwa	Omkareshwar Temple
Shahdol	Amarkantak (origin of river Narmada)
Ujjain	Mahakaleshwar Temple, Jantar-Mantar
Bawangaja (Near Indore)	Jain Pilgrim Place
Chitrakoot	Legendry Place
Khajuraho	Artistic Temple
Meihar	Temple of Maa Sharda
Sanchi	Buddh Pilgrim Place (famous stupa)
Maheshwar (Near Indore)	Huge Temple Ghat
Mukta Giri (Betul)	Jain Pilgrim place
Jabalpur	Dhuadhar waterfall
Shahdol	Kapil dhara waterfall
Rewa	Chechai, Kewati and Ahuti waterfall
Panchmarhi	The only hill station of state
Bheraghat (Near Jabalpur)	Natural sight and famous marble rocks

Highest, Lowest and the Only Place in M.P.

Population	
Smallest district	Harda
Smallest division	Narmadapuram
Biggest district	Indore
Population Density	
Biggest district	Indore
Others	
Only hemp (Ganja) producing district	Khandwa
Only opium producing district	Mandsaur
Only district where diamond is found	Panna
Only district where white lions are found	Rewa
Maximum circulated newspaper	Nai Dunia
First national park	Kanaha-kisli
Biggest railway junction	Itarsi
Maximum amount of coal deposits	Sohagpur
Longest bridge	Mahanadi bridge (Tawa) (Near Hoshangabad, 1322.56 metre)
First university	Dr. Hari Singh Gaur University, Sagar
Biggest mosque	Tajul Mosque (Bhopal)
First medical college	Gajra Raje Medical college established at Gwalior in 1946
First tribal communication research centre	Jhabua
First state to nationalise the forests	Madhya Pradesh

Miscellaneous Facts

- In India, Madhya Pradesh is known as the "Heart of India".
- Re-organisation of Madhya Pradesh was done on 1st November, 1956.
- At the time of state re-organisation, Bhopal province was merged into Madhya Pradesh.
- On 1st November, 1956, Bhopal was declared the capital of Madhya Pradesh.
- From the Geo-scientists' point of view, Madhya Pradesh is the part of oldest land of Gondwanaland.
- The temples of Khajuraho were constructed by Chandellas.
- Doodh Raj (Paradise fly catcher) is the state bird of Madhya Pradesh.
- Madhya Pradesh produces 51.4% of the country's production of soyabean, that's why it is known as a soyabean state.
- Observatory, to the data related to weather is situated at Indore.
- The lowest temperature is at Shivpuri in Madhya Pradesh.
- 25% of the country Tendu leaf (Biri Patta) is produced in Madhya Pradesh.
- For wildlife protection, the training is provided at "Kanha National Park".
- Rashtriya Chambal of Morena is the biggest bird sanctuary in Madhya Pradesh.
- Sailana Florican of Ratlam is the smallest bird sanctuary.
- 14% of the world's tigers are found in Madhya Pradesh.
- Mahakaleshwar temple of Ujjain is situated on the bank of the Shipra river.
- 11.7 carat diamond from every 100 ton rocks is found from Majhgaon mines.
- The depth of Singrauli coal field is 136 metres, which is second in the world.
- National Soyabean Research Centre (N.S.R.C.) and Central Agriculture Engineering Institute are situated at Bhopal.
- The Horticulture College of Madhya Pradesh is situated in Mandsaur.
- The agriculture engineering college of Madhya Pradesh is situated at Jabalpur.
- There are three agriculture universities in Madhya Pradesh—two in Jabalpur and one in Gwalior.
- Paper for making the currency notes (Rs) is prepared in Hoshangabad, while mint is at Dewas.
- Jabalpur is the important centre of Biri-industry.
- At a distance of few kilometres from Shahdol that Amlai paper factory has been established by Birla group.
- A factory of chip board and particle board is in Itarsi.
- In cotton textile production, Madhya Pradesh ranks seventh.

- Match Box manufacturing factory is in Gwalior.
- Madhya Pradesh Industrial Development Corporation, situated at Bhopal, was established in 1965.
- First T.V. studio was established at Bhopal.
- In Fourteenth century, the fort of Mandsaur was constructed by Alauddin Khalji.
- Madhya Pradesh Election Commission was formed on 19th January, 1994.
- Madhya Pradesh Panchayat Raj Act was installed on 25th January, 1994.
- Pattabhi Sita Ramaiya was the first governor of Madhya Pradesh.
- Ravi-Shankar Shukla was the first chief minister of Madhya Pradesh.
- The minimum period of a chief minister of Madhya Pradesh was of Raja Naresh Chand Singh only for 13th days.
- Virendra Kumar Saklecha was the 1st non-congress chief minister of the state.
- Training regarding different regulations of traffic to the traffic police is provided by Police Traffic Training Institute, Bhopal.
- B.G. Ghate was the first I.G. Police of Madhya Pradesh.
- Armed police training centre is at Indore.
- Pt. Kunji Lal Dubey was the first Chairman of Madhya Pradesh Vidhan Sabha.
- Vishwa Nath Tamaskar was the first opposition leader of state assembly.
- Madhya Pradesh High court is located at Jabalpur.
- Honourable Justice Mohd. Hidayathullah was the first chief justice of newly formed Madhya Pradesh High Court.
- Smt. Sarojini Saxena was the first woman Justice of Madhya Pradesh High Court.
- Mustaq Ali the famous cricketer of M.P. made a century for India in 1936. It was the first century made by an Indian, playing against England.
- Sharad Joshi the famous comic writer was first associated with Journalism. He wrote books—Parikrama, Rah Kinare Baith, Kisi Bahane, Tilism, Dushri Satah.
- Snigdha Mehta is a famous international table tennis player.
- Subba Rao, the famous Congress leader as well as social worker played an important role and worked with Sri Jaiprakash Narain while making the dacoits to surrender.
- Different art exhibitions of Maqbul-Fida-Hussain, the famous painter have been arranged not only in India, but also in different countries of world. So Hussain was awarded Padam Shree in 1966, Padam Bhusan in 1973 and Kalidas Samman in 1987 alongwith different other awards and continued the processes of its developed painting.
- Narsimhapur district, the Hindi speaking area achieved the glory of being 100% literate.
- Planning for establishing the first Dry port is at Indore in Madhya Pradesh.

- The first jewel purifying centre of Madhya Pradesh has been established at Jabalpur.
- Petro-chemical Industry based on Mathura refinery is being established at Morena.
- State government established Baba Saheb Ambedkar National Social Science Institute at Mahu, the birth place of Ambedkar.
- The first Sailrich organic fertilizer plant, established by Madhya Pradesh Agriculture Industrial Development Corporation is in Bhopal.
- The first national youth festival of India was arranged in January 1995 in Bhopal.
- Programme "Operation Faith" launched under the leadership of "Bardu Rajan" to make ineffective the poisonous gas produced under the "Bhopal Gas Tragedy. (2nd December, 1984).
- Programme known as "Operation Play Fields" was launched in the state for making more facilities and their optimum use in sports.
- The new name of Narmada Valley Development Project is Indira Sagar Project.
- Madhya Pradesh High Court was established in 1956.
- Madhya Pradesh High Court benches are at Indore and Gwalior.
- Lok-Adalat in Madhya Pradesh was started on 13th April, 1986.
- Indore, Bhopal, Gwalior, Jabalpur and Khajuraho are the five aerodromes in Madhya Pradesh.
- Separate Post and Telegraph division in Madhya Pradesh was formed on 1st July, 1962.
- Relay programmes of All India Radio (Akashvani) in Madhya Pradesh was started on 22nd July, 1955.
- T.V. relay centre in Madhya Pradesh was started in 1972-73. The first T.V. Relay centre was started in Raipur (Chhattisgarh).
- Centre for making of Doordarshan Programme in Madhya Pradesh is being established at Bhopal.
- Gwalior fort was constructed by Raja Suraj Sain in 525 AD.
- In Madhya Pradesh Gwalior fort is known as the fort of Jewels.
- The fort of Raisain was constructed by king Raj Basanti in 16th century.
- Sultan Mohammad Tughlaq made the construction of Dhar fort in 1344 in Madhya Pradesh.
- The fort of Aseergarh was constructed by king Asha Ram Ahir. The temple of Asha Devi is in this fort.
- Kirti Pal, Pratihar king has made the construction of Chanderi fort in 11th century. Johar kund, Hawa Mahal and Naukhand Mahal are the worth seen places in this fort.
- The fort of Ginnaur was constructed by Maharaja Udai Burman in 13th century.

- The fort of Bandhavagarh was constructed in the 14th century.
- The fort of Ajaigarh was constructed by Ajaipal. The palace of Raja Aman in this fort is worth seen. It has a beautiful pattern of fine stone engraving.
- Right to Information Act was made effective on 31st January 2003 in Madhya Pradesh. The main objective of this was to bring transparency in administration, to protect the human rights and check the corruption.
- Deen Dayal Rojgar Project has been implemented in Madhya Pradesh by the state government in order to encourage self employment (Swarojgar Yojana) programme of unemployed youths in Madhya Pradesh.
- Melody queen late Lata Mangeshkar belonged to Indore and famous playback singer late Kishor Kumar belonged to Khandwa.
- Greatest vocalist of all time Lt. Pt. Kumar Gandharva belonged to Dewas.

Districts of Madya Pradesh

S.No.	Districts	Area (sq. km)	Headquarters
1.	Agar	—	—
2.	Ashoknagar	4674	Ashoknagar
3.	Alirajpur	2,165	Alirajpur
4.	Anuppur	3746	Anuppur
5.	Balaghat	9,229	Balaghat
6.	Barwani	5,422	Barwani
7.	Betul	10,043	Betul
8.	Bhind	4,459	Bhind
9.	Bhopal	2,772	Bhopal
10.	Burhanpur	2,473	Burhanpur
11.	Chhatarpur	8,687	Chhatarpur
12.	Chhindwara	11,815	Chhindwara
13.	Damoh	7,306	Damoh
14.	Datia	2,038	Datia
15.	Dewas	7,020	Dewas
16.	Dhar	8,153	Dhar
17.	Dindori	7,427	Dindori
18.	Guna	11,065	Guna
19.	Gwalior	5,214	Gwalior
20.	Harda	3,339	Harda
21.	Hoshangabad	10,037	Hoshangabad
22.	Indore	3,898	Indore
23.	Jabalpur	10,160	Jabalpur
24.	Jhabua	6,782	Jhabua
25.	Katni	4,947	Katni
26.	Khandwa (E. Nimar)	10,779	Khandwa
27.	Khargone (W. Nimar)	13,450	Khargone
28.	Mandla	13,269	Mandla
29.	Mandsaur	9,791	Mandsaur

S.No.	Districts	Area (sq. km)	Headquarters
30.	Morena	11,594	Morena
31.	Narsinghpur	5,133	Narsinghpur
32.	Neemuch	4,267	Neemuch
33.	Niwari	—	—
34.	Panna	7,135	Panna
35.	Raisen	8,446	Raisen
36.	Rajgarh	6,154	Rajgarh
37.	Ratlam	4,861	Ratlam
38.	Rewa	6,134	Rewa
39.	Sagar	10,252	Sagar
40.	Satna	7,502	Satna
41.	Sehore	6,578	Sehore
42.	Seoni	8,758	Seoni
43.	Shahdol	14,028	Shahdol
44.	Shajapur	6,196	Shajapur
45.	Sheopur	6,585	Sheopur
46.	Shivpuri	10,278	Shivpuri
47.	Sidhi	10,256	Sidhi
48.	Singrauli	—	Singrauli
49.	Tikamgarh	5,048	Tikamgarh
50.	Ujjain	6,091	Ujjain
51.	Umaria	4,026	Umaria
52.	Vidisha	2,742	Vidisha

❑❑❑

History

Early History

The history of Madhya Pradesh can be traced from very early times. In 1867-68, A.C. Carllyle discovered a large number of pigmy flints of the neolithic age in Rewa. Earlier in 1866, W.L. Wilson of the Geological Survey of India collected a number of paleolithic tools from the trap area forming the Southern boundary of the Sagar District. Before 1952, it was known from the work of the Yale-Cambridge Expedition that man had inhabited the Narmada Valley between Hoshangabad and Narsimhapur in the Middle Pleistocene period (about 2,00,000 years ago). A man who chipped tools with the help of other stones lived on its bank. Discovery of similar tools in similar contexts at Maheshwar, Mandasaur and Nahargadh on the Sivna, and other places on the Chambal points to the fact that this region was also inhabited during the stone Age. Moreover, judging from the types of tools, it appears that the man on the Narmada was not different from one who lived on the Chambal. Recent excavations at Bhimbetka in the Raisen District have brought to light the earliest sequence of paleolithic times and the residential cave floor of Acheulian hunters (more than 50,000 years ago). Earlier, the excavations at Maheshwar, Kayatha, Nagda, Eran and Navdatoli have yielded sufficient traces of chalcolithic culture. The excavations at Ujjain, however, have not yielded any chalcolithic material, while Ujjain is surrounded, like an island, by the chalcolithic sites.

The riddle of haematite drawings discovered in the caves or rock-shelters along with interesting relics in the various districts of Madhya Pradesh, indicate the habitations of the 'primitive people' and their movements in those areas. Of the two forest sites in the Raisen District, 152 painted rock-shelters at Barkhera and 55 at Kharwai have been discovered.

The earliest stratum yielded a few paleolithic tools. This was followed by those using smaller stone tools, microlithic implements and, finally, pottery. Recently, ten rock-shelters have been discovered in the Itar-pahar hill, 36 km from Rewa. Besides Raisen and Rewa the rock-paintings and engravings have also been discovered in the districts of Mandsaur, Narsinghagarh, Bhopal, Hoshangabad, Sagar, Panna, Ambikapur and Raigarh. Stone implements, bones and pot-sherds have been obtained in several of the rock-shelters. These relics, along with the paintings have been found useful for the study of the material culture of the people inhabiting the rock-shelters.

Great centres of culture and civilization gradually developed in the valleys of the Narmada, Chambal, Betwa and other rivers. The stone age people first settled in these valleys, where they found moderate climate and abundant resources for livelihood. Later on, the chalcolithic people made their homes near the banks of the rivers. Among the chalcolithic sites, Maheshwar and Navdatoli, Eran, Kayatha, Nagda are very important. They found the river banks convenient for making pottery, and for cultivation. In course of time important cities like Ujjayini, Mahismati, Vidisa, Dasapura, Airikina, Tripuri, etc., sprang up on left their mark in the history of ancient India.

Mahajanpadas

The *Anguttaranikaya* mentions what appears to be a stereotyped list of the *Sodasa-Maha-Janapada*, i.e. 'the Sixteen Great States'. Of these, Avanti which includes the two well-known divisions—the northern division, called Avanti with its capital of Ujjayini (Ujjain) and the southern division, called Avanti-Daksinapath with its capital at Mahissati (Mahismati)—was one, while the other parts of Madhya Pradesh were occupied by the kingdoms of the Vatsas, Kausambi (modern Kosam, U.P.), as their chief town, and of the Cetis with their capital at Sotthivati (Suktimati city). The Ceti (Caidya or Cedi) country corresponds roughly to the modern Rewa Division.

Dasarna was also mentioned as one of the Great States of India. It was one of the old names of East Malwa, with its capital at Vidisa (modern Besnagar in the Vidisha district) in Madhya Pradesh.

About the beginning of the fifth century B.C., Avanti became a very important power in India under the rule of Pradyotas. According to the early Buddhist traditions, the three rivals of Avanti were (1) Magadha, with its capital at Girivraja-Rajagraha, (Patna), (2) Kosala with Sravasti (Set-Mahet) as its capital, and (3) Vatsa with its capital at Kausambi (Kosam).

Early traditions suggest Pradyota's protracted warfare with king Udayana of Vatsa.

After Pradyota, his son Palaka came to the throne of Ujjayini probably after supplanting his elder brother, Gopala. Palaka was not a popular ruler, he was ousted by Aryaka, who was probably the son of Gopala. Pradyota had two great grandsons (i.e. grandsons of his son Palaka), viz., Avantisena and Maniprabha the former ruling over Ujjayini and the latter over Kausambi.

Mauryas

The emergence of Chandragupta Maurya is an important episode in the political history of India. With the help of Kautilya, son of a Bahmana of Taxila, he is said to have overthrown the infamous Nanda. The story of the emergence of Chandragupta Maurya and the subsequent overthrow of the Nandas by him is essentially obscure. But Plutarch states that Chandragupta overran and subdued the whole of India with an army of 6,00,000 men. This would suggest that he had to recover the various provinces of the Nanda empire gradually after consolidating his position in Magadha. In the days of Asoka, there were at least five provinces under the Mauryas, of which four undoubtedly formed part of Chandragupta's empire. These are Avantirattha i.e. Avantirastra (capital-Ujjayini), Daksinapatha (capital-Suvarnagiri), Uttarapatha (capital-Taksasila) and Pracya (capital-Pataliputra). The fifth province was Kalinga, which was the only conquest of Asoka.

According to Buddhist traditions, the Avantirastra with its headquarters at Ujjayini was also one of the provinces of the Maurya empire under Bindusara and Asoka, the son and the grandson of Chandragupta Maurya, respectively. Asoka himself was for a time his father's viceroy at Ujjayini. In the inscriptions of Asoka, official injustice and corruption are referred to in connection with Taksasila, Ujjayini and other places of the empire. From the first of the Kalinga edicts it is clear that Ujjayini was one of the most important centres of Maurya administration and that it was governed by a *Kumara* (i.e. a prince of the royal blood, often a son or a brother of the emperor).

On becoming an ardent Buddhist a few years after his accession, Asoka erected some stupas and railings at Sanchi, possibly about 250 B.C. The Sanchi edict is one of the four minor pillar edicts of Asoka dealing with the penalty for creating schism in the Buddhist Church. The rock edicts of Asoka have also been discovered from other parts of Madhya Pradesh, one at Rupnath in the Jabalpur district, and another from the Datia District.

Shunga Dynasty

Pushyamitra overthrown Mauryan Dynasty and became new King of Magadh. His empire ultimately extended to the Narmada, and included some cities like Pataliputra, Ayodhya, Vidisa, and perhaps also Jalandhara and Sakala. Merutunga incorporated Avanti into the dominions of Pushyamitra.

Vidisa (modern Besnagar) was governed by prince Agnimitra, as the Viceroy (*goptr*) of his father Pushyamitra. One of the brothers-in-law of Agnimitra was placed in charge of a frontier fortress on the bank of the Narmada. From the text it appears that the king of Vidarbha, Yajnasena, was a natural enemy (*prakrtyamitra*) of Pushyamitra's family. Yajnasena's cousin, Madhavasena, a friend of Agnimitra, was captured and incarcerated in Vidarbha, while he was secretly on his way to Vidisa. Consequently, Agnimitra declared war against the Vidarbha king and defeated him. The kingdom of Vidarbha was ultimately divided between Yajnasena and Madhavasena, both of whom acknowledged the suzerainty of the house of Pushyamitra.

Satavahanas

While the Magadha empire was in the process of dissolution, the Andhras (Satavahanas) emerged as the most important power in trans-Vindhyan India.

Simuka, originally a feudatory of the Kanvas, overthrew his overlord, Susarman who was probably ruling over Malwa and the adjoining regions about the third quarter of the first century B.C.

Simuka was succeeded by his brother Krisna, and he, in turn by his son Satakarni-I. Satakarni-I was a powerful ruler. The Nanaghat inscription states that he performed one *Rajasuya* and two *Asvamedha* sacrifices. The inclusion of Sanchi within his dominion is perhaps suggested by a record discovered from there. The discovery of coins of the type called 'the Malwa fabric', bearing the name of king Sata also points to the early Satavahana rule in Malwa. These coins are similar to the early cast and punch-marked coins of Eran, Besnagar and Ujjain, i.e., both East and West Malwa. They might belong to Simuka-Satavahana or Satakarni-I.

Kusanas/Sakas

It is not definitely known how far the Kusana influence was extended to the south of Mathura and Benaras, both of which formed parts of Kaniska I's empire. But the inscription of Vaskusana of the year 22 (100 A.D.) found at Sanchi, possibly indicates that the Kusana hegemony was established in that region even at the time of Kaniska-I, who reigned at least upto the years 23. The discovery of the Sanchi image inscription of the year 28 (106 A.D.) of Vasiska also proves the continued Kusana occupation of East Malwa.

During the weak rule of the successors of Kaniska-I, Sakas gradually began to rule almost independently.

Bhumaka was the earliest Ksaharata Satrap, who was placed in charge of the south-western part of the Kusana empire. Bhumaka's association with West India including Malwa has been proved by the evidence of coins. He seems to have been succeeded by another Satrap named Nahapana belonging to the same Ksaharata family. Nahapana is known to have reigned between 119 and 124 A.D., and it appears from a number of his coins and inscriptions that he had been ruling almost independently over a vast region. His dominions comprised wide areas including Malwa. His kingdom undoubtedly included Western Malwa, since places like Dasapura (Mandasaur in West Malwa), Ujeni (Ujjain) and rivers like Tapi and others figure in his inscriptions. The case of East Malwa is not certain, but Sircar points out the probabilities of Nahapana's rule over that region. The Puranic chroniclers describe a Naga king of Vidisa of about the third century A.D. as the second Nakhavat (i.e. Nahapana). It shows the great impression Nahapana had created on the people.

The Junagarh inscription of Rudradaman-I (150 A.D.) tells that the Sakas (i.e. the Kardamaka rulers) reconquered no fewer than six countries from the Satavahanas, which included the Akara-Avanti-Anupa regions. These conquests, according to some, were probably made when Rudradaman was a Kshatrapa under his grandfather Castana who was the viceroy of the south-eastern province of the Kusana empire. The same inscription also tells that Rudradaman defeated Satakarni of the Deccan twice, but did not destroy him on account of their close relationship.

Thus, it appears from the inscriptional evidence that both East and West Malwa became an integral part of Rudradaman's kingdom.

Guptas

During the first half of the fourth century A.D., the Guptas consolidated their position and made their power felt in different parts of India. Among the rulers of Aryavartta who were defeated by Samudragupta, Rudradeva had been identified with the Saka king Rudrasena-III (348-78 A.D.) of Ujjain. Rudrasena-III succeeded in asserting his independence after a period of 13 years (from 351 A.D. to 364 A.D.) but he was not powerful enough to issue coins. Ganapatinaga and Nagasena who were extirpated by Samudragupta, ruled from Padmavati (modern Pawaya or Padma-pawaya) near Narwar of the Sindh river, between Gwalior and Jhansi. Among the republican States that offered allegiance to the Gupta Emperor, the Malavas possibly lived in Rajasthan and parts of Malwa, the Prarjunas in the Narsingpur (Narsimhapur) District, the Sanakanikas in East Malwa, and the Kakas in the Kakanadabota (Sanchi) region.

Samudragupta also subdued the forest kingdoms about Dabhala (the Jabalpur District). His Eran inscription testifies to his conquest of East Malwa. Probably Samudragupta annexed the eastern part of the Saka dominions, but kept Rudrasena-III in possession of the western districts as his feudatory.

Again, as to his South Indian conquests we find the names of the regions like Kosala and Mahakantara which may be located in Madhya Pradesh. Kosala i.e. the South Kosala was comprised of the modern Bilaspur and Raipur Districts of Madhya Pradesh and the Sambalpur District of Orissa, Mahakantara (which is the same as Kantara of the *Mahabharata*) included a wild tract between the valley of the Wainganga and Eastern Kosala.

About the close of the fourth century A.D., the Saka King, Rudrasimha-III, or one of his successors was overthrown by Samudragupta's son and successor, Chandragupta-II Vikramaditya (C. 376-413 A.D.) who annexed the rest of the Saka dominions (i.e. West Malwa) to the Gupta Empire. This is suggested by the inscriptions and coins of the Gupta emperor. It appears that Chandragupta-II's son, Govindagupta, was placed at Ujjayini (Ujjain) as the Viceroy of Western India probably comprising Malwa, Gujarat (including Kathiawar) and Rajasthan.

Post-Gupta Age

Harsavardhana, brother of Rajyavardhana, came to the throne of Thanesvar in 606 A.D., and fought against Devagupta and Sasanka. He succeeded in driving out the enemies from the present Uttar Pradesh and Bihar and became the master of former Maukhari Kingdom.

The Kalachuris might have been ousted from East Malwa by Harsavardhana who is known to have led a successful expedition against the Maitraka king of Valabhi in Kathiawar, and an unsuccessful one apparently in Southern Gujarat against the Chalukya King, Pulakesin-II (610-42 A.D.) before 634 A.D. Harsa's presence in the Gujarat-Kathiawar region presupposes his occupation at least of parts of Malwa and Rajasthan.

Towards the close of the eighth century, the Gurjjara-Pratiharas of Rajasthan, the Rastrakutas of the Deccan, and the Palas of the East India began their three cornered struggle for paramountcy. The Gurjjara-Pratiharas came into prominence in the second quarter of the eighth century A.D. by the successful resistance they offered under Nagabhata-I to the Arabs.

Vatsaraja, son of a nephew of Nagabhata I, became a powerful ruler. Vatsaraja's kingdom comprised both Malwa and Rajasthan. He, however, suffered a defeat at the hands of Rastrakuta Dhruva and had to take refuge in the 'trackless desert' of Rajasthan.

Nagabhata II, the son and successor of Vatsaraja, retrieved the fallen fortunes of his family. He defeated Chakrayudha and the lord of Vanga, and forcibly seized the hill-forts of the kings of Anartta, Malava, Kirata, Turuska, Vatsa and Matsya.

The next Pratihara king Ramabhadra had a brief period of reign. He was succeeded by his illustrious son, Bhoja I, who held over a mighty empire in Northern India right from the Sutlej and the foothills of the Himalayas to the Narmada.

According to a Rastrakuta record, Indra III crossed the Yamuna, and completely devastated the city of Kanauj during the reign of Mahipala-I. But, as on previous occasions, the Rastrakutas did not stay long, and Mahipala-I re-established the fortunes of his family. The success in Malwa is hinted at by the claim made by Bhamana, the feudatory Kalachuri chief of Gorakhpur, that he conquered Dhara.

The Paramara King Vakpati-II Munja is known to have made Ujjayini his residence as early as 975 A.D.

Harsa Siyaka, grandson of Vakpati-I and the father of Vakpati-II, claims to have defeated the Rastrakuta king Khottiga (968-73 A.D.). He was known as the king of Malava or of the Malavas.

Chandellas of Bundelkhand

With their capitals at Mahoba and Kalanjara the Chandellas or Chandratreyas held sway over Bundelkhand (the West Rewa Division). The Chandellas became very powerful under Yashovarman (925 A.D.). Yashovarman has been described as the conqueror of the hill-fort of Kalanjara (*Kalanjaradri*), which is known to have been within the Gurjjara-Pratihara empire.

Dhanga (950-1000 A.D.), son and successor of Yashovarman, acknowledged the supremacy of the Pratiharas at least in 954 A.D., when Gwalior, the Yamuna, Kalanjara, the northern border of the Jabalpur District, and Vidisha were the extreme limits of the Chandella kingdom. He obviously inherited this kingdom from his father. His feudatory Vajradaman of the Kacchapaghata family invaded Gwalior and captured it before 977 A.D. It is claimed that Vajradaman conquered Gopagiri, defeating the king of Kanauj. Dhanga also claims to have attained supreme lordship after inflicting a defeat over the King of Kanyakubja.

Kalachuris

The Kingdom of the Chandellas was bordered on the south by that of the Kalachuris of Chedi. The Kalachuris are sometimes referred to as the Kings of the Dahala-mandala, whose capital was Tripuri, now a village known as Tewar, 6 miles west of Jabalpur in Madhya Pradesh. The earliest known king of the dynasty is Kokkala-I (880-910 A.D.) who was considered to be one of the greatest generals of his time.

Kokkala-I made his younger sons the rulers of the different divisions of his kingdom. A descendant of one of them founded a kingdom in Daksina-Kosala, with the capital at Tummana.

Sankaragana succeeded his father Kokkala-I and fought against a Somavamsi ruler of Kosala and conquered Pali, 12 miles north-west of Ratanpur, in the Bilaspur District of Madhya Pradesh. He made an alliance with the Rastrakuta King Krisna-II, against the Eastern Chalukya King Vijayaditya-III, but was defeated with great loss. He was succeeded by his younger brother, Yuvaraja-I, in the second quarter of the tenth century A.D. He inherited the military skill of his father and grandfather, and made extensive conquests.

Medieval Period

In 1022 A.D., Mahmud invaded the Chandella territory. However, after obtaining a nominal submission of the Raja of Gwalior, the Sultan proceeded to invade Kalanjara. But like the Gwalior fort, Kalanjara also could not be stormed by Mahmud. Rather a friendly relation was established between the two rivals.

In 1309, 'Ala-ud-din Khalji wrested the Damoh District from the Chandella King. After that, the Chandellas, like the other contemporary clans, paled into insignificance.

With the decline of the Chandella power, the whole of Madhya Pradesh was practically parcelled out into a number of petty states, of which a few became prominent in the course of time.

Rewa

The Rewa Chiefs claims to be Vaghela Rajputs, tracing their descent from the Chalukya or Solanki rulers of Anahila-pataka. Baghelkhand was named after the ruling house of Rewa. It was, however, known to the Muhammadan historians as Bhata or Bhatghora.

Lavanaprasada of the village Vyaghrapalli or Vaghela (Gujarat) was the governor of Udayagiri and Vidisha under the rulers of Anhilapataka. From the

State record of Rewa, it appears that Viradhavala, the son of Lavanaprasada, migrated to Marpha, 18 miles north-east of Kalanjara in 1233-34 A.D. He was succeeded by his eldest son, Karnadeva, who married the daughter of the Kalachuri ruler of Ratanpur and received the Bandhogarh fort as dowry. Karnadeva moved from Marpha and established himself at Bandhogarh.

The earliest historical reference to a Vaghela Chief of Rewa is in the time of Bahlol Lodi (1451-89). The Vaghela Chief was Raja Bhira or Bhaira at that time, and he assisted Hussain Shah of Jaunpur against Bahlol Lodi. Raja Bhira is said to have offered allegiance to Sikandar Lodi (1489-1517) who attacked Bandhogarh in the reign of Salivahana Vaghela, but failed to capture it, and later 'sacked the country' as far as Banda.

Salivahana was succeeded by his son Virasimha about 1500 A.D., who was on good terms with Sikandar Lodi. From the *Akbarnama* of Abul Fazal, we know that he gave asylum to Aman Das, who later became famous as Sangram Shah, the father-in-law of the celebrated Durgavati. Virasimha is the 'Narasimha' who was mentioned by Babur as assisting Rana Sangramasimha at the battle of Kanwah (March 16, 1527) with 4,000 horse men. He later received the Bhata territories as *Nankar jagir* (maintenance grant) from Babur.

In the time of Akbar, the Baghelkhand region fell partly in the Bhatghora and partly in the Kalanjara Sarkar of the Allahabad Subha. Maharaja Ramachandra Vaghel of Bandhogarh is said to have presented his celebrated court musician Tansen Kalawant to the Mughal emperor Akbar. Aurangzeb is said to have separated the districts round Rewa from Bhat-ghora and included them together with Sohagpur in Kalanjara Sarkar.

After the death of Aurangzeb, Avadhutasimha, the minor Vaghela Chief was ousted by Hirde (Hrdaya) Shah of Panna. An appeal was made to the Emperor Bahadur Shah who at once sent troops and reinstated the Vaghela Chief to his former place. In 1755 Avadhutasimha was succeeded by Ajitasimha. During his time, the royal State Exchequer was put to severe strain owing to the Maratha incursions. But the Raja is said to have rejected an offer of alliance with the British Government. On Ajitasimha's death, Jayasimha accepted the protection of the British Government by a treaty of 1812 and another of 1813.

Gond

The earliest known Gond Kingdom to emerge into prominence was that of Kherla, near Betul. Narasimha Rai, the Raja of Kherla, enjoyed great wealth and power in 1398, and his kingdom included all the hills of Gondwana and other adjoining regions. He took part in the wars between the Bahmani Kings and the rulers of Malwa and Khandesh, and was finally defeated by Hoshang Shah of Malwa.

In the sixteenth century, Sangram Shah, the 47th Raja of the Gond line of Garhamandla, extended his dominion over 52 *garhs* or districts, comprising Saugor (Sagar), Damoh and, possibly Bhopal, the Narmada Valley, and Mandla and Seoni on the Satpura highlands.

About 200 years after Sangram Shah's time, Bakht-Buland, the chief of a Gond principality, established his headquarters at Deogarh in Chhindwara, and also founded the city of Nagpur, to which his successor removed the capital. The Deogarh Kingdom extended over the modern districts of Betul, Chhindwara and Nagpur and portions of Seoni, Bhandara, and Balaghat.

Bundelas

The Bundelas appeared at Garh Kander and ruled the surrounding country from the eleventh to the fifteenth centuries. Rudrapratapa moved from Garh Kander to Orchha in the beginning of the sixteenth century during the disturbed conditions resulting from Babur's invasion. Champat Rai, Jagirdar of Mau Mahowa, fought against the Mughals, and his son Maharaja Chatrasal joined hands with the Marathas in liquidating the Mughal empire.

Duing the seventeenth century Chatrasal wrested a part of the Vindhyan plateau and the Narmada Valley from the Mandla territories. But in 1733, finding himself hard pressed by the Muhammadan governors of Allahabad and Malwa, he called for the help of the Peshwa. On his death in 1735, Chatrasal left one-third of his Kingdom to the Peshwa who sent an agent to take charge of the territory and founded the Maratha Subah of Saugor (Sagar).

Marathas

In 1737, Raghoji Bhonsla, the founder of the Bhonsla State, received an order from the Peshwa to collect the *Chauth* from Berar and Gondwana, and in the following year, he went to Nagpur. By 1743, he acquired the Gond principality of Deogarh, penetrated into Chhattisgarh and rendered it a tributary. In the following decade, Chhattisgarh, Sambalpur and even Cuttack were added to the Bhonsla State, to which the kingdom of Chanda was also merged.

The set back of the Marathas in the third battle of Panipat in 1761, however, for a time stopped their encroachment. But in 1781, the land of the Gonds became a part of the Maratha principality of Saugor (Sagar). Ten years later, the Bhonsla Raja of Nagpur drove out the Saugor (Sagar) Marathas from the greater part of the Narmada Valley. In 1799, he also gained possession of Mandla.

Malwa

The province of Malwa was conquered by Ala-ud-din in 1305 and thus remained a part of the Sultanate of Delhi till 1398. Its governor, Dilawar Khan, threw off Delhi's allegiance after Timur's invasion, and became the *de facto* monarch. His son Alp Khan, later known as Hushang Shah, ascended throne in 1406. He was a powerful king. After Hushang Shah's death, his son Ghazi was deposed by his minister Mahmud Khan in 1436, and he founded the Khalji dynasty of Malwa. Mahmud enlarged his dominions to a great extent, but during the reign of Mahmud-II, a later ruler of the line, the independence of Malwa came to an end (1531) and the kingdom became a part of Gujarat. In 1562 Malwa was annexed to the Mughal Empire.

Malwa was used as the highway to the south both by the Mughals and the Marathas. It formed a *Subah* under the Mughal Emperors. After the death of Aurangzeb, the Marathas made a bid for the conquest of northern India, and in the latter part of the eighteenth Century, Malwa came to be divided between the Maratha rulers of Gwalior and Indore, belonging to the Scindia and Holkar families, respectively.

Gwalior and Indore

Gwalior and Indore were perpetually at war. It has been said that the history of India might have been different if the rulers of these two States could have presented a united front to the British in the beginning of the nineteenth century. The Third Anglo-Maratha War of 1817-18 finally broke the power of the Marathas.

Bhopal

There were constant wars between the rulers of Bhopal and the Maratha generals. In 1805, the Scindia invaded Hoshangabad, and for some time held part of the district, and finally came the scourge of the Pindharis who devastated the country for several years. In 1818, the overthrow of the Peshwa gave the British all the territories in Saugor (Sagar) and the Narmada Valley which nominally belonged to him. The same year also saw the distubances in Nagpur and the flight of Appa Sahib. All the Bhonsla possessions about the Narmada were ceded to the British by treaty, and what remained of the Bhonsla State was taken under their management during the minority of the young Raja who had been placed upon the throne. In 1830, the reins of Government were assumed by the Raja himself; but on his death in 1853, without a heir the State became a British possession in accordance with the Doctrine of Lapse.

Modern Period

Revolt of 1857

The great Revolt of 1857 was the first agitation of an all-India character. It affected an extensive region from Meerut to Kolhapur and involved both Hindus and Muslims. Only a month after its start in the Meerut-Delhi area, the Sagar-Narmada territory and Nagpur were swept by the waves of the Revolt. The spirit of restless independence in the Sagar-Narmada territory could not be curbed easily.

Soon after the spread of the Revolt in Jhansi early in June 1857, it spread like a wild fire in the Sagar-Damoh region. Almost the entire area north of the Narmada was in arms against the British. The Rajas of Banpur and Shahgarh took leading parts and imprisoned the Europeans of their areas, who were later on permitted to go to Sagar. By August 1857, practically the entire area to the north of Narmada, except Jabalpur and Mandla, went in the possession of the freedom forces. Soon after, in Jabalpur also these forces found in the Gond Raja Shankar Shah their leader. This Raja belonged to the family of the brave Rani Durgavati of Garh Mandla, who had fought for the independence of her kingdom against the Mughal-army of Akbar.

The Rani of Ramgarh a small estate in the Mandla district, took heroic part in the freedom movement. She herself used to lead her army on the battlefield, clad in full military dress, armed with a sword. Like Rani Durgavati, she met with a heroic death on the battle-field fighting for independence till her last breathe.

The counter-offensive, severely launched by Hugh Rose in the Sagar-Narmada territory, began to turn the tide in favour of the British. But the freedom fighters continued their struggle undeterred. Tatya Tope, the great general of Nana Saheb, now came to their help. The chivalrous deeds of Tatya Tope in Bundelkhand are well-known. After the deah of Rani of Jhansi in June 1857, Tatya Tope continued his guerilla warfare against the British for several months. At long last, he unfortunately fell victim to a betrayal and was hanged at Shivpuri on the 18th April, 1859.

But the most historic and heroic effort was made from Rani Laxmi Bai of Jhansi when she attacked Gwalior along with Tatya Tope and shook the foundation of Britishers in the region. Though she was killed during war and the attempt failed but she left an unprecedented example of bravery and Nationalism. A similar effort came from Rani Avanti Bai at Rewa, but she also died. These acts of nationalism set the tone for future course of action to achieve independence from foreign rule. It marked an unmatched unity between people of the state without any discrimination of caste or creed. It left the people with a ray of light that the unity and more coordinated efforts could win them freedom. Some of the prominent activities that took place after the 1857 revolution are discussed below:

Flag (Jhanda) Satyagrah: It began in 1923 from Jabalpur when the Police Commissioner insulted our national flag. Then national flag was hoisted in every part of the state and Sarojini Naidu and Maulana Azad hoisted the national flag at the town hall of Jabalpur. For some time Flag Satyagrah was also launched at the national level.

Salt Satyagrah: It was launched at Jabalpur under the leadership of Pt. Govind Das for the same cause as done by the Gandhiji.

Jungle Satyagrah: It was launched by the Betul region for the protection of their land and forest from the encroachment of Britishers.

Charan Paduka Massacre: It is also known as the Jaliyanwala Bagh massacre of Madhya Pradesh. Police opened fire on the peaceful meeting of freedom fighters at Chattarpur, in which six persons were killed and many were wounded.

Individual Satyagrah: Gandhiji launched the nationwide Individual Satyagrah at Jabalpur, and Shri Vinoba Bhave became the first Individual Satyagrahi.

Madhya Pradesh: After Indian Independence

Madhya Bharat was created in 1950 out of the former British Central Provinces and the princely States of Makrai and Chhattisgarh, with Nagpur as the capital of the State. The new States of Madhya Bharat, Vindhya Pradesh and Bhopal were formed out of the Central India Agency. In 1956, the States of Madhya Bharat,

Vindhya Pradesh and Bhopal were merged into Madhya Pradesh, and the Marathi speaking southern region Vidarbha, which included Nagpur, was ceded to Bombay State. Bhopal became the new capital of the State. In November 2000, as follow up of the Madhya Pradesh Reorganisation Act, the south-eastern portion of the State was split off to form the new State of Chhattisgarh. It is the 26th state of the Union of India.

TEST YOUR SELF

1. Who of the following revolted after the 'Treaty of Durlabh' with British?
A. Jawahar Singh B. Vinay Singh
C. Pratap Singh D. None of these

2. Hunas attacked central India during the reign of
A. Samudragupta B. Skandagupta
C. Chandragupta II D. Chandragupta Maurya

3. Rudradaman was a ruler of which of the following dynasties?
A. Satavahana B. Chandella C. Kalchuri D. Sakas

4. Which of the following rulers made Orcha the capital of Bundelkhand?
A. Bundela B. Chandella C. Mughal D. Scindia

5. Before independence which of these rulers ruled at Indore?
A. Holkar B. Maratha C. Scindia D. Malwa

6. Bharhut stupa is situated at
A. Chhatarpur B. Sidhi C. Satna D. Vidisha

7. Parmars were the rulers of
A. Kalinga B. Madhya Pradesh
C. Bengal D. Andhra

8. In the Mahajanapad yug the Ujjain was capital of
A. Matsya B. Avanti C. Ashok D. Vajji

9. At which of the following places the stone paintings of early man have been found?
A. Bhartrihari caves B. Udaygiri caves
C. Bagh caves D. Bhimbetka caves

10. Under the region of which rulers the famous Khajuraho temples were built?
A. Chola B. Chandella C. Chalukya D. Chera

11. The historical place Chitrakoot is situated in
A. Satna B. Sidhi C. Dindori D. Mandala

12. In the ancient India the proofs of the aestone of 'sati' are found at which of the following sites?
A. Sanchi B. Vidisha C. Eran D. Tigwan

13. Which of the following regions of India was known as 'Avantika'?

A. Bundelkhand B. Dandkaranya
C. Malwa D. Nimarh

14. Among the following which one was not an active centre of rebel during the first freedom struggle for independence in 1857?

A. Mahu B. Neemuch C. Murar D. Nagda

15. Which of the following freedom fighters is not related to Rewa?

A. Dinesh Chandra Pandey B. Tribhuvan Nath Tiwari
C. Bhairav Prasad D. Veer Narayan Pandey

16. The 'Jhanda Satyagraha' started from Jabalpur, which later spread in the whole state was in

A. 1907 B. 1923 C. 1917 D. 1919

17. Pt Nehru inaugurated the Central India State on

A. 1st November, 1956 B. 26th January, 1950
C. 28th May, 1948 D. 15th August, 1947

18. At which of the following places, the British did not make a cantonment for better control?

A. Agra B. Neemuch C. Mahu D. Satna

19. The mighty ruler of Vidarbha, Bheemrath, married her daughter .... with Nala—the king of Nalpur.

A. Kalawati B. Rajvasanti C. Damyanti D. Durgavati

20. The Gupta ruler Samudragupta who is often known as the Napoleon of India ruled on the Northern part of which river?

A. Narmada B. Mahanadi C. Tapti D. Chambal

ANSWERS

1	2	3	4	5	6	7	8	9	10
A	B	D	A	A	C	B	B	D	B
11	**12**	**13**	**14**	**15**	**16**	**17**	**18**	**19**	**20**
A	C	C	D	D	B	B	D	C	A

❑❑❑

Physiographic Features

Madhya Pradesh (including what is now Chhattisgarh) was constituted on recommendations of the State Re-organisation Commission on 1st November 1956. The Mahakoushal and Chhattisgarh part of the Old Central Provinces (CP) and Berar, Vindhya Pradesh, Madhya Bharat and Bhopal were merged to form the new state. Some districts of Central Provinces and Berar were transferred to Maharashtra and there were a few minor adjustments with Rajasthan, Gujarat and Uttar Pradesh. From 1st November 2000 Chhattisgarh was carved out of Madhya Pradesh. The state is endowed with rich natural resources, salubrious climate and fertile agro-climatic conditions. At present Madhya Pradesh consists of 10 divisions and 52 districts. As per 2011 census, it has a population of 72 million with a population density of 236 persons per sq.km.

Madhya Pradesh lies between latitude 21°6′ and 26° 54′ N and longitude 74° and 82° 47′ E. It covers a geographical area of 308,000 sq.km which is about 9.38% of the total area of India. The State is land - locked and at no point is the sea less than 300 kms away. Uttar Pradesh, Chhattisgarh, Maharashtra, Gujarat and Rajasthan surround it.

Most of the State lies on the tableland of Central India bounded by the Upper Gangetic plains in the north; the Godavari valley in the south; the plains of Gujarat in the west; and plateau of Bundelkhand and Chhattisgarh in the east. The State is traversed by the Vindhya, Satpura and Maikal hill ranges running east west. The highest point is at Dhupgarh near Pachmarhi in Hoshangabad district, at 1,350 m. Most of the State has an elevation of between 305 to 610 m above Mean Sea Level (MSL). Low-lying areas are in the narrow Narmada valley in the central southern parts. In general, the State stretches across a geographically elevated position. Based on its topography, the state can be divided in to the following natural regions :-

The Plateau of Malwa

Covering almost the entire western region of Madhya Pradesh, the plateau, formed by the Deccan trap rocks, starts north of the Narmada and Betwa rivers and found in Guna, Rajgarh, Mandsaur, Jhabua, Dhar, Ratlam, Dewas, Ujjain, Sehore, Vidisha, Shajapur, Raisen and Sagar districts. Its average height is normally 350 to 450 m but some peaks have attained a height of even more than 800 m. Chambal, Mahi, Kshipra, Betwa and Parvati are the main rivers of this region.

The Plateau of Central India

This region covers the northern part of the lower basin of Chambal river. It is formed by the Vindhyan rock groups with the Deccan trap in the south and the Bundelkhand gneiss rocks in the east. The Bundi and Karauli hills form its western boundary. The region presents an amalgam of low land and upland topography. The area is marked by deep ravines of the Chambal, Kalisindh and Parvati rivers. This region spreads in Morena, Bhind, Gwalior, Shivpuri, Sheopur, Guna and Mandsaur districts. Maximum height of the region is 500 m., however, the plain situated to the north and north east has a height between 150 – 300 m.

The Plateau of Bundelkhand

It lies to the east of the Central India Plateau and is bound on the northeast by the Rewa – Panna plateau. The area consists of granite rocks of the Arabian era. Generally, the plateau is flat with marginal slopes and the topography is smooth and undulating. One-third of the northern plain area is monotonously flat and is in strong contrast to the Vindhyan tableland which rises in three well – marked escarpments roughly delineated by the Betwa, Dhasan, Ken and Sindh rivers. This region in Madhya Pradesh is spread over in Tikamgarh, Chhatarpur, Datia, Gwalior and Shivpuri districts. The height of this region is between 150 to 450 m. Sidhababa hills (1172 m) constitute the highest peak.

The Plateau of Rewa and Panna

This is also known as Vindhyan plateau and lies to the northeast of the Bundelkhand plateau. The maximum height of the plateau is 750 m. The Bhander hills of the Vindhya State group and the Kymore ranges have a number of waterfalls with heights up to 450 m. The area is drained by the Ken, Sonar, Berma and Tons rivers. The covered area has most of its spread in Damoh, Panna, Satna and Rewa districts.

The Narmada-Sone Valley

It is drained by the Narmada and Sone rivers and extending from the northeast to west with an average height of 300m. It is bounded by the Vindhyan, Bhander and Kymore hills in north of the valley; the Satpura and the Maikal hills in the south; and the Bagholkhand highlands in the east. The valley is narrow, and the trap falls in the Narmada River do not allow much navigation. The districts included are Mandla, Jabalpur, Hoshangabad, Raisen, East Nimarh, West Nimarh, Barwani, Harda, Dhar and Dewas of Madhya Pradesh. Part of Rewa, Shahdol, Umaria and Sidhi districts form the part of Sone valley.

The Satpura and Maikal Region

The region south of Narmada Valley has an average height of only 300m though it contains the highest point in the State, the peak of Dhupgarh. The Satpura slope is sharp on the south face and gentle on the north. The region is drained by Tawa, Johila, Denwa, Wainganga and Vardhan rivers. The area includes Chhindwara, Betul, Seoni, Balaghat, Mandla and parts of Khandwa and Khargone districts.

The Eastern Plateau

This region has a spread in the eastern districts of Madhya Pradesh, which is called Baghelkhand Plateau in Sidhi district. In this region, the height of plateau varies from 400 to 1000m.

Mountain Ranges of Madhya Pradesh

S. No.	Mountain Ranges	Position	Elevation
1.	Aravalli Range	North-West of Madhya Pradesh	1158 m
2.	Vindhyachal Range	North of Narmada	900 m
3.	Satpura Range	South of Narmada	700 to 1350 m
4.	Maikal Amarkantak	South-East extension of Satpura	—
5.	Mahadev	Eastern extension of Satpura	—
6.	Kaimur-Bhander	Eastern extension of Vindhyachal	450-600 m

Test Your Self

1. The highest peak of Madhya Pradesh 'Dhupgarh' is in
   A. Hoshangabad B. Satna
   C. Rewa D. Mandsaur
2. Which division of Madhya Pradesh has the maximum number of districts?
   A. Indore B. Jabalpur C. Bhopal D. Ujjain
3. The height of the highest point of Malwa Plateau Sigar is
   A. 881 m B. 870 m C. 860 m D. 877 m
4. The height of the highest peak of Madhya Pradesh, Dhupgarh of Satpura Range is
   A. 1250 m B. 1350 m C. 1450 m D. 1650 m
5. Vindhya range is made up of
   A. Quartz B. Sand C. Granite D. A and B
6. Satpura range is made up of
   A. Graphite B. Basalt C. Quartz D. A and B
7. Which of the following states does not share its boundary with Madhya Pradesh?
   A. Uttar Pradesh B. Bihar
   C. Chhattisgarh D. Maharashtra
8. Match the following

List I (Rocks)	List II (Region)
(a) Archaean Times	1. Narmada Valley
(b) Dharwar	2. Gwalior
(c) Cuddapah	3. Balaghat
(d) Tertiary Rock	4. Bundelkhand

Codes

	(a)	(b)	(c)	(d)		(a)	(b)	(c)	(d)
A.	4	3	2	1	B.	3	4	2	1
C.	4	1	2	3	D.	3	2	1	4

9. Which one of the following is not a part of the central highlands of the State of Madhya Pradesh?

A. Bundelkhand plateau
B. Satpura maikal range
C. Malwa plateau
D. Narmada-Son valley

10. Chhindwara, Khandwa, Betul are major towns of which of the following regions of the state?

A. Central highland
B. Satpura-Maikal range
C. Baghelkhand plateau
D. None of the above

ANSWERS

1	2	3	4	5	6	7	8	9	10
A	A	A	B	D	D	B	A	B	B

❑❑❑

Drainage System

As Madhya Pradesh is located in the centre of India, most of the rivers are interstate rivers. The rivers namely Chambal, Sindh, Betwa, Ken flow northward and meet with Yamuna whereas the river Sone falls directly into Ganga. Narmada, Tapti and Mahi rivers flow westward and meet Arabian Sea whereas Wainganga and Pench rivers meet Godavari in the south. Rivers in Madhya Pradesh are mostly seasonal and rainfed, receiving maximum water flow during the monsoon season. The non-monsoon flow in some perennial rivers is mainly due to flow from groundwater. Due to varied topographical, rainfall and climatic conditions in the State, the availability of water is not uniform spatially or temporally. There is an increasing demand of water for human consumption, agriculture and industrial purposes, etc.

The drainage system of the state is governed by six major river basins, the details of which are as follows :

Ganga Basin

River Ganga originated from the hills of Himalayas at Gangotri and meets Bay of Bengal. The basin extends into 11 states viz. Uttarakhand, Himachal Pradesh, Uttar Pradesh, Haryana, Delhi, Rajasthan, Madhya Pradesh, Bihar, Jharkhand, Chhattisgarh and West Bengal. In Madhya Pradesh, the basin extends up to the districts of Mandsaur, Ujjain, Shajapur, Rajgarh, Neemuch, Vidisha, Guna, Shivpuri, Datia, Gwalior, Morena, Sheopur, Bhind, Tikamgarh, Chhatarpur, Panna, Satna, Rewa, Ashoknagar, Dindori, Dhar, Ratlam, Indore, Dewas, Sehore, Raisen, Sagar, Bhopal and Damoh. The Ganga Basin can be further sub-divided into three sub-basins viz. Yamuna, Tons and Sone, details of which are discussed below :

Yamuna Sub-Basin

Total geographical area of Yamuna sub-basin in Madhya Pradesh is 1,42,250 sq.km, out of which the area available for Agriculture is estimated as 90,105 sq.km and water available at 75% dependability is 27,627 hm. Total water available for use of the State after deducting for interstate agreements is 23,642 hm only. The major rivers of this sub-basin in Madhya Pradesh are Chambal, Ken, Dhasan, Betwa, Kunwari, Sindh, Paisuni and Jamni details of which are as under:

- **Chambal sub-sub Basin:** It originates from Indore districts and meets river Yamuna near Bhind. Total length of the river 965 km, out of which initial length of 320 km lies in Madhya Pradesh, 226 km in Rajasthan, 216 km makes the boundary between Madhya Pradesh and Rajasthan, 112 km makes the boundary between Madhya Pradesh and Uttar Pradesh and 64 km in Uttar Pradesh before confluence with Yamuna river. Kalisindh, Parvati, Kuno and Sip are the main tributaries of the river Chambal.

- **Betwa sub-sub Basin:** It originates near Bhopal and meets Yamuna near Hamirpur. Total Basin area in Madhya Pradesh is 19,365 sq.km. Total length of river is 575 km, out of which 216 km lies in Madhya Pradesh, 98 km common boundary between the two states and 261 km in Uttar Pradesh. The major tributaries are Kaliasote, Halali, Bah, Sagar, Budhna, Jamni Bina.
- **Dhasan sub-sub Basin:** It originates in Raisen district of Madhya Pradesh. Total basin area in Madhya Pradesh is 8,291 sq.km. Total length of the river is 365 km, out of which 240 km lies in Madhya Pradesh, 54 km common boundary between Madhya Pradesh and Uttar Pradesh and 71 km in Uttar Pradesh.
- **Ken sub-sub Basin:** It originates in Jabalpur district. Total basin area in Madhya Pradesh is 24,785 sq.km. Total length of river is 427 km, out of which 292 in Madhya Pradesh and Uttar Pradesh and 51 km makes the common boundary between the two states.
- **Kunwari Sindh sub-sub Basin:** it originates in Vidisha district. Total catchment area of the river in Madhya Pradesh is 26,699 sq.km and total length is 470 km. A length of 461 km of the river falls in M.P. and 9 km in Uttar Pradesh. Major tributaries of Sindh are Mahuar, Parbati, Pahuj, Kunwari.
- **Jamni sub-sub Basin:** It originates in Sagar district. Total catchment area in Madhya Pradesh is 1,235 sq.km and total length is 201 km. In Madhya Pradesh the river flows for 29 km, for 85 km river makes boundary between Madhya Pradesh and Uttar Pradesh and last 87 km flows in Uttar Pradesh.
- **Paisuni and Badhain sub-sub Basin:** Total basin area of river Paisuni in Madhya Pradesh is 416 sq.km and of Baidhain river is 1504 sq.km in Madhya Pradesh. These two rivers originate in Satna and Panna district and meet river Yamuna below Banda district.

Tons Sub-Basin

River Tons originates in Satna district. Total basin area in Madhya Pradesh is 11,974 sq.km. The river meets Ganga after flowing 246 km in Madhya Pradesh, 7 km making boundary between Madhya Pradesh and Uttar Pradesh and finally 67 km in Uttar Pradesh. Total land put to use for agriculture purpose in Tons basin is 8,460 sq.km in the State for which 2,244 hm of water is available for its use against total available water at 75% dependability is 2,244 hm.

Sone Sub-Basin

Total length of the river is 784 km. In Madhya Pradesh the river flows for 470 km. The river meets Ganga in Bihar state near Patna. The major tributaries of river

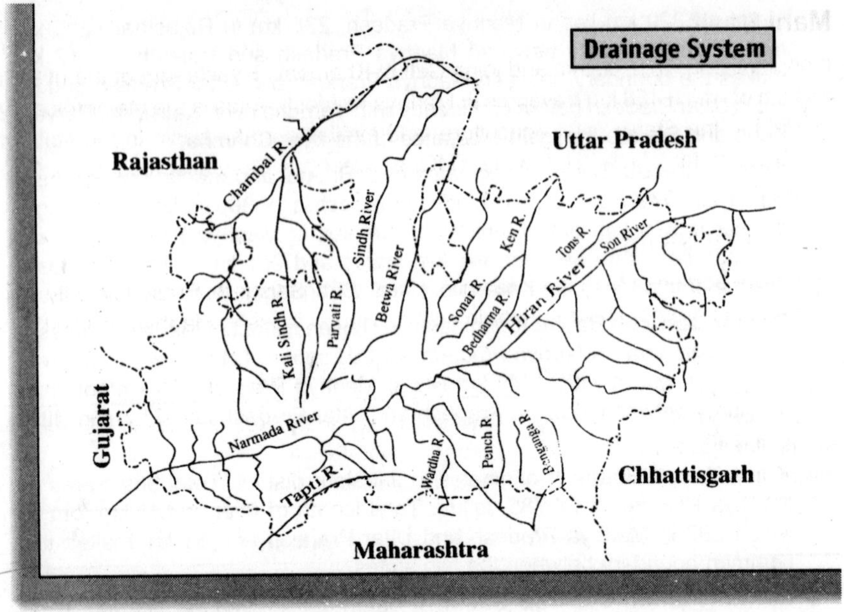

Sone are Johilla, Mahanadi, Gopad, Rehar, Kanhar, Banas. As interstate agreement between Madhya Pradesh, Uttar Pradesh and Bihar, Madhya Pradesh can use 5.25 MAF (6,475.77 hm).

Narmada Basin

It originates from Amarkantak and flows from east to west and joins Arabian Sea. Total length of river is 1312 km and in Madhya Pradesh the river flows for a length of 1077 km. As per Narmada award of Tribunal Madhya Pradesh has been allocated 18.25 MAF of water. Major tributaries of the river Narmada are Banjar, Heran, Kolar, Sukta, Tawa, Tendoni, Beda, Sher, Shakkar, Man, Jobat and Goi rivers.

Godavari Basin

In Madhya Pradesh, only the river Wainganga, Wardha and Pench originate in district Seoni and Chhindwara respectively. Total drainage area of these rivers in Madhya Pradesh is 23,388 sq.km.

Tapti Basin

It originates from Multai in Betul district. This river also flows from east to west. Total length of the river is 724 km. In Madhya Pradesh the length of river is 332 km. Total agriculture land available in the State is 6,330 sq.km. Water available at 75% dependability in the state is 2,401 hm. Madhya Pradesh can use 1,646 hm as per agreement with the Maharashtra state.

Mahi Basin

It originates in Dhar district and joins Gulf of Khambat. Total length of the river is 583 km of which 158 km traverses in Madhya Pradesh. Anas is the major tributary of Mahi in the State. Total agriculture land available in the basin in the state is 3,450 sq.km for which 338 hm (12 TMC) of water has been allocated to Madhya Pradesh.

Mahanadi Basin

The major portion of Mahanadi basin now lies in Chhattisgarh. Presently, only 154 sq.km basin area of Hasdeo river in district–Anuppur lies in Madhya Pradesh.

Direction of Flow of Rivers

Rivers flowing Northward	—	Chambal, Sone, Betwa, Ken, Kali Sindh and Parvati
Rivers flowing Southward	—	Wainganga and Pench
Rivers flowing Westward	—	Narmada, Tapti and Mahi

Rivers in Madhya Pradesh

S.No.	Rivers	Length (kms)	Originates at
1.	Narmada	Total-1312 in MP-1077	Amarkantak (District-Anuppur)
2.	Tapti	724	Near Multai (District-Betul)
3.	Chambal	965	Janapav Mountain (Vindhya Range) (District Indore)
4.	Sone	784	Amarkantak (District Anuppur)
5.	Betwa	575	Kumra Village (District Raisen)
6.	Tawa	—	Pachmarhi (Mahadev Hills)
7.	Kshipra	195	Kaka Bardi (Indore)
8.	Kali Sindh	150	Bagali Village (Dewas)
9.	Small Tawa	—	Betul
10.	Ken	—	Vindhyachal Mountain
11.	Wainganga	—	Plateau to Paraswada
12.	Kunwari	—	Plateau/Shivpuri
13.	Wardha	—	Vardhan Hill (District Betul)
14.	Kunu	—	Shivpuri District
15.	Parvati	—	Sehore District
16.	Sindh	—	Sironje (Guna)
17.	Gaar	—	Lakhar (Shivni)
18.	Tons	—	Kainur Hills (Satna)
19.	Dhasan	—	Sagar District

Cities and their River Bank

City	River	City	River
Jabalpur	Narmada	Mahu	Chambal
Bundelkhand	Betwa	Hoshangabad	Narmada
Dhar	Narmada	Shajapur	Parvati
Maheshwar	Narmada	Omkareshwar	Narmada
Rajgarh	Parvati	Multai	Tapti
Burhanpur	Tapti	Dewas	Kali Sindh
Orchha	Betwa	Shivpuri	Sindh
Balaghat	Wainganga	Ujjain	Kshipra
Datia	Sindh	Panchmarhi	Tawa
Badwani	Narmada	Sonekach	Kali Sindh
Sanchi	Betwa	Guna	Betwa
Sheopur	Chambal	Ratlam	Chambal
Vidisha	Betwa	Mandla	Narmada
Nimarh	Narmada	Jhabua	Narmada

Rivers and their Place of Confluence

S.No.	River	Place of Confluence
1.	Narmada	Gulf of Khambat
2.	Chambal	Yamuna River (Etawa)
3.	Tapti	Gulf of Khambat
4.	Kali Sindh	Chambal River (Rajasthan)
5.	Betwa	Yamuna River (Hamirpur)
6.	Kshipra	Chambal River
7.	Ken	Yamuna River
8.	Parvati	Chambal River
9.	Sindh	Chambal River
10.	Tawa	Narmada River
11.	Kunwari	Chambal River
12.	Kunu	Chambal River
13.	Wardha	Wainganga River (Maharashtra)
14.	Wainganga	Godawari River

Rivers and their Major Tributaries

River	Tributaries
Narmada	Left bank—Barnar, Banjar, Tawa, Small Tawa, Kundi, Dev, Doodhi, Sher, Shakkar, Right bank—Hiran, Tindoni, Barna, Chandra Keshar, Kanar, Maan, Uuti, Hathani
Chambal	Banas, Parvati, Kali Sindh
Sone	Johila
Tapti	Poorna
Betwa	Dhasan, Beens, Sindh
Tawa	Malini, Denwa, Sukhtawa, Kalibhit
Shipra	Khan
Wainganga	Pench, Kanan

Major Waterfalls

S.No.	Waterfall	River (Place)
1.	Dhuandhar Waterfall	Narmada (Jabalpur)
2.	Dugdh Dhara Waterfall	Narmada (Anuppur)
3.	Mandahar Waterfall	Narmada (Khandwa)
4.	Kapildhara Waterfall	Narmada (Amarkantak)
5.	Sahasra Dhara Waterfall	Narmada (Maheshwar)
6.	Dardi Waterfall	Narmada (Khandwa)
7.	Chachai Waterfall	Beehad (Rewa)
8.	Pandav Waterfall	Ken (Panna)
9.	Chulia Waterfall	Chambal (Mandsaur)
10.	Rahatgarh Waterfall	Chambal (Sagar)
11.	Patalpani Waterfall	Chambal (Indore)
12.	Jhadidaha Waterfall	Chambal (Indore)
13.	Kevati Waterfall	Beehad (Rewa)
14.	Bahuti Waterfall	Beehad (Rewa)
15.	Bhalkunda Waterfall	Sagar
16.	Dutchess Waterfall	Panchmarhi
17.	Piyawan Waterfall	Near Rewa
18.	Shankar Kho Waterfall	Jamner
19.	Apsara Waterfall	Panchmarhi
20.	Rajat Waterfall	Panchmarhi
21.	Kedarnath Waterfall	Aravalli Ranges
22.	Purva Waterfall	Near Rewa
23.	Belohi Waterfall	Near Rewa

TEST YOUR SELF

1. Narmada originates at
A. Amarkantak B. Mandsaur
C. Mahu D. Shahdol

2. The longest river of Madhya Pradesh is
A. Narmada B. Chambal C. Sone D. Betwa

3. The highest waterfall of Madhya Pradesh is
A. Bahuti B. Dhuandhar C. Kapildhara D. Chalia

4. Ujjain is situated on the bank of
A. Khan river B. Bichia river C. Parvati river D. Kshipra river

5. The longest dam in Madhya Pradesh has been built at
A. Betwa B. Tawa C. Narmada D. Chambal

6. Chachai fall is on river ....
A. Narmada B. Chambal C. Beehad D. Ken

7. Which rivers emerge from Amarkantak?

A. Chambal – Sone B. Betwa – Tawa
C. Narmada – Sone D. Sone – Tawa

8. Which of the following rivers forms ravines due to erosion?

A. Chambal B. Narmada C. Sone D. Ken

9. Which of the following rivers form estuary?

A. Narmada – Tapti B. Narmada – Sone
C. Narmada – Ken D. Narmada – Chambal

10. Which is the second longest river of the state?

A. Chambal B. Kshipra C. Betwa D. Tapti

11. River Tawa originates at

A. Mahadev hills B. Amarkantak
C. Bagoli village D. Sehore village

12. The direction of flow of river Mahi is in

A. Westward direction B. Southward direction
C. Eastward direction D. Northward direction

ANSWERS

1	2	3	4	5	6	7	8	9	10
A	A	A	D	A	C	C	A	A	A
11	**12**								
A	A								

❑❑❑

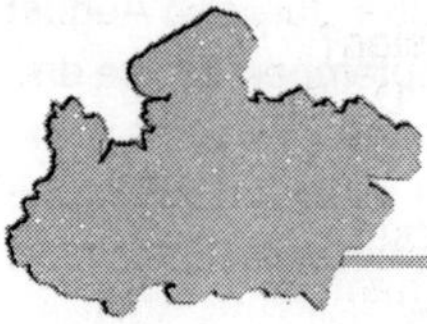

Climate

The climate variations in the State of Madhya Pradesh are obviously due to different physical and natural phenomena. The rainfall in the districts of the State is variable. There are three main seasons in the State. The summer season starts from March till June, rains from mid-June till October and winter from November till next February.

The agriculture is mostly based on the mercy of rains which depend upon the monsoons. When monsoons are delayed the rains are affected and the State has a drought as irrigation facilities are very scarce.

Summer Season

Throughout the Indian subcontinent the summer in general is from March to June. Similarly in Madhya Pradesh, the temperature progressively rises from March till June. Till May the temperature crosses the mark of 30°C. During this time the temperature in Gwalior, Morena, Datiya and Southern Balaghat is around 42.5°C. In this season the isotherm of 40°C divides the state in two equal halves. The places laying to the East of this are Mandla, Shahdol, Shivni, Chhindwara, and Betul and places towards the West are Dewas, Shajapur, Indore, Dhar, Ujjain, Jhabua, Ratlam and Mandsaur. This season is normally dry with very low humidity. The sky is generally clear across the state and sometimes also faces sand blowing winds known as Loo locally.

Winter Season

In Madhya Pradesh, the winter season is from November to February. From 23rd September, as soon as the sun starts moving towards South the average temperature starts falling. During October, the temperature of whole Madhya Pradesh remains in between 20.9 to 26.6° C. During this season, the sky is generally clear. Colder nights, sometimes cause a fog and mist on high plateaus or hilly regions. During December-January there could be some rain because of the Western disturbances which is locally called as 'Maawath'. These rains sometimes lead to sudden fall in the temperature. As soon as the March comes the temperature again starts rising and in the onset of summer.

Rainy Season

The rainfall in the State varies from 700 mm to 1800 mm on the average. The monsoon arrives in the State in the second or third week of June. July and August experience very heavy rainfall. There are sporadic rains in September. By the end of September and the beginning of October the monsoon recedes. The rains in the State arrive through south-west monsoon which provides the major rainfall of the total annual rainfall in the State. The winter rains usually come between December and February. Scanty rains are received during the summers.

Areas with More than Average Rainfall

Narsimhapur, Betul, Chhindwara, Shivni, districts come under such areas. Because of being on the Eastern side of the state, these places receive more rainfall due to more humidity. The average rainfall in these areas is 125 cm to 150 cm.

Areas with Average Rainfall

The North-Eastern places of the state comes under this section. Central highlands, plateau of Bundelkhand, Rewa-Panna Plateau are these areas which receive lesser rainfall due to the lack of humidity and their physical features. Place receiving the least rainfall in the state is Gohad in Bhind district which receive an average rainfall of 55 cm.

Areas with Minimum Rainfall

The main reason behind the minimum rainfall is the absence of humidity. Till the South-Western monsoon reaches here, it either becomes void of moisture or has a very low humidity. Places coming under this zone are Neemuch, Mandsaur, Ratlam, Dhar, Jhabua etc.

Madhya Pradesh Average Rainfall (area wise)

Region	Rainfall (in cm)
Panchmarhi	212.3
Sidhi	165.1
Mahadev Hills	150
Mandla	152.4–165
Balaghat	153.4–165
Malwa Plateau	76–114
Bundelkhand Plateau	76–114
Western Central Plateau	76.2
Central Highlands	62.5–114.3

TEST YOUR SELF

1. The maximum rain in Madhya Pradesh occurs at
   A. Panchmarhi B. Bhind
   C. Hoshangabad D. Betul
2. Which of the following months is also known as the second summer in Madhya Pradesh?
   A. September – October B. August – September
   C. May – June D. June – July
3. 'Maawath' are
   A. rain caused by Western disturbances
   B. rain with snow fall and thunderstorm
   C. summer rain
   D. landslide
4. How many climatic zones are found in Madhya Pradesh?
   A. 5 B. 6 C. 4 D. 2
5. The climate of the state of Madhya Pradesh is generally characterised as
   A. Tropical B. Sub-tropical C. Continental D. None of these
6. The average weather conditions of a place for a longer period of time refers to as
   A. Monsoon B. Climate C. Humidity D. Weather
7. Which part of Madhya Pradesh has a moderate climate?
   A. Northern Plains B. Malwa Plateau
   C. Vindhyan Hills D. Narmada Valley
8. Which among the following districts gains more than average rainfall?
   A. Betul B. Shivni C. Chhindwara D. All of these
9. Panchmarhi receives an average annual rainfall of ....
   A. 200 cm B. 212 cm C. 185 cm D. 228 cm
10. Which district of Madhya Pradesh receives maximum temperature during summer?
    A. Gwalior B. Morena C. Datia D. All of these

ANSWERS

1	2	3	4	5	6	7	8	9	10
A	A	A	A	B	B	C	D	B	D

❑❑❑

Soils

The agriculture of any state depends upon the type of Soils it has. Soils are formed due to the breakage of rocks. The top most layer of the Soils consists of rocks and living organisms. It is the combination of many chemical complexes.

In Madhya Pradesh almost all the variety of soils can be seen.

Red Soil

This type of soil can be seen in the majority portion of the state. It is found in Vindhya Pradesh, Mahakoshal and south Madhya Bharat regions. Red soil is of three types : (a) Red soil; (b) Red and Yellow; and (c) Mixed red and black.

Red soil is deficient in phosphates. The red and yellow soil may be light or medium or heavy. It is suitable for rice cultivation and is found in Raipur, Bilaspur, Durg, Rajnandgaon, Balaghat districts and parts of Surguja, Mandla and Bastar districts. The mixed red black soil is generally deficient in nitrogens, phosphoric acid, organic matter and lime. It is found in Rewa, Satna, Panna, Chhattarpur, Tikamgarh and Datia districts and parts of Shivpuri district.

The Black Soil

Also known as the "Black Cotton Soil" is most suited for growing cotton, wheat and millets. This type of soil has a basic feature of retaining water and moisture. Phosphates, nitrogen and humus are less in this type of soil but at certain places the potash may be high. The Malwa and Mahakoshal regions consist of such type of soil. The districts of Shahdol, Betul, Chhindwara, Seoni and Mandla also consists of such type of soil.

Deep Black Soil: It is found in Narmada region, Narsimhapur, Hoshangabad and Jabalpur districts and is very much suited for wheat, cotton and jowar.

Medium Black Soil: A number of crops can be grown in such type of soil and is found mostly in Malwa region and Vindhya ranges.

Layered Black Soil: It is usually found on hills and plateau. It is found in the stony areas of Vindhya ranges and Satpura ranges and parts of Shahdol, Mandla, Surguja, Raigarh, Bastar and Jhabua districts.

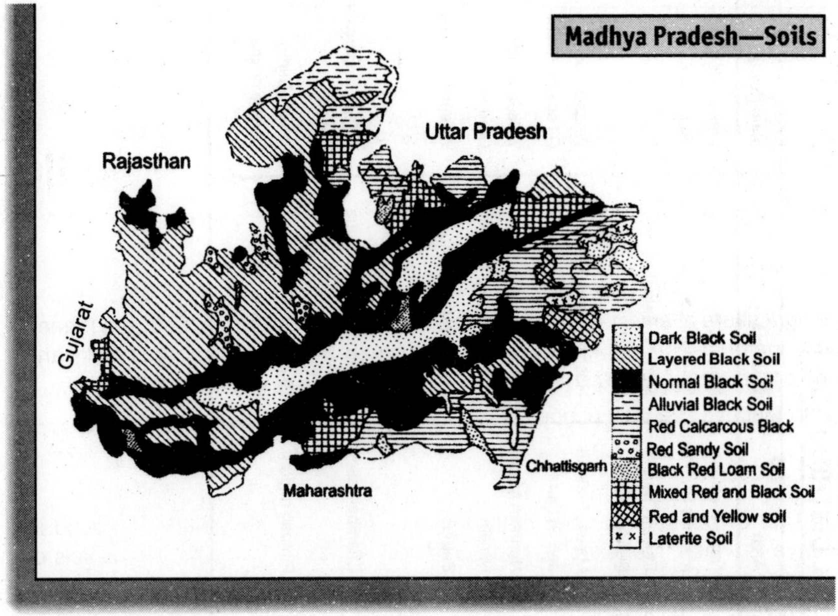

Alluvial Soil

This soil has been found out of the eroded form of Bundelkhand, Niece rocks and sediments of Chambal. Itis found in the Morena, Bhind, Gwalior and Shivpuri districts in about 30 lakh acres. This soil also lacks humus, organic material, nitrogen and phosphorus. The ratio of sand, slit and dirt in the soil is 50 : 19.6 : 29.4. Because of the excess of sand in the soil, it is less prone to erosion. The soil is suitable for the cultivation of wheat, cotton and sugarcane.

Laterite Soil

Laterite soil is a bi-product of the sediments of rives. In Madhya Pradesh, it is found in Gwalior, Bhind and Morena. it is suitable for the cultivation of wheat, sugarcane and cotton.

Mixed Soil

In different regions of the state red, yellow and black soils are found in mixed forms. This soil lacks in phosphates, nitrogen and carbonic compounds and is not so fertile. It is majorly used for the cultivation of coarse grains like jowar, barely etc.

MADHYA PRADESH : SOIL DISTRIBUTION

S.No.	Soil	Main Constituent	Lacks	Nature	Area	Districts	Main Crops
1.	Alluvial Soil	Carbonates	Phosphorus, Humus	Neutral	North-Western Madhya Pradesh	Morena, Bhind, Gwalior, Shivpuri, Sheopur	Wheat, Cotton, Sugarcane
2.	Red-Yellow Soil	Iron Oxides, Calcium	Nitrogen, Humus	Acidic to Basic	Eastern part of Bundelkhand	Mandla, Balaghat, Shahdol	Rice
3.	Dark Black Soil	Iron, Lime and solubles of HCl	Phosphorus, Nitrogen, Humus	Acidic	Malwa, Plateau and Satpura	Hoshangabad, Harda	Wheat, Jowar, Oil seeds, Gram
4.	Normal Black Soil	Iron, Lime and solubles of HCl	Phosphorus, Nitrogen, Humus	Acidic	Northern Malwa, Nimarh	Guna, Shajapur, Sehore, Ujjain, Vidisha, Bhopal	Wheat, Cotton, Groundnut
5.	Layery or Layered Black Soil	Iron, Lime and solubles in acidic HCl	Phosphorus, Nitrogen, Humus	Acidic	Satpura	Chhindwara, Shivni, Betul	Wheat and Rice
6.	Laterite Soil	—	Phosphorus, Nitrogen	Acidic	Chambal valley	Gwalior, Bhind, Morena	Wheat, Sugarcane, Cotton
7.	Mixed Soil	—	Phosphorus, Nitrogen, Organic compounds	—	Plateau region	Tikamgarh, Panna, Satna, Rewa, Sidhi	Jowar, Barley, Coarse grains

Soil Beds in Madhya Pradesh

Soils	Districts
Laterite Soil	Morena, Bhind, Gwalior, Sheopur
Alluvial Soil	Morena, Bhind, Gwalior, Shivpuri
Red-Yellow Soil	Mandla, Balaghat, Shahdol, Sidhi
Calcareous Soil	Mandla
Black-yellow Soil	Balaghat
Dark Black Soil	Hoshangabad
Layery Black Soil	Chindwara, Betul, Shivni
Normal Black Soil	Jhabua, Mandsaur, Khargone, Khandwa, Indore, Dewas, Sehora, Shajapur, Damoh, Jabalpur etc.
Mixed Soil	Panna, Tikamgarh, Chhatarpur, Satna, Rewa, Sidhi etc.

Soil Erosion

Soils erosion is the phenomenon of continuous deterioration in the soil due to the shifting of soil through various environmental forces, one of the main factors of soil erosion is Deforestation. Roots of the plants and trees hold the soils in its place and they also sustain the adverse effects of atmospheric forces and therefore prevent soil erosion. But due to extensive deforestation soil erosion is becoming a grave danger to the human civilization, especially in the areas where soils are of light and medium texture. The scene is no different in Madhya Pradesh, which is facing rapid soil erosion in its northern part along the Chambal and its tributaries. Large scale gully erosion can be seen in the belt around the districts of Gwalior, Morena and Bhind. Since the soils of this area are light and lack vegetation thus water takes away soils with its flow and results is erosion.

Soils erosion not only disturbs to pographic and ecological balance but large part of fertile sub surface land also goes waste through run off. Thus it is social, environment and economical problem of the present era. The only way to centre this menace is to create a healthy nature friendly ecological environment around us.

TEST YOUR SELF

1. Which of the following districts is affected mostly by soil erosion?
   A. Morena B. Bhind C. Guna D. Shivpuri
2. The parent material of black soil is
   A. Basalt rocks B. Sedimentary rocks
   C. Aplite rocks D. Andesite rocks

3. Madhya Pradesh soils can broadly be classified into

A. 9 categories
B. 5 categories
C. 8 categories
D. 16 categories

4. Black soil lacks minerals like

A. iron and nitrogen
B. phosphorus and iron
C. nitrogen and phosphorus
D. iron

5. Which of the following soils is the most abundant soil type in the Madhya Pradesh?

A. Normal black soil
B. Layered black soil
C. Dark black soil
D. None of these

6. The pH of black soil is

A. 7.5–8.5
B. 6.5–8.5
C. 6.5–7.5
D. 7.5–9.5

7. Match the following

List I	List II
(a) Dark Black soil	1. Mandala
(b) Calcareous Soil	2. Balaghat
(c) Layered Black Soil	3. Hoshangabad
(d) Black Yellow Soil	4. Chhindwara

Codes

	(a)	(b)	(c)	(d)		(a)	(b)	(c)	(d)
A.	1	2	3	4	B.	3	2	1	4
C.	4	3	2	1	D.	3	1	4	2

8. Mixed soils are majorly used in cultivation of

A. cash crops
B. cotton
C. coarse grains
D. sugarcane

9. Laterite soil is

A. found in Gwalior, Bhind and Morena district
B. found in the areas of Chambal valley
C. lacking in phosphorus and nitrogen
D. acidic in nature

10. Match the following

List I	List II
(a) Alluvial Soil	1. Humus
(b) Red Yellow Soil	2. Nitrogen
(c) Black Soil	3. Phosphorus and Humus
(d) Laterite Soil	4. Phosphorus and Nitrogen

Codes

	(a)	(b)	(c)	(d)		(a)	(b)	(c)	(d)
A.	1	2	3	4	B.	4	3	2	1
C.	3	1	4	2	D.	2	4	1	3

11. Which of the soils is preferred for the cultivation of wheat and rice?

A. Layered black soil
B. Red soil
C. Alluvial soil
D. Normal black soil

12. Which of the following soils generally has high contents of lime and iron?

A. Black soil
B. Laterite soil
C. Alluvial soil
D. Red Yellow soil

13. Which of the following soils is a by-product of the sediments of rivers?

A. Red Yellow soil
B. Alluvial soil
C. Laterite soil
D. Mixed soil

ANSWERS

1	2	3	4	5	6	7	8	9	10
A	A	B	C	A	A	D	C	A	C
11	**12**	**13**							
A	A	C							

❑❑❑

Forests & Wildlife

Madhya Pradesh is the second largest state of the country with an area of 3,08,000 km^2 constituting 9.38% of the geographical area of the country. Physiographically, the state can be divided into four regions, viz., the low lying areas in north and north-west of Gwalior, Malwa Plateau, Satpura and Vindhyan Ranges. Chambal, Betwa, Sone and Narmada are four important rivers of the State. The rainfall decreases from south-east and east to north-west and west. The average annual rainfall varies from 800 mm to about 1,800 mm. The annual temperature ranges from 22.5°C to 25°C.

Recorded Forest Area

Recorded Forest Area (RFA) in the State is 94,689 sq km of which 61,886 sq km is Reserved Forests, 31,098 sq km is Protected Forests and 1,705 sq km is Unclassed Forests. In Madhya Pradesh, during the period 1st January 2015 to 5th February 2019, a total of 12,785.98 hectares of forest land was diverted for nonforestry purposes under the Forest Conservation Act, 1980 (MoEF & CC, 2019).

Protected Areas

Ten National Parks and 25 Wildlife Sanctuaries constitute the Protected Area network of the State covering 3.51% of its geographical area. There are 6 Tiger Reserves in the State covering an area of 6117.26 sq km. Eco-sensitive zones have been declared for 19 protected areas. The State with a population of 526 Tigers, is recognized as Tiger State of India, as per the 'All India Tiger Estimation 2018'.

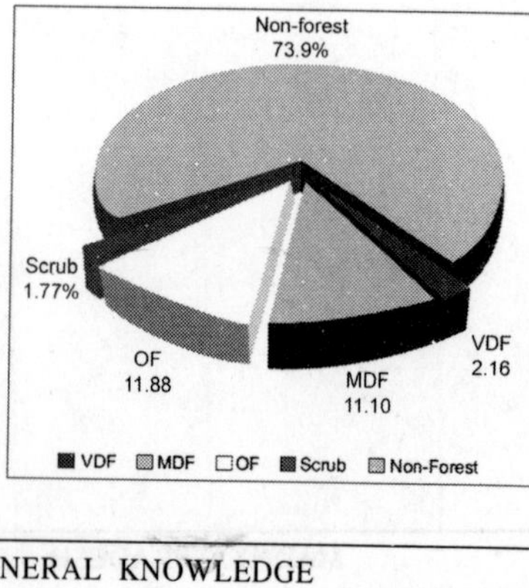

Forest Cover

Based on the interpretation of IRS Resourcesat-2 LISS III satellite data of the period Oct 2019 to December 2020, the Forest Cover in the State is 77,492.60 sq km which is 25.14 % of the State's geographical area. In terms of forest canopy density classes, the State has 6,664.95 sq km under Very Dense Forest (VDF), 34,209.02 sq km under

Moderately Dense Forest (MDF) and 36,618.63 sq km under Open Forest (OF). Forest Cover in the State has increased by 10.11 sq km as compared to the previous assessment reported in ISFR 2019.

District-wise forest cover in different canopy density classes are given below:

District-wise Forest Cover (Area in km^2)

District	Geographical Area	2021 Assessment				Percent of GA
		Very Dense Forest	Mod. Dense Forest	Open Forest	Total	
Alirajpur	3,182	0.00	207.29	474.06	681.35	21.41
Anuppur	3,747	108.31	337.50	411.66	857.47	22.88
Ashoknagar	4,674	0.00	265.93	421.32	687.25	14.70
Balaghat	9,229	1,407.64	2,630.88	884.26	4,922.78	53.34
Barwani	5,427	0.00	186.79	717.57	904.36	16.66
Betul	10,043	230.11	1,922.32	1,510.36	3,662.79	36.47
Bhind	4,459	0.00	28.08	198.48	226.56	5.08
Bhopal	2,772	0.00	120.77	207.79	328.56	11.85
Burhanpur	3,427	57.92	625.89	603.75	1,287.56	37.57
Chattarpur	8,687	184.01	817.24	755.89	1,757.14	20.23
Chhindwara	11,815	575.68	2,021.61	2,010.84	4,608.13	39.00
Damoh	7,306	2.00	844.92	1,739.79	2,586.71	35.41
Datia	2,902	0.00	91.13	121.65	212.78	7.33
Dewas	7,020	12.00	935.21	1,000.06	1,947.27	27.74
Dhar	8,153	0.00	115.64	528.62	644.26	7.90
Dindori	7,470	1,084.98	1,271.24	666.21	3,022.43	40.46
East Nimar	7,352	147.80	1,153.11	784.48	2,085.39	28.36
Guna	6,390	2.00	414.00	911.50	1,327.50	20.77
Gwalior	4,560	1.00	323.69	902.14	1,226.83	26.90
Harda	3,334	19.00	523.70	396.61	939.31	28.17
Hoshangabad	6,703	271.64	1,366.15	783.41	2,421.20	36.12
Indore	3,898	0.00	348.10	326.51	674.61	17.31
Jabalpur	5,211	40.26	501.04	560.53	1,101.83	21.14
Jhabua	3,600	0.00	30.69	189.52	220.21	6.12
Katni	4,950	93.90	607.87	654.85	1,356.62	27.41
Mandla	5,800	691.78	1,092.55	792.65	2,576.98	44.43
Mandsaur	5,535	0.00	42.01	198.67	240.68	4.35
Morena	4,989	0.00	96.12	665.55	761.67	15.27
Narsimhapur	5,133	61.00	655.81	623.97	1,340.78	26.12
Neemuch	4,256	0.04	119.22	669.74	789.00	18.54
Panna	7,135	82.95	1,476.06	1,189.59	2,748.60	38.52
Raisen	8,466	22.55	1,302.18	1,346.59	2,671.32	31.55
Rajgarh	6,153	0.00	37.86	133.94	171.80	2.79
Ratlam	4,861	0.00	2.53	72.63	75.16	1.55
Rewa	6,314	60.91	377.18	363.11	801.20	12.69

District	Geographical Area	2021 Assessment				Percent of GA
		Very Dense Forest	Mod. Dense Forest	Open Forest	Total	
Sagar	10,252	1.00	1,138.81	1,645.43	2,785.24	27.17
Satna	7,502	12.00	904.19	835.33	1,751.52	23.35
Sehore	6,578	20.70	614.84	714.61	1,350.15	20.53
Seoni	8,758	237.07	1,787.12	1,038.84	3,063.03	34.97
Shahdol	6,205	122.03	818.26	1,014.41	1,954.70	31.50
Shajapur	6,195	0.00	2.44	59.47	61.91	1.00
Sheopur	6,606	6.00	1,394.25	2,043.66	3,443.91	52.13
Shivpuri	10,066	18.00	779.39	1,749.14	2,546.53	25.30
Sidhi	4,851	315.96	881.29	805.27	2,002.52	41.28
Singrauli	5,675	393.73	992.29	776.84	2,162.86	38.11
Tikamgarh	5,048	1.00	89.73	295.58	386.31	7.65
Ujjain	6,091	0.00	2.60	34.10	36.70	0.60
Umaria	4,076	377.98	1,092.66	530.60	2,001.24	49.10
Vidisha	7,371	1.00	344.52	431.24	776.76	10.54
West Nimar	8,025	1.00	474.32	825.81	1,301.13	16.21
Grand Total	**3,08,252**	**6,664.95**	**34,209.02**	**36,618.63**	**77,492.60**	**25.14**

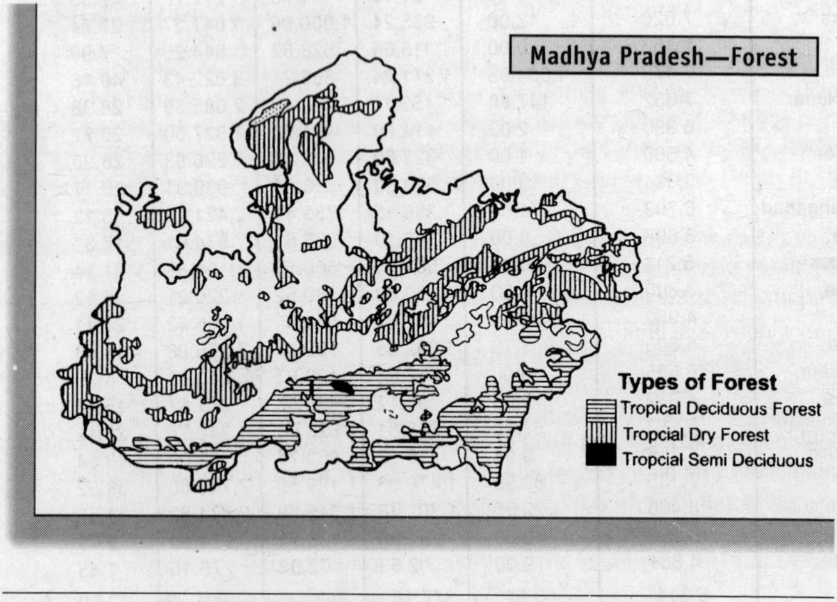

Forest Cover Inside and Outside Recorded Forest Area (or Green Wash)

The forest Cover inside and outside Recorded Forest Area (RFA) has been analysed in different categories and presented in Table given below:

Forest Cover Inside and Outside Recorded Forest Area or (Green Wash) in Madhya Pradesh

(in sq km)

Forest Cover Inside the Recorded Forest Area (or Green Wash)			Forest Cover Outside the Recorded Forest Area (or Green Wash)		
VDF	MDF	OF	VDF	MDF	OF
6,251 9.65%	30,195 46.62%	28,326 43.73%	414 3.25%	4,014 31.56%	8,293 65.19%
Total	64,772		Total	12,721	

Tree Cover

In 2021 Tree cover in Madhya Pradesh is 8,054 sq km. Tree cover of Madhya Pradesh has decreased by 285 sq km as compared to the previous assessment reported in ISFR 2019.

Forest Product

Forest product plays an important role in the socio-economic development of the state. In addition to the meeting bonafide needs of the villagers residing in and around forest areas, sale of forest products contributes substantially to the state exchequer. Important forest products are timber, small timber, fuel wood, bamboo and many non forest products like Tendu Patta, Harra, Sal Seed, etc. Teak (Tectona grandis), Sal (Shorea vodusta). Bija (Pterocarpus marsopium), Saja (Terminalia), Haldu (Adina cordifdia), Lendia (larger stroemia parviflora) are the main tree species which are harvested annually from the forest. Timber and bamboo harvesting is carried out departmentally in selected coupes annually as per the provisions laid down in the working plans in force. The working plans prescribe specific treatments for specific areas for getting sustained yield.

Important Trees found in Madhya Pradesh

Name of Trees	Districts
Saal	Mandla, Umaria, Shahdol, Balaghat, Dindori, Sidhi
Teak (Sagaun)	Jabalpur, Hoshangabad, Betul, Sagar, Chhindwara, Mandla
Bamboo	Balaghat, Seoni, Mandla, Dinsori, Betul, Jabalpur, Sagar
Catechu Trees	Jabalpur, Sagar, Damoh, Umaria, Hoshangabad, Sidhi
Lakh	Umaria, Jabalpur, Mandla, Seoni, Shahdol, Hoshangabad
Gum	Sidhi, Shahdol
Tobacco Leaves	Jabalpur, Sagar, Rewa, Shahdol
Dhobi's Marking Nut (Bhilava)	Shahdol, Mandla, Chhindwara
Myrobalam (Harra)	Chhindwara, Mandla, Balaghat, Sheopur, Shahdol

Various Programmes

The government of Madhya Pradesh has off lately sensed the urgency to reform forest resources and have therefore launched many schemes and projects in this direction. Some of the major programmes going on this direction are:

1. **Drought Prone Areas Programme:** Under this scheme the drought prone districts of Madhya Pradesh namely Dhar, Jhabua, Betul, Sidhi, Shahdol and Khargone etc. are being focused. Plantation, development of grass lands and other such activities are being taken in these areas.
2. **Panch Van Yojana:** It aims at increasing the forest cover to 33 per cent of the total land of the state.
3. **Social Pores Try Scheme:** Under this scheme state government is promoting the people towards tree farming, hedge plantation and to promote private nursery.
4. **Tree Plantation Programme:** It aims at increasing forest cover in the state and to create a cleaner environment, especially in the urban areas. This programme are run by public participation and by mutual support. NGOs are also actively engaged in this field by creating awareness amongst the people towards important of forest in our lives.

Greening of Non-forest Lands: Lok Vaniki

In the state of MP, there are large number of small patches of private tree-clad areas and forests. They have not been yielding any income to the owners. Such private landholdings of the thousands of farmers are small, generally ranging from 0.5 ha to 15 ha.

The owners of such private forests are tempted to somehow get rid of the standing tree crop and convert the land into agricultural fields or they become indifferent to their forests. In order to achieve the overall goal of conservation and sustainable development, a scheme based on private forestry, called *Lok Vaniki* was launched by the Government of MP in April 1999 on a pilot basis. The scheme envisages that felling of trees in private forests of willing owners, will take place as per a duly approved management plan. Such management plans would prescribe multi-tier scientific management of privately held forest. The management plan is to be prepared for each private holding to ensure continuity of management and improvement of the area.

The bhumi swami or the lok vaniki beneficiary has to sell the timber growing on his or her land to the forest department only, and the price of the timber so sold is paid to the bhumi swami as per the rates fixed by the state government.

The MP Lok Vaniki Act, 2001

The state of Madhya Pradesh has enacted the MP Lok Vaniki Act, 2001 (MP Act No. 10 of 2001) to give a boost to scientific management of privately owned 'forests' and other 'tree-clad areas' in the state. The Act provides an opportunity to the willing landholders to take up management of their tree-clad holdings for optimising economic returns to themselves and simultaneously ensuring environmental benefits to the society.

Madhya Pradesh New Forest Policy-2005

The new forest policy-2005 has been announced after 53 years, since the last forest policy was announced in 1952. The new forest policy declared by the state government envisages a more close co-ordination between people and state in order to make state clean and rein. It presents the relationship between environment and society in a new perspective.

The main objectives of the forest policy-2005 are as follows:

1. Proper management of forests, while taking care of situational, social, economical and technical aspects of the area.
2. To protect and develop the forest products.
3. To take care of the interest of the group depending on forest produce while maintaining the aim of the policy.

Indian Institute of Forest Management (IIFM), Bhopal

The Indian Institute of Forest Management (founded 1982) is an autonomous institution located at Bhopal in Madhya Pradesh established by the Ministry of Environment and Forest, Government of India with financial assistance from the Swedish International Development Corporation Agency (SIDA) and course assistance from the Indian Institute of Management Ahmedabad. IIFM has been established with the following objectives:

1. Provide training in management and related subjects for persons from the Indian Forest Service, Forest Departments, Forest Development Corporation and Forest related industries with a view to equip them to practice the art and profession of management of forestry development.
2. Select and prepare outstanding and talented young persons for careers leading to management responsibility in forestry and the forest-related system.
3. Meet the need of Indian forestry and forest-related industry and commerce in respect of upto-date information on forestry management through research, consulting and publication.

4. Assist, institute and carry out research in matters concerning the use of management and allied techniques and methods conductive to the development of forestry in the country.

Major Forest Institutions of the State

Institution	Head Quarters	Role
Madhya Pradesh Eco Tourism Development Board	Bhopal	To develop eco-tourism
Sanjivani Sansathan	Bhopal	Trade of forests herbs development
Bharatiya Van Anusandhan Sansathan	Jabalpur	Research of plants
Indian Forest Management Institution	Bhopal	Forest produce and forest management related training
Van Rajik Mahavidyalaya	Balaghat	Forest related training
Van Rajik Mahavidyalaya	Betul	Forest related training
Van Vikas Nigam	Bhopal	Conservation and development of forests

Wildlife

The state of Madhya Pradesh is highly rich in flora and fauna due to the availability of dense forests. To save and protect this biodiversity, the regions are divided into wildlife sanctuaries, national parks and forest reserves.

The Wildlife Sanctuaries in the State

S.No.	Name	Area Covered (sq. km.)	District	Fauna
1.	Chambal	3902.00	Morena	Ghariyal, Crocodile, Turtle, Otter Dolphin, Migratory Birds
2.	Nauradehi	1034.52	Sagar	Tiger, Leopard, Chital, Sambar, Nilgai
3.	Panchmarhi	461.85	Hoshangabad	Tiger, Leopard, Sambar, Chital, Gaur, Chinkara, Bear, Nilgai
4.	Panpatha	245.84	Shahdol	Tiger, Leopard, Chital, Sambar, Muntjac, Nilgai, Chousingha Deer, Bear
5.	Kuno	345.00	Sheopur	Tiger, Leopard, Sambar, Chital, Nilgai, Chinkara, Black Buck
6.	Pench	449.39	Seoni	Tiger, Leopard, Chital, Gaur, Sambar, Nilgai, Jungle Fowl
7.	Ratapani	688.79	Raisen	Tiger, Leopard, Sambar, Chital, Nilgai, Chinkara
8.	Sanjay Dubri	364.59	Sidhi	Tiger, Leopard, Sambar, Chital, Gaur, Chinkara, Nilgai, Muntjac

S.No.	Name	Area Covered (sq. km.)	District	Fauna
9.	Singhori	287.91	Raisen	Gharial, Crocodile, Turtle, Migratory Birds
10.	Son-Ghariyal	209.00	Sidhi/Shahdol	Kharmor
11.	Sardarpur	318.12	Ratlam	Kharmor
12.	Sailana	12.96	Ratlam	—
13.	Ralamandal	234.55	Indore	—
14.	Orchha	45.00	Tikamgarh	—
15.	Gangav	—	Panna	—
16.	Durgawati	—	Jabalpur	—
17.	Bori	518.00	Hoshangabad	Tiger, Leopard, Sambar, Chital, Gaur, Bear, Wild Boar
18.	Bagdara	478.90	Sidhi	Leopard, Chital, Black Buck, Sambar, Chinkara, Nilgai
19.	Phen	110.74	Mandla	Tiger, Leopard, Chital, Sambar
20.	Ghatigaon	512.00	Gwalior	Chinkara, Nilgai, Sambar, Great Indian Bustard
21.	Gandhisagar	368.62	Mandsaur	Leopard, Chital, Chinkara, Nilgai, Barking Deer, Water Bird
22.	Karera	202.21	Shivpuri	Black Buck, Sambar, Chital, Chinkara, Great Indian Bustard
23.	Ken-ghariyal	45.00	Chhatarpur/Panna	Gharial, Crocodile
24.	Kheoni	122.70	Dewas	Leopard, Bear, Chital, Sambar, Nilgai
25.	Narsinghgarh	57.19	Rajgarh	Leopard, Chital, Sambar, Wild Boar, Peacock, Grey Hornbill

National Parks

The numero uno State of India in terms of the area under forests is also a pioneer in the field of conservation and preservation of these forests and flora and fauna in them. For insite conservation of this biodiversity, the national parks and sanctuaries have been developed as under the Wildlife (Protection) Act, 1972. As of now, there are 10 National Parks and 25 Sanctuaries spread over an area of about 11000 sq. km.

National Parks and Sanctuaries	Area (sq. km.)	Location	Establishment	Fauna
Kanha National Park	940	Mandla	1995	Tiger, Leopard, Gaur, Chital, Sambar, Nilgai, Chinkara, Barking Deer, Barasingha, Wild Boar and variety of upland birds

National Parks and Sanctuaries	Area (sq. km.)	Location	Establishment	Fauna
Sanjay National Park	838	Sidhi/Sarguja (CG)	—	Tiger, Panther, Sambar, Chital, Gaurete
Mandala Plant Fossils	0.27	Mandla	—	Plant, Fossils
Panna National Park	543	Panna/ Chhatarpur	1981	Leopard, Sambar, Nilgai, Chital Deer, Tiger, Wild Bear
Satpura National Park	524	Hoshangabad	1981	Tiger, Leopoakig, Nilgai, Four horned antelope, Chinkara, Wild Boar, Wild Dog, Bear, Black Buck, Fox, Mouses, Deer, India joint squirrel etc.
Pench National Park	293	Seoni/ Chhindwara/ Nagpur	1983	Tiger, Panther, Bison, Chital, Sambar, Nilgai, Chinkara, Barking, Deer, Chousingha Deer, Wild Boar and variety of upland birds
Van Vihar National Park	445	Bhopal	1983	Tiger, Panther, Lion, Bear, Hyena etc.
Madhav National Park	354	Shivpuri	1959	Panther, Chital, Sambar, Nilgai, Chinkara, Black Buck, Chausingha Deer, Wild Boar, Crocodile
Bandhavgarh National Park	437	Umaria	1968	Tiger, Panther, Gaur, Chital, Sambar, Nilgai, Chinkara, Barking Deer, Wild Boar and variety of upland birds

Project Tiger

Government of India with WWF launched the 'Project Tiger' in 1973. Initially, it was launched in the nine protected areas across India selected under the scheme, and Kanha National Park was one of them. At present, six national parks are under Project Tiger—Kanha, Panna, Bandhavgarh, Pench, Sanjay and Satpura.

Biodiversity Conservation

1. The biodiversity of Madhya Pradesh is extremely rich with a wide variety of species. The conservation and sustainable use of biodiversity is fundamental to ecologically sustainable development.
2. There is a need for conservation of state's rich biodiversity. Its sustainable use and equitable sharing of benefits arise out of its use, and are achieved in such a manner that empowers people.

Panchmarhi Biosphere Reserve

1. The biosphere reserve's total area is 4926.28 km. It includes three wildlife conservation units, the Bori Sanctuary, Satpura National Park and Panchmarhi Sanctuary.
2. The Panchmarhi Biosphere Reserve is a conservation area in the Satpura Range of Madhya Pradesh and covers parts of Hoshangabad, Betul, and Chhindwara districts.
3. The forests are dominated by teak and sal.
4. The reserve is mostly covered in forest and an important transition zone between the forests of Western and Eastern India.

Social Forestry

By the mid-seventies, the realisation became clear that if peoples' demands were not met, it would be impossible to save forests. This was to be achieved through social forestry on village and private lands. As such, a Five-Year Social Forestry Project was launched in Madhya Pradesh in 1981-82 and continued up to 1985-86, in 21 districts. Plantations were raised over 41,875 ha of village common lands and 2,328 ha of such land was brought under pasture development. In all, nearly 31 million seedlings were distributed, mainly to the agriculturists.

Social forestry was not tried on forest lands, as such lands were sought to be used for producing timber and pulpwood and people's participation on such lands was not encouraged. Thus, social forestry was seen as a programme which would release industrial forestry from social pressures. But in order to keep people out, it was necessary to make them produce what they consumed free of charge using community and private lands to draw off the pressure on forest lands.

Joint Forest Management (JFM)

After experiencing from the past that government alone cannot effectively protect and manage the forest resources, the state government decided to take the co-operation of people living adjoining to the forest area and finally introduced the concept of participatory management in forestry sector. With a view to involving local people in forest management, not only to check further degradation of forest for their basic needs, but also to introduce the concept of sustainable forest development together with village development, the Government of India issued a circular on 01/06/90 supporting joint planning and management of degraded forests in all parts of India. The state of Madhya Pradesh took a lead in JFM.

JFM is the best way to protect, regenerate and manage forests. The basic object behind it is to create awareness in local people that they are the owners of the forests collectively and the forest department is only a manager.

In order to reduce the dependence of the villagers on forests, village resource development programmes/eco-development programmes have been taken up as one of the important activities of the JFM. Eco-development is based on the belief that if foresters support village development—resources, cattle, veterinary inputs, schools, health, water, roads, etc.—then the people will appreciate the role of forests and help in its protection.

Forest Department Initiatives under State Plan Development Funds

PPA or the People's Protected Areas

This new initiative undertaken by the MP State Minor Forest Produce Co-operative Federation is based on sustainable livelihood approach with biodiversity conservation (SLAB) and involves conservation and development along with non-destructive and sustainable harvesting of non-wood forest products (NWFP).

People and Forest Management

With livelihood forestry, subsistence and consumption would be met more from forest land, and market demand would be met more from private land. Using private lands for short rotation products will permit the large area of forest lands to be used for long gestation trees, which enrich the environment and provide a range of products to the poor. Choice of species and management practices should be radically changed to suit the new policy. In Madhya Pradesh, the changes at policy level has allowed government to harness the tremendous attachment of the tribals for forests. The schemes have been conceived to demonstrate that the development of forests also bestowed benefits on the tribals, and this has initiated a new era of partnership between the tribals and the government.

TEST YOUR SELF

1. Indian Forest Management Institute is located at

A. Bhopal
B. Indore
C. Gwalior
D. Jabalpur

2. What is the primary role of Sanjivani Sansthan established in Bhopal?

A. Conservation and development of forests
B. To develop eco-tourism
C. Trade of forest herbs development
D. Forest related training

3. When was the forest policy for Madhya Pradesh constituted?

A. 1963
B. 1950
C. 2005
D. 1951

4. Match the following

List I	List II
(a) Sanjivani Sansthan	1. Betul
(b) Van Rajik Mahavidyalaya	2. Bhopal
(c) Indian Forest Management Institution	3. Jabalpur
(d) Bhartiya Van Anusandhan Sansthan	4. Bhopal

Codes

	(a)	(b)	(c)	(d)		(a)	(b)	(c)	(d)
A.	1	3	2	4	B.	1	4	3	2
C.	4	3	2	1	D.	2	1	4	3

5. What is the forest area of Madhya Pradesh as per 2021 assessment?
A. 60,580 sq km
B. 90,760 sq km
C. 77,492.60 sq km
D. None of these

6. When was the 'Lok Vaniki' programme launched by Government of Madhya Pradesh?
A. 1998 B. 1999 C. 1997 D. 1992

7. Bori Wildlife Sanctuary is in which district?
A. Jhabua B. Rajgarh C. Hoshangabad D. Dhar

8. Ghatigaon Wildlife Sanctuary is located in district ....
A. Sidhi B. Gwalior C. Jhabua D. Bhopal

9. Phen Wildlife Sanctuary is located in which district?
A. Mandla B. Jhabua C. Jabalpur D. Dhar

10. National Chambal Wildlife Sanctuary is located in which district?
A. Morena B. Jhabua C. Raisen D. Sidhi

11. Match the following

List I (Sanctuary)	List II (District)
(a) Panchmarhi	1. Jabalpur
(b) Ratapani	2. Tikamgarh
(c) Orchha	3. Hoshangabad
(d) Durgawati	4. Raisen

Codes

	(a)	(b)	(c)	(d)		(a)	(b)	(c)	(d)
A.	3	4	2	1	B.	4	2	3	1
C.	1	2	3	4	D.	4	3	2	1

12. How many national parks are there in Madhya Pradesh?
A. 3 B. 10 C. 8 D. 4

13. How many sanctuaries are there in Madhya Pradesh?
A. 16 B. 20 C. 22 D. 25

14. "Mandla Plant Fossils" is a
A. Biological Park
B. Sanctuary
C. National Park
D. Tiger Reproduction Centre

15. When was the Madhav National park established?
A. 1959 B. 1969 C. 1971 D. 1974

16. Match the following

List I	List II
(a) Panna National Park	1. 1981
(b) Kanha National Park	2. 1995
(c) Van Vihar National Park	3. 1983
(d) Satpura National Park	4. 1981

Codes

	(a)	(b)	(c)	(d)
A.	3	2	4	1
B.	1	2	3	4
C.	1	4	2	3
D.	2	3	4	1

17. The state animal of Madhya Pradesh is
A. Musk deer
B. Swamp deer
C. Tiger
D. Crocodile

18. When was the 'Project Tiger' launched?
A. 1973 B. 1985 C. 1995 D. 1972

19. How many parks of Madhya Pradesh are under project tiger?
A. 4 B. 5 C. 6 D. 7

20. Which of the following is the only biosphere reserve located in Madhya Pradesh?
A. Panchmarhi
B. Betul
C. Panna
D. Madhavgarh

ANSWERS

1	2	3	4	5	6	7	8	9	10
A	C	C	D	C	B	C	B	A	A
11	**12**	**13**	**14**	**15**	**16**	**17**	**18**	**19**	**20**
A	B	D	C	A	B	B	A	C	A

❑❑❑

Agriculture

Agriculture is the basis of Madhya Pradesh's economy. Less than half of the land area is cultivable, however, and its distribution is quite uneven because of variations in topography, rainfall, and soils. The main cultivated areas are found in the Chambal valley, the Malwa Plateau, the Rewa Plateau, and the Chhattisgarh Plain. The Narmada valley, covered with river-borne alluvium, is another fertile area.

The most important crops are rice, wheat, sorghum (jowar), corn (maize), pulses (legumes such as peas, beans, or lentils), and peanuts (groundnuts). Rice is grown principally in the east, where there is more rainfall, while in western Madhya Pradesh wheat and sorghum are more important. The state is the largest soybean producer in India. Other crops include linseed, sesame, sugarcane, and cotton, as well as inferior millets, which are grown in hilly areas. The state is a large producer of opium (in the western district of Mandasaur, near Rajasthan) and marijuana (in the southwestern district of Khandwa [East Nimarh]).

Major Produce of Madhya Pradesh

Cereals : Wheat, Rice, Pulses, Jowar.

Oilseeds : Soyabean, Niger, Mustard.

Vegetables : Green Peas, Cauliflower, Okra, Tomato, Potato, Eggplant, Onion, Gourd.

Fruits : Mango, Guava, Orange, Melon, Papaya, Banana.

Spices : Garlic, Coriander, Ginger, Tur

Flower : Tube Rose, Roses, Marigold, Gladiolus

Land Holding Pattern

Size of land holding	% to total
Less than 1 ha.	44
1-2 ha	27
More than 2 ha	29
Total	**100**

Cropping Pattern

Madhya Pradesh is predominantly Kharif Crops growing State. Kharif Crops occupies about 59% whereas Rabi Crops occupies about 41% area out of the total cropped area in the State.

About 41% of cropped area generally occupied by cereal crops, while pulses occupied 21% area and oilseed occupied about 27% area. Rest 11% area is occupied by vegetables, fruits, fodder and other horticultural crops.

Wheat

India has the largest area in the world under wheat. However, in terms of production, we are only the second largest behind China. MP is one of the main wheat producing states with total production of 35,669 thousand Mt. tonnes (2020-21). The major districts in the state which produces wheat are Shivpuri, Guna, Vidisha, Raisen, Narsimhapur, Chhindwara, Hoshangabad and Betul.

The state enjoys distinct advantage due to production of specialized wheat varieties. Madhya Pradesh is a major producer of Durum Wheat in the country. Durum Wheat commands a higher price as compared to non durum wheat mainly on account of its use in processing wheat products.

Durum wheat has great demand in the international market; Durum which is one of the most important species of Wheat offers vast potential for its exports. Indore has developed a number of varieties like HI-8381 (Malvashree) and HI-8498 (Malvashakti) which are high yielder. Few varieties have also come from Maharashtra like MACS-2846 and MACS-2694, which offer good potential.

The State government is keen to promote organic production of wheat which had a substantial demand in the international market, and has already worked out a plan for this purpose.

Main Varieties of Wheat Grown in the State of Madhya Pradesh

Types of Wheat	Varieties
Sharbati	Sujata, Kalawal, Narmada-4, Narmada-Bara, 306
Duplicate Sharbati	147, Lok-van
Durum	Malavraj, Malavratna, Malavshri, Malavshakti, PBW-34, PDW-233. WH-896, HD-2189, K-9107, DWR-549 and HI varieties MPO-1106 - latest, commercial production to commence from current wheat year i.e. 2001-02.

Rice

In Madhya Pradesh, rice is cultivated in 41 districts, out of which only two districts are under medium productivity group (yield 2,000-2,500 kg/ha) and there is no area/district under high productivity group.

Recently, basmati varieties have been successfully grown in Gwalior and Morena districts of the state.

Varieties of Basmati/Aromatic Rice in MP

Small Grain	Chinore, Dubrej, Kalimooch, Bishnubhog, Badshah Bhog, Tulsi-Manjari
Medium Grain	Chatri, Modhuri, Vishnu Parag
Long Grain	Laloo

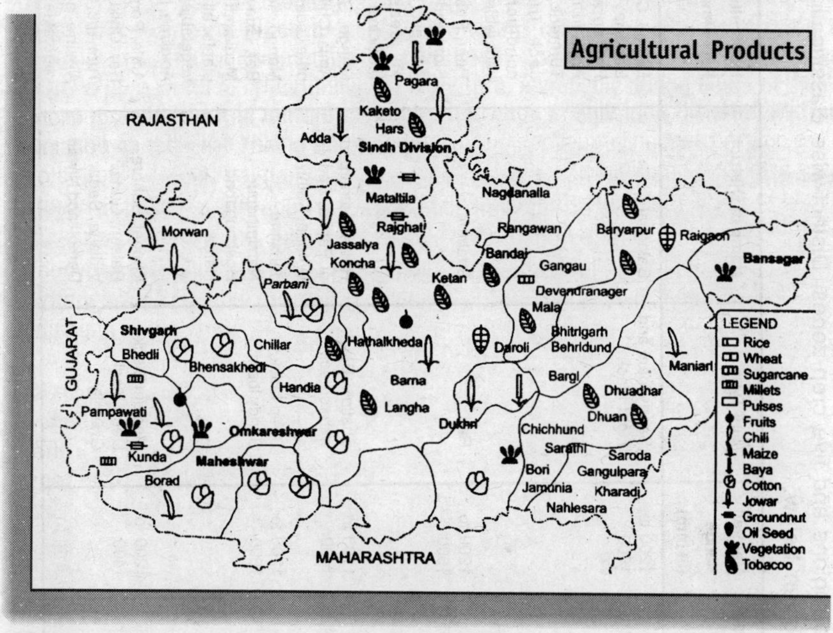

Oilseeds

India is the leading consumer of oilseeds in the world. Although India is the third largest producer of oilseeds in the world, yet it is also one of the largest importers of edible oils. Oilseeds, although occupying only 10 percent of the country's total cultivated land, play a dominant role in Indian economy. A very wide range of oilseeds produced in the state including mustard, groundnut, sunflower, sesame, rapeseed, safflower, soyabean, linseed and castor, gives a wide scope for an oil refining units and thus one unit for vegetable oil refining is also proposed.

Madhya Pradesh being the leading producing state of Soyabean in India contributes to around 51.4% of the total Indian production and is also called the soybean bowl in India.

Over the year, oil availability from soyabean has grown remarkably. Soyabean oil accounts for 13% of the total domestic oil production.

Agro-Climatic Regions and Crop Zones in the State

The state can be divided in 11 agro-climate regions and five crop zones. District-wise classification along with the soil type and normal rainfall range is given below:

S. No.	Crop Zone	Name of Agro-Climatic Region	Temperature	Rainfall Range (in mm)	Soil Type	Name of District	Horticulture Crops Recommended
1.	Rice Zone	Chhattisgarh plain Balaghat district	Min. Temp 2.5° C to 5° C	1200 to 1600	Sandy loam and Light black	Balaghat	Mango, Chiku, Guava, Lime, Banana, Papaya, Munga, Pomegranate, Colocasia, Amla in irrigated condition, Turmeric, Chillies, Ginger, Jack fruit, Ber in arid condition (all type of vegetables)
	Wheat Zone	Northern Hill region of Chhattisgarh	Min. Temp 0° C to 2.5° C	1200 to 1600	Red	Shahdol	Pear, Peach Litchi, Mango, Sidhi and Jack fruit, Coffee, Turmeric, Ginger, Tree spices off season vegetables, Medicinal and Aromatic crops
2.	Wheat and Rice Zone	Kymore plateau Satpura hills	Min. Temp 0° C to 2.5° C	1100 to 1400	Shallow, Black with red soil	Rewa, Satna part of Panna, Seoni, Umaria, Katni	Mango, Guava, Lime, Ber, Amla, Chillies, Coriander and other seasonal vegetables
3.	Wheat Zone	Central Narmada Valley	Min. Temp 2.5° C to 5° C	1200 to 1600	Deep black, Sandy loam	Jabalpur, Narsimhapur, Hoshangabad, Harda	Mango, Acidlime, Mandarin, Ber, Guava, Amla, Papaya, Medicinal and Aromatic plants, all types of seasonal vegetables, Mandarin, Acidlime, Mosambi
		Vindhya Plateau	Min. Temp 0° C to 2.5° C	1200 to 1400	Medium Black Deep black, Gravelly	Bhopal, Sehore, Raisen, Guna, Vidisha, Sagar, Damoh and Niwari	Amla, Pomegranate, Mango, Ber, Chiku, Papaya, Turmeric, Chillies, Coriander, Ajwine and all seasonal vegetables

S. No.	Crop Zone	Name of Agro-Climatic Region	Temperature	Rainfall Range (in mm)	Soil Type	Name of District	Horticulture Crops Recommended
4.	Wheat Jowar Zone	Grid region	Severe winter temperature below 0° C	800 to 1000	Alluvial, Loamy loam, Loamy light	Bhind, Morena, Sheopur, Gwalior Shivpuri	Mandarin and Sweet orange, Lime, Under assured irrigation and Guava, Ber, Amla, Custardapple under rainfed condition Coriander, Chillies, Garlic and seasonal vegetables
		Bundelkhand	Min. Temp	800 to 1400	Mixed red and black (medium)	Chhatarpur, Datia, Tikamgarh, part of Panna, (with protection in winter in early stages)	Orange, Mosambi, Acidlime, Amla, Mango, Chiku, Karonda, Ginger, Turmeric, Dioscoria, Colocasia
		Satpura Plateau	Min. Temp upto 0° C to 2.5° C	1000 to 1200	Shallow black gravelly	Betul and Chhindwara	Orange, Mosambi, Acidlime, Mango, Guava, Ber, Chillies, Turmeric, Flower Marigold, Colecrops and other vegetables
5.	Cotton-Jowar Zone	Malwa plateau	Min. Temp upto 0° C	1000 to 1200	Medium black gravelly	Shivpuri (partial), Guna, Ratlam, Ujjain, North part of Jhabua, Dhar, Indore and Dewas	Orange, Acidlime, Mosambi, Grape, Chiku, under irrigated conditions, Ber Guava, Pomegranate, Coriander, Fenugreek and vegetables
		Nimarh plains	Min. Temp 2.5° C to 5° C	800 to 1000	Medium black	Khandwa, Khargone, Kukshi, Manawar tehsil of Dhar district	Mango, Banana, Grape, Papaya, Chiku, Lime, Guava and Pomegranate in irrigated condition, Turmeric, Chillies, Colocasia, Fennel and seasonal vegetables

In Jowar production, Madhya Pradesh ranks after Andhra Pradesh, Maharashtra, and Karnataka, Jowar is a crop of moist climate and dryness (hot), Light loam soil is suitable of it.

Gram is a specific cereal which is also used as pulse. It is a Rabi Crop, sown in the month of October and harvested in March. In the beginning this crop requires moist climate but later on it requires dry season. Hoshangabad, Narsimhapur, Harda, Guna, Vidisha, Ujjain, Mandsaur, Neemuch, Indore, Dewas, Bhind, Morena, Raisen, Sheopur are the main grain producing areas.

Among the pulses—Tuar is an important crop. It is sown in entire state with Cotton and Jowar in Kharif season. Prabhat, Khargon-2, Type-21, Mukta, Gwalior-3, J. A.-3, C-11 are the types of Tuar sown in Madhya Pradesh, Chhindwara, Gwalior, Bhind, Morena, Sagar, Indore, Ujjain, Rewa, Khandwa and Narsimhapur districts of Southern and Eastern Madhya Pradesh are its main producing areas.

Groundnut is a Kharif Crops, which is grown both for oil and cereals. In Madhya Pradesh the groundnut is produced in Malwa Plateau and lower area of Narmada Valley. From the area as well as production of groundnut, point of view Madhya Pradesh ranks sixth.

Horticulture

Horticulture is an integral part of agriculture and an important source of income for the small and marginal farmers as the productivity and production of Horticulture crops are much more than the Agriculture. MP is endowed with varied agro-climatic conditions that offer immense scope for cultivation of various kinds of horticulture crops. This provides an excellent platform for MP to emerge as a leading producer of horticulture crops.

Horticulture in MP has achieved considerable growth rate during the last five years. The major fruit crops grown in the state are Banana, Orange, Guava, Lemon, Mango and Papaya. Most seasonal vegetables are grown extensively throughout the state.

Spices

MP is leader in seed and bulbous spices being the largest producer of Garlic and second largest producer of coriander and chillies in India.

Among spices, maximum area is under coriander followed by chillies and garlic. They together account for 85% of the total area under spices in MP.

Spices

S.No.	Name of Spices	Major Districts
1.	Turmeric	Tikamgarh, Khandwa, Badwani
2.	Garlic	Mandsaur, Ratlam, Ujjain, Dewas
3.	Coriander	Guna, Mandsaur, Rajgarh, Vidisha
4.	Chillies	Khargone, Dhar, Indore, Betul
5.	Ginger	Tikamgarh, Chhindwara, Khargone, Dewas
6.	Other spices	Ujjain, Shajapur, Sagar

Fruits

S.No.	Name of Fruits	Major Districts
1.	Banana	Khandwa, Rajgarh
2.	Guava	Hoshangabad, Badwani, Dhar
3.	Papaya	Dhar, Khandwa, Khargone, Hoshangabad
4.	Grapes	Guna, Mandsaur, Indore, Khandwa
5.	Mango	Rewa, Jabalpur, Shahdol, Katni
6.	Orange	Chhindwara, Mandsaur, Shajapur, Rajgarh
7.	Mosambi	Hoshangabad, Shajapur
8.	Lime	Hoshangabad, Khargone, Ujjain
9.	Other fruits	Indore, Hoshangabad, Khargone, Satna

Vegetables

S.No.	Name of Vegetables	Major Districts
1.	Tomato	Bhopal, Datia, Chhatarpur
2.	Brinjal	Sagar, Jabalpur, Bhopal, Khandwa
3.	Cabbage	Indore, Betul, Hoshangabad
4.	Cauliflower	Chhindwara, Indore, Hoshangabad
5.	Okra	Balaghat, Hoshangabad
6.	Pea	Ujjain, Indore, Hoshangabad
7.	Potato	Indore, Dewas, Ujjain
8.	Sweet potato	Surguja, Chhatarpur, Hoshangabad
9.	Onion	Khandwa, Shajapur, Sagar, Indore
10.	Other vegetables	Indore, Ujjain, Hoshangabad

Flowers

Name of Flowers	Major Districts
Medicinal and Aromatic Plants	Ujjain, Indore, Dewas, Ratlam, Shivpuri, Khargone

Contract Farming

Contract farming is a well established concept in developed nations. Although relatively new in India, it is rapidly gaining popularity and is being increasingly practised across the Country. Leading industrial houses, especially for whom agriculture produce forms an integral part of processing functions, has evinced significant interest in the practice.

With a well established agriculture practice, India presents vast opportunities for contract farming industry and companies across the globe are keenly evaluating the value proposition offered by various States in the country to practice contract farming.

To assist Madhya Pradesh realize present and upcoming opportunities in contract farming, the Government of Madhya Pradesh is keen to facilitate the development of a thriving contract farming industry in the State.

In this regard, the Government of Madhya Pradesh invites participation from the leading national and international agro products companies, agri-export houses, food processing, and pure play contract farming firms to engage in mass practice of contract farming in Madhya Pradesh.

Under the development option, the private player would enter into "Contract agreement" with individual farmers (with substantial land holding) or with a consortium of small farmers. The contract would unambiguously specify the terms and conditions pertaining to contracted acreage, quantity, price schedule, payment modalities, delivery schedule and other relevant concerns.

The farmers entering into contractual arrangement would dedicate their farms for specific crops and would be responsible for their cultivation, harvesting, primary processing and delivery. They would also be responsible for the day to day functioning and management of the farm.

The private partner would be responsible for planning in terms of crop rotation, product selection, grading & quality control, final procurement, logistics etc. Further, the private partner would assist the farmers by disseminating modern farming techniques providing access to high-end tools and machineries to facilitate mechanized farming on large scale.

Further, financial support and vital technical know how's (to improve quality & quantity of produce) would also be provided to the farmers by partnering with financial institutions, insurance firms and agriculture technology companies.

Following would be the key activities practised under contract farming:

- Seed multiplication
- Organic foods, vegetables and fruits
- Aromatic, herbal and medicinal plants
- Floriculture
- Exports specific crops

Animal Husbandry

Livestock sector alone contributes 8.05% of the state GDP. The 11 agroclimatic zones and rich biodiversity makes the Madhya Pradesh conducive for development of not only dairy and poultry but also for rearing of sheep, goat and pig.

Native breeds of Nimarhi, Kenkatha and Malvi are known for their superior drought power. Bhadawari breed of buffalo from northern parts of the state has been the champion in fat content of milk. The cross bred cows of Jersey and Holstein Friesen and pigs of white Yorkshire breed have very well acclimatized themselves to the state.

There are seven government cattle breeding farms and one bull rearing farm in the State.

Government Cattle Breeding Farms in the State

S.No.	Name	District
1.	Cattle Breeding Farm, Garhi	Balaghat
2.	Cattle Breeding Farm, Imlikheda	Chhindwara
3.	Cattle Breeding Farm, Minora	Tikamgarh
4.	Cattle Breeding Farm, Ratona	Sagar
5.	Cattle Breeding Farm, Bhadbhada	Bhopal
6.	Cattle Breeding Farm, Agar	Shajapur
7.	Cattle Breeding Farm, Rodia	Khargone
8.	Bull Rearing Farm, Amanala	Jabalpur

Sheep Breeding Farm

Four government sheep breeding farms are functioning in the state. The local sheep in the state produces poor quality of wool, so in order to improve the quality of wool of local sheep, the Rambullete are introduced in the farms. By this, the Rams are produced and distributed to the shepherds for breeding during breeding season.

Sheep Breeding Farms in the State

S.No.	Name	District
1.	Sheep Breeding Farm, Padora	Shivpuri
2.	Sheep Breeding Farm, Minora	Tikamgarh
3.	Sheep Breeding Farm, Bansakhedi	Mandsaur
4.	Sheep Breeding Farm, Shivpuri	Shivpuri

Madhya Pradesh State Cooperative Marketing Federation (MARKFED)

The Madhya Pradesh State Cooperative Marketing Federation (MARKFED) is an Apex level Federation of Cooperative Marketing Societies in the State of Madhya Pradesh. The Society is registered under the Madhya Pradesh Cooperative Societies Act 1960. Federation represents the numerous marketing and allied societies of the state. With the creation of the Chhattisgarh state the business activities of MARKFED have been bifurcated. M.P. MARKFED has an extensive network of branches in the state-

i. Zonal Offices - 7 ii. District Marketing Offices - 45

Objectives

1. To assist and strengthen its member marketing and other marketing societies in the state

2. To provide agricultural inputs to the farmers through member of societies numbering over six thousand to promote the production of their agricultural produce
3. To procure the agricultural produce from farmers in regulated Markets
4. To carry out welfare activities as per the state government directives
5. To construct godowns to increase the storage facilities in the state

The Madhya Pradesh State Agro-Industries Development Corporation Ltd.

The Madhya Pradesh State Agro-Industries Development Corporation Ltd. is a wholly Government company headquartered at the State Capital Bhopal which is actively engaged in promoting the agro potential of Madhya Pradesh.

Major Activities of Madhya Pradesh Agro are:

1. Marketing of Agricultural inputs such as Seeds, Pesticides, Agricultural Machineries, and Tractors, Irrigation systems such as Pump sets, Sprinkler and Drip system and Chemical Fertilizers.
2. Manufacture of High Quality Bio-Fertilizers such as Rhizobium, Azatobacter and PSB.
3. Promotion of Agro Processing Industries in Madhya Pradesh with special emphasis on units for Pulping, Brining and Freezing of Fruits, Vegetables and Floriculture.
4. Procurement and marketing of Vegetables and Fruits in raw and processed form for the Domestic and International market.
5. Providing incentives declared by the Central Government as well as State Government on different Incentive Schemes.

Madhya Pradesh State Seed Certification Agency

Madhya Pradesh State Seed Certifying Agency was established in 1980. It conducts certification for seeds production.

The purpose of seed certification is to maintain and make available to the public, through certification, high quality seeds and propagating materials of notified kind and varieties so grown and distributed as to ensure genetic identity and genetic purity. Seed Certifications also designed to achieve prescribed standards.

Madhya Pradesh State Livestock and Poultry Development Corporation

The MP State Livestock and Poultry Development Corporation was established 19th November 1982.

Vision

To improve, enrich and enhance Livestock and Poultry production in the state and increase the income levels of farmers involved in animal husbandry, particularly women. To get M.P. declared as a Goat state of the country.

Objectives

Production, procurement, collection, rearing and marketing of livestock and livestock products (except milk and milk products) poultry and poultry products.

Activities

- Supply of genetically superior animals to beneficiaries under different Govt. Schemes.
- Implementation of breed improvement Programme in the state.
- To increase the milk production in the state through National Programme on Cattle & Buffaloes breeding.
- To protect the Farmers from losses due to death of animals through livestock insurance scheme.
- Production and to market poultry and animal feed.

20th Livestock Census

- As per Livestock census 2019 total livestock in M.P. is 363.3 lakhs.

20th Livestock Census 2019

(in million)

S.No.	Livestock	Livestock Census 2019	% Increase Decrease
1.	Cattle	18.7	–4.42
2.	Buffaloes	10.3	25.88
3.	Goats	11.06	38.07
4.	Horses & Poneys	0.13	–29.48
5.	Donkeys	0.03	–063.61

Fisheries Sector

Inland fishery is an integral component of rural development programme in Madhya Pradesh. It is gaining increasing importance for its potential for employment and income generation. It caters primarily to the needs of socio-economically weaker and backward communities of fishermen, scheduled tribes and scheduled castes, which constitute the poorest section of the society. Fish is an important source of protein rich food.

Madhya Pradesh possesses 4.04 lakh hectares of water area in the form of large, medium and small irrigation reservoirs, village's ponds and private ponds. The river and their tributaries form a network of 17088 km. The tributaries of Ganges, Yamuna like Chambal, Betwa, Ken, Sone and Sindh have their origin in the state. Under NVDA some newly constructed reservoir having about 0.83813 lac ha. water area are also available for development of fishery activities.

TEST YOUR SELF

1. Highest percentage of land holdings in Madhya Pradesh lies in

A. less than 1 hectare
B. 1-2 hectares
C. more than 2 hectares
D. none of these

2. Highest percentage of land occupied in Madhya Pradesh by

A. cereals
B. pulses
C. oilseeds
D. vegetables

3. *Sujat, Kalawal* and *Malavraj* are varieties of which crops produced in Madhya Pradesh?

A. Jowar
B. Wheat
C. Bajra
D. Rice

4. *Laloo* is a variety of

A. small grain rice
B. medium grain rice
C. long grain rice
D. both B and C

5. Balaghat district in Madhya Pradesh lies in agro-climatic regions of

A. Wheat zone
B. Rice zone
C. Wheat-Rice zone
D. Wheat-Jowar zone

6. Khandwa and Rajgarh are main producers of

A. Lime
B. Orange
C. Banana
D. Papaya

7. Turmeric in Madhya Pradesh is mainly produced in

A. Khandwa, Badwani
B. Guna, Mandsaur
C. Ujjain, Shajapur
D. Rajgarh, Chhindwara

8. The Madhya Pradesh state Agro-Industries Development Corporation Ltd. is headquartered at

A. Jabalpur
B. Bhopal
C. Satna
D. Indore

9. Madhya Pradesh Seed Certification Agency was established in

A. 1963
B. 1972
C. 1980
D. 1985

10. Madhya Pradesh State Livestock and Poultry Development Corporation was established in

A. 1871
B. 1975
C. 1978
D. 1982

11. Madhya Pradesh is divided into how many agricultural zones?

A. 9
B. 8
C. 7
D. 11

12. Which district of Madhya Pradesh produces maximum soyabean?
A. Hoshangabad
B. Ujjain
C. Mandla
D. Vidisha

13. Which district of Madhya Pradesh produces maximum opium?
A. Khandwa
B. Satna
C. Mandsaur
D. Mandla

14. Which district of Madhya Pradesh has maximum net agricultural land?
A. Ujjain
B. Hoshangabad
C. Neemuch
D. Morena

15. Which of the following crops is produced maximum in Madhya Pradesh?
A. Flower
B. Paddy
C. Wheat
D. Gram

ANSWERS

1	2	3	4	5	6	7	8	9	10
A	A	B	C	B	C	A	B	C	D
11	**12**	**13**	**14**	**15**					
D	B	C	A	C					

❑❑❑

Irrigation

Introduction

Although most of the agriculture in India depends upon rain for the water supply, but the cropping which is done in non-rainy season or the crops which could not get enough water through rain have to be supplied water through artificial means. To ensure this water supply for agriculture artificially is known as irrigation. In terms of availability of irrigation, Madhya Pradesh comes under backward states. The total irrigated areas in the state is 125.15 lakh hectares (2019-20), which is 80.6% of the cropped area. At the district level, the maximum irrigated area is under Hoshangabad district *i.e.*, 87% and the minimum is in Dindori district, *i.e.*, just 0.6%.

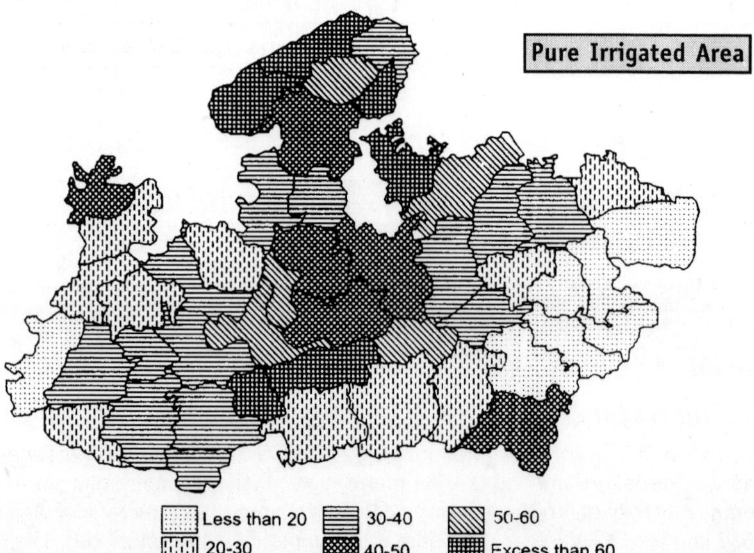

Sources of Irrigation

The total irrigated area of Madhya Pradesh is 125.15 lakh hectares out of which around 78.56% is irrigated through wells, handpumps and borewells. Hence, these remain the most important sources of irrigation in the state. Alongwith this, canals and ponds are the other major sources for irrigation. The various means of irrigation and their distribution as per area is as:

Wells and Tubewells: These are the major sources of irrigation as around 78.56% area of net irrigated zone are irrigated through these traditional means. These are most popular sources of irrigation in the Western districts. To draw the water from wells, electricity run motors and diesel pump sets are used. Being cheap and easily available, these are most common among small farmers.

Canals: Canals irrigate the 22.11% area of the net irrigated area. Although, a good network of canals has improved the picture of agriculture in the state upto a good extent, but their contribution in the net irrigated area is continuously decreasing because of high rate of investment and time taking development of projects.

Ponds: Around 3.79% of the net irrigated area is irrigated through ponds. In the Balaghat, Shivni and Panna districts major irrigation is done through the ponds.

Other Sources: Other sources like rivers, drains, etc irrigate the 13.03% area of the state. Such traditional means are majorly popular among small farmers in Sagar, Damoh, Panna, Katni, Umaria, Shahdol etc.

Major Sources of Irrigation

S.No.	Source	Irrigated Area (000 Hec.)
1.	Wells and Tubewells	9831.9
2.	Canals	2766.8
3.	Ponds	474.4
4.	Others	1630.9

Major Irrigation Projects

As Madhya Pradesh has a vast network of small and big rivers, many irrigation projects have been developed over them. The major projects of these are:

Chambal Valley Project

Gandhi Sagar Dam

This is the first of the four Chambal Valley Projects, located on the Rajasthan-Madhya Pradesh border. It is a 64-metre high masonry gravity dam, with a live storage capacity of 6,920 mm^3 and a catchment area of 22,584 km^2, of which only 1,537 km^2 are in Rajasthan. The dam was completed in the year 1960. The hydro-power station is located at the dam site and comprises five generating units, four of 23 MW each and one 27 MW capacity. The water released after power generation is utilised for irrigation through Kota Barrage. Rajasthan has a 50% share in the power generation of this station.

Rana Pratap Sagar Dam

It is located 52 km downstream of Gandhi Sagar dam across the river Chambal in Rajasthan. This dam was completed in the year 1970.

It is a straight masonry gravity structure, 54 metres high. The power house is located on the left side of the spillway and consists of 4 units of 43 MW each, with firm power generation of 90 MW at 60% load factor. The total catchment area of this dam is 24,864 km^2, of which only 956 km^2 are in Rajasthan. The free catchment area below Gandhi Sagar dam is 2,280 km^2. The live storage capacity is 1,566 mm^3. Rajasthan State has a 50% share in the power generation of this station.

Jawahar Sagar Dam

It is located 29 km upstream of Kota city and 26 km downstream of Rana Pratap Sagar dam, across the river Chambal. It is a concrete gravity dam, 45 metre high and 393 m long, generating 60 MW of power with an installed capacity of 3 units of 33 MW. The work was completed in 1972. The total catchment area of the dam is 27,195 km^2, of which only 1,496 km^2 are in Rajasthan. Rajasthan has a 50% share in the power generation of this station.

Kota Barrage

It is located about 0.8 km upstream of Kota City in Rajasthan. Water released after power generation at Gandhi Sagar, Rana Pratap Sagar and Jawahar Sagar Dams, is diverted by Kota Barrage for irrigation in Rajasthan and in Madhya Pradesh through canals on the left and the right sides of the river. The work on this dam was completed in 1960.

The total catchment area of Kota Barrage is 27,332 km^2, of which the free catchment area below Jawahar Sagar Dam is just 137 km^2. The live storage is 99 mm^3. It is an earthfill dam with a concrete spillway. The right and left main canals have a headworks discharge capacity of 188 and 42 m^3/sec, respectively. The total length of the main canals, branches and distribution system is about 2,342 km, serving an area of 229 kha of CCA. 50% of the water intercepted at Kota Barrage has been agreed to be diverted to MP for irrigation.

Halali Project

The Samrat Ashok Sagar (Halali Project) is constructed across river Halali, a tributary of Betwa. The dam is located near village Khowa at border of Raisen and Vidisha district in Madhya Pradesh. The project comprises of an earthen dam 945 metre long with maximum height of 29.57 metre above foundation level. The left bank canal 3.24 km long with head discharge capacity of 22.64 cumec, bifurcates into right bank and left bank canal of length 17.61 km and 23.43 km respectively to irrigate 37,636 hectare annually in Raisen and Vidisha district.

Narmada Valley Project

Rani Avanti Bai Lodhi Sagar (Bargi)

The Rani Avanti Bai Lodhi Sagar (Bargi) project is major multipurpose project across river Narmada in Madhya Pradesh. The main dam is located at a distance of about 45 km from Jabalpur city. The project has a composite earthen and masonry dam with a canal system on the left bank to provides annual irrigation of 2,19,000 hectare in Jabalpur and Narsimhapur district. It also provides water supply of 54 Mcum to Jabalpur city. The project has also hydro power generation capacity of 100 MW.

Tawa Reservoir

Tawa Reservoir is also known as the Tawa Dam. It is located at the confluence of the Denwa and Tawa rivers. The reservoir is considered to be the third largest reservoir of the Narmada Valley Project, which provides water for irrigation of the nearby farming lands. This dam was constructed over a period of two decades, extending between 1958 and 1978.

Maan Dam

The Maan dam is one of the biggest project in the Narmada Valley Development Project, built on the river Maan in Dhar district in Madhya Pradesh. River Maan is one of the tributaries of Narmada river.

Shahid Chandra Shekhar Azad Sagar (Jobat)

The Shahid Chandra Shekhar Azad Sagar (Jobat) project in Madhya Pradesh is an irrigation project envisaging construction of a composite dam across river Hathni, a tributary of river Narmada, which is near village Waskal, 24 km from Kukshi town. The Jobat Irrigation Project is planned to benefit the drought prone area declared by Government of India and tribal areas of Kukshi Tehsil in Dhar District of Madhya Pradesh. The dam is in Jhabua District, while the command is located in Dhar District.

Indira Sagar Project

Indira Sagar Project is a Multipurpose project which will have the largest storage capacity in the country. It will have an installed capacity of 1000 MW and annual irrigation of 27.5 lakh hectare.

Omkareshwar Dam

The Omkareshwar Dam is one of the major down stream dam of Indira Sagar Project, lies along the bank for the Narmada and Kaveri. Omkareshwar Jyotirlinga, one of the 12 Jyotirlinga is situated on the confluence of river Narmada and Kaveri.

Maheshwar Dam

Maheshwar is one of the planned large dams on the Narmada Valley to provide 400 MW electricity. The town of Maheshwar is situated in Khargone district of Madhya Pradesh on the bank of Narmada River and famous for Maheshwar fort, Rammandir, Ahalya fort and Ek Mukhi Datta Temple.

Parbati-Kalisindh-Chambal Link

Parbati-Kalisindh-Chambal link project envisages the diversion of surplus waters of Parbati and Kalisindh sub-basins to Gandhisagar dam /Rana Pratap Sagar dam across Chambal River. The water will be utilized for irrigation in the new command areas enroute the link canal & the existing command of Chambal system at Kota barrage. Water of the Chambal thus saved by way of substitution will be tapped in the upper reaches and will be utilised in the drought prone districts of Upper Chambal sub-basin, where the present level of irrigation is 5.44% of culturable area.

Irrigation Projects in Madhya Pradesh

Project	River	Description	Areas under these Projects
Narmada Valley Project (Omkareshwar, Maheshwar, Sardar Sarovar, Indira Sagar)	Narmada and its 41 tributaries	There are 29 large, 135 medium and 3600 small projects under this project. An amount of 2600 MW of electricity is produced and 27.5 lakh hectare is being irrigated by the Indira Sagar Project in MP and the same work is done by the Sardar Sarovar Project near Bhadoch at Gujarat. Another Indira Sagar Project is at Punasa of Khandawa. Mrs Indira Gandhi inaugurated this plant on 23rd October, 1984. The Indira Sagar and Omakareshwar Projects are two large projects under which about 3-lakh hectare area will be irrigated.	All the districts from the beginning to the end of Narmada, Gujarat, Rajasthan, Maharashtra and Madhya Pradesh

Project	River	Description	Areas under these Projects
Chambal Valley Project	Chambal	This project is the joint venture of Rajasthan and Madhya Pradesh. This project started into three stages in 1954. (i) The Gandhi Sagar Project completed in 1960 (ii) Rana Pratap Sagar (iii) Jawahar Sagar (Kota bairaj) The canals on the left side irrigates Rajasthan.	Bhind, Morena, Gwalior, Shivpuri
Halali Project	Halali	This dam was built in the year 1973-76. It is 29.57 m high and 945 in long, it irrigates about 37,636 hectare of land.	Vidisha, Raisen
Pench	Pench	It is a joint project of MP and Maharashtra, it irrigates 63.388 hectare of land.	Balaghat, Chhindawara
Baansagar	Sone	It is a joint project of Madhya Pradesh, Uttar Pradesh and Bihar. The contribution of these three is in the ratio 50 : 25 : 25 respectively, it produces 405 MW of electricity.	Districts of Rewa and Sidhi in Madhya Pradesh
Bargi Project (*Rani Avantibai Sagar Project*)	Bargi (Jabalpur)	The dam was built in the year 1917. It is 69 it high, it irrigates 2.5-lakh hectare of land.	Jabalpur, Mandla, Seoni
Matatila Dam (*Rani Laxmibai Project*)	Betwa	It is a joint project of Madhya Pradesh and Uttar Pradesh, it irrigates 1.09 hectare of land and 1.16 hectare of land in Madhya Pradesh.	6 districts of Uttar Pradesh and 4 districts of MP
Baandh Project	Baandh	This dam is at the border of Madhya Pradesh. It is built to irrigate the areas of Madhya Pradesh.	Madhya Pradesh and Maharashtra

Project	River	Description	Areas under these Projects
Bawanthadi	Bawanthadi	It is a joint project of Madhya Pradesh and Maharashtra. It irrigates 17357 hectare of land in Maharashtra and 18615 hectare of land in Madhya Pradesh.	Madhya Pradesh and Maharashtra
Tawa	Tawa (Hoshangabad)	Capacity—it has the capacity to irrigate 3.33-lakh hectare of land. At present 2.47-lakh hectare of land is irrigated.	Hoshangabad
Barana	Barana	This dam is situated near village Bari. It irrigates 60290 hectare of land.	Raisen
Ken Multipurpose Project	Ken	It is a joint project of Madhya Pradesh and Uttar Pradesh, it generates 50 MW of electricity.	Chhatarpur, Panna
Singhpur Barrage	Urmil	This is a proposed project. The canals at to be made by Madhya Pradesh and the dams are to be built by Uttar Pradesh.	Chhatarpur
Urmil	Urmil	The water distribution ratio from this dam to Madhya Pradesh and Uttar Pradesh is 60 : 40. The length of canal in Madhya Pradesh is 137 km.	Chhatarpur
Kaali Sagar	Supplementary of Bandh	This dam is supplementary of river Bandh. It irrigates 1174 land of MP and 3522 hectare land of Maharashtra.	Madhya Pradesh and Maharashtra
Kolardam	Kolar	It is the irrigator of Sehore and the water supplier of Bhopal. It irrigates 60887 hectare of land.	Sehore
Maahi	Maahi	It has two dams and two canals. The canal at Dhaar lengths 137 km, irrigates 7913 hectare of land. The canal at Jhabua irrigates 18517 km.	Dhaar, Jhabua

Project	River	Description	Areas under these Projects
Bhander Canal	Betwa	Length-57.6 km irrigates 44535 hectare of land.	Datia, Gwalior, Bhind
Upper Baanganga (*Sanjay Sarovar*)	Baanganga	Capacity-irrigates 103722 hectare of land.	Balaghat, Seoni
Thavar	Thavar	Capacity-irrigates 18212 hectare of land	Mandla
Sukta	Sukta (Khandwa)	Capacity-irrigates 15583 hectare of land.	Water supplier of Khandwa
Sindhu	Sindh	Water supplier of Gwalior, it irrigates 35200 hectare of land.	Shivpuri, Gwalior
Dejla Dewara	Yoral	Capacity-irrigates 9000 hectare of land.	Khargone
Choral	Choral (Indore)	Capacity-irrigates 5000 hectare of land of Mau.	Mau
Narganva	Auxiliaries of Ken river	This is a joint project of Madhya Pradesh and Uttar Pradesh, it irrigates 16190 hectare of land at Chhatarpur.	Chhatarpur

Canals of Madhya Pradesh

1. **Mahanadi Project Canals:** The Mahanadi canals have been constructed fewer than three stages providing irrigation to about 3.4 lakh hectares of land. The scheme involves construction of barrage across the Mahanadi at Rudri across the Sandur River under Ravishankar Sagar Project, feeder canal, Pairi dam and 1,145 km long irrigation canals.
2. **Wainganga Canal:** It takes off from the Wainganga River (length 45 km) to irrigate about 4,000 hectares of land in Balaghat, Seoni (Madhya Pradesh) and Bhandara (Maharashtra) districts.
3. **Tandula Canal:** Under this scheme two earthen dams have been built near the confluence of the Tandula and Sukha rivers. Canals taken out from these are providing irrigation to about 66,000 hectares of cropland in Raipur and Durg districts.
4. **Chambal Project Canals:** This scheme involves construction of three dams. Canals under this scheme irrigate about 5.15 lakh hectares of agricultural land in Gwalior, Bhind, Morena and Datia districts. The main branches of the canal are the Ambah and the Morena.

5. **Barna Project Canals:** The Barna project involves the construction of a barrage across the Barna river (a tributary of the Narmada) and canals which irrigate about 64,400 hectares of land in Raisen district.
6. **Tawa Project Canals:** Canals originating from the barrage across the Tawa River with total length of 197 km irrigate about 3 lakh hectares of area in Hoshangabad district.
7. **Halali Project Canals:** Under this project canals have been taken out from the barrage built across the Halali River to irrigate about 73,500 hectares of cropped area in Vidisha district.

Major Canals of Madhya Pradesh

S.No.	Canal	River	Districts benefiting
1.	Chambal canal	Chambal river	Morena, Bhind, Gwalior, Sheopur, Neemuch, Mandsaur
2.	Wainganga canal	Wainganga river	Balaghat and Bhandara district of Maharashtra
3.	Halali canal	Betwa river	Raisen, Vidisha
4.	Tawa canal	Tawa river	Hoshangabad
5.	Barna canal	Barna	Hoshangabad

TEST YOUR SELF

1. The total irrigated area in Madhya Pradesh is
   A. 33 per cent B. 80.6 per cent
   C. 42 per cent D. 47 per cent
2. The maximum irrigated area in Madhya Pradesh is under the district of
   A. Dindori B. Umaria C. Shahdol D. Hoshangabad
3. The minimum irrigated area in Madhya Pradesh is under district of
   A. Panna B. Katni C. Dindori D. Shivni
4. Which among the following is the major sources of irrigation in Madhya Pradesh?
   A. Canals B. Wells and Tubewells
   C. Ponds D. Other sources
5. Which among the following districts of Madhya Pradesh is not benefitted from Wainganga canal?
   A. Balaghat B. Morena C. Gwalior D. Both B and C
6. Halali canal in Madhya Pradesh emerges from river
   A. Chambal B. Barna C. Halali D. Wainganga

7. Gandhi Sagar Dam is located on the river
   A. Wainganga B. Chambal
   C. Betwa D. Barna

8. Samrat Ashok Sagar is constructed across the river
   A. Halali B. Chambal C. Narmada D. Barna

9. Which among the following is not a part of Narmada Valley Project?
   A. Tawa Reservoir
   B. Maan Dam
   C. Rani Avanti Bai Lodhi Sagar Project
   D. Omkareshwar Dam

10. Baansagar project is located on river
    A. Peuch B. Sone C. Bargi D. Betwa

11. 'Narmada Bachao Andolan' is associated with
    A. JP Narayan B. Medha Patkar
    C. P Chidambaram D. HN Bahuguna

12. Which district is highly dependent on ponds for irrigation?
    A. Harda B. Shivni C. Dindori D. Hoshangabad

ANSWERS

1	2	3	4	5	6	7	8	9	10
B	D	C	B	D	C	B	A	D	B
11	12								
B	B								

❑❑❑

Mineral Resources

Madhya Pradesh is one of the most important states regarding mineral production. The State has vast resources of coal. Most of the coal available is of low grade, has high ash content and is of non-cooking type. Chhindwara, Balaghat, Shahdol, Rajgarh, Jabalpur, Sidhi and Betul are important coal producing districts of the State. Coal produced in the State is not suited for metallurgical purposes.

Iron deposits are found in the district of Khandwa, Khargone, Hoshangabad, Betul, Narsimhapur, Sagar, Gwalior and Jabalpur.

Bauxite is used for producing aluminium. It is found in Amarkantak region, Katni in Jabalpur, Baihar in Balaghat and also in Raigarh, Mandla, Seoni, Chhindwara, Guna, Jhabua and Gwalior districts.

Manganese ore is used for making steel, colouring glasses, chemical production, etc. Balaghat is the most important manganese producing district. Besides this, it is also found in Chhindwara, Jabalpur and Indore districts.

Diamonds are produced in the district of Panna. The Majhgawan area is the richest diamond producing area in the Panna district.

Limestone has a variety of uses. The State is rich in limestone deposits. The Chhattisgarh region and Jabalpur-Satna belt have rich deposits of limestones. Limestones are also found in Rewa, Morena, Raigarh and Narsimhapur districts.

Quartz and Silica sand are used in manufacturing glasses and telecommunications. It is found in parts of Morena, Dewas, Satna, Gwalior, Jabalpur, and Vidisha districts.

Dolomite is used in paints and rubber industries and pharmaceutical industries. It is found in Jabalpur districts. The dolomite of Bhedaghat is of very pure variety. It is now also found in Mandla, Narsimhapur and Morena districts.

Corundum is used in optical industries. It is found in Sidhi district only.

Copper is very important mineral used in variety of industries. They are found in Malanjkhand in Balaghat district.

Fire Clay is used in the establishment of all kinds of furnances in steel, cement and other industries. The State is rich in fire clay and is found in Jabalpur, Chhindwara, Shivpuri, Gwalior, Satna, Shahdol, Hoshangabad and Jhabua districts. High quality clay is found in parts of Narsimhapur, also found in Morar (Gwalior) and Mandsaur.

Phosphorite deposits are found in Sagar, Jhabua and Chhattarpur districts.

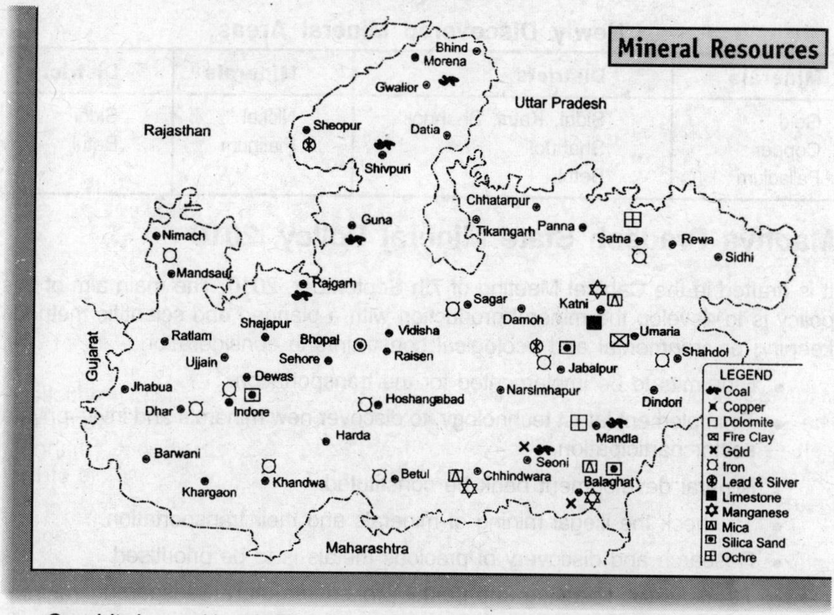

Graphite is used in number of industries. Small deposits of graphite are located in Betul district.

Soap and Talc Stone are found in Jabalpur and Jhabua districts. *Felspar* is located in Jabalpur and Chhindwara districts. *Sillimanite* deposits are located in Sindhi and Rewa districts. *Lead* deposits are found in Hoshangabad, Jabalpur, and Shivpuri districts. *Mica* is found in Chhindwara and Balaghat districts.

Madhya Pradesh : Mineral Producing Districts

Minerals	Districts
Diamond	Panna, Satna, Jabalpur
Manganese	Balaghat, Chhindwara, Jhabua, Khargone
Iron ore	Balaghat, Mandla, Jabalpur, Vidisha
Copper	Balaghat, Jabalpur, Hoshangabad, Sagar
Coal	Shahdol, Chhindwara, Hoshangabad, Betul
Limestone	Jabalpur, Mandsaur, Satna, Katni
Bauxite	Mandla, Jabalpur, Rewa, Satna, Shahdol, Sidhi
Dolomite	Balaghat, Narsimhapur, Shivni, Chhindwara, Jabalpur
Tungsten	Agargaon (Hoshangabad)
Asbestos	Balaghat, Chhindwara, Hoshangabad, Jhabua, Mandsaur
Pyrite	Surajpur, Devas, Dhar, Jhabua, Shivpuri
Slate	Mandsaur
Antimony	Jabalpur
Talc	Jabalpur, Jhabua, Narsimhapur
Caoline	Rewa, Antri, Gwalior

Newly Discovered Mineral Areas

Minerals	Districts	Minerals	Districts
Gold Copper Palladium	Sidhi, Katni, Shahdol Shahdol Betul	Nickel Platinum	Sidhi Betul

Madhya Pradesh State Mineral Policy, 2010

It is drafted in the Cabinet Meeting of 7th September, 2010. The main aim of this policy is to develop the mineral production with a planned and scientific methods keeping environmental and ecological constraints in consideration.

- E-permits to be implemented for the transportation.
- To implement latest technology, to discover new minerals and invite private sector participation.
- Mineral development bank be constituted.
- To check the illegal mining of minerals and their transportation.
- Research and discovery of precious metals is to be prioritised.
- To make the licensing and permit procedures more transparent.

TEST YOUR SELF

1. Copper is mainly found in ....
A. Balaghat B. Satna C. Rewa D. Betul

2. In which district of Madhya Pradesh, antimony is found?
A. Balaghat B. Jabalpur C. Datia D. Morena

3. The only diamond producing state of India is
A. Madhya Pradesh B. Andhra Pradesh
C. Rajasthan D. Bihar

4. Diamond is found in the district of ....
A. Dewas B. Panna C. Jhabua D. Shivni

5. Platinum is found in
A. Jhabua B. Balaghat C. Betul D. Mandsaur

6. Tungsten is found in the Agargaon region of
A. Betul B. Hoshangabad
C. Jhabua D. Jabalpur

7. Gondwana group of rocks are rich in ....
A. sandstone and coal B. granite
C. diamonds and coal D. limestone

8. Sidhi, Katni and Shahdol are famous for
A. diamond B. platinum C. gold D. nickel

9. Which of the following rocks in the State of Madhya Pradesh are devoid of any fossils?
A. Dharwar
B. Archaean
C. Cuddapah
D. Vindhyan system of rocks

10. Which region of Madhya Pradesh is called Gondwana?
A. Narmada Valley
B. Chambal Valley
C. Northern Region
D. South-East Region

ANSWERS

1	2	3	4	5	6	7	8	9	10
A	B	A	B	C	B	A	C	B	D

❑❑❑

Industry

Madhya Pradesh is endowed with rich mineral, forest and agricultural resources.

All these factors provide a sound base for a establishment and development of various type of industries in the state yet Industries have come up only in selected pockets. Such as Indore, Bhopal, Ujjain, Jabalpur, Gwalior, Satna etc. whereas the rest of the state is industrial backward.

Constant efforts are being made by the state government for planned growth of Industries, specially medium and large scale industries. In the state for removing regional imbalances and dispersal of Industries in backward districts areas. Some time back the state government had taken a decision to promote large/medium Industries in those districts where such industries did not exist. As a large result of the various incentives provided by the state government's intensive efforts and persuasion, there has been a very good response from the entrepreneurs to establish industries is backward district/areas also.

A good number of new units have been established in these areas and a large number of proposals has been received and processed for establishments of large, medium and small scale industries.

Cement Industry: Limestone is found in abundance in Madhya Pradesh. The first cement factory was built at Banmore (Morena) by ACC Cement way back in 1922-23. At present there are more than 23 such factories at Kemur, Satna, Maihar, Neemuch etc.

Sugar Industry: The first sugar mill in the state was established at Jawra (Ratlam) in 1934. Since sugarcane is cultivated majorly in the Western districts of the state, major sugar mills are situated in the Western districts of the state. The largest sugar mill of the state is at Barlai in Sehore. Other major sugar mills of the state are Bhopal Sugar Mill (Sehore), Dabra Sugar Mill (Gwalior), Jivajirao Sugar Company (Mandsaur) and Jaura Sugar Mill (Ratlam) etc.

Paper Industry: The first paper mill in the state was National News Print and Paper Mill established at Nepanagar in 1956 near Khandwa. Today there are nine registered paper mills in the state. Orient Paper Mill established at Amlai near Shahdol district is most important of all.

Cotton-based Industry: First cotton mill of the state was established in 1906 at Burhanpur. Indore is the largest centre of production of cotton in the state. The other cotton centres are at Gwalior and Ujjain.

Artificial Thread Industry: This is comparatively a recent industry in the state. For these the raw material is procured from Mumbai, Gwalior and Dewas situated artificial thread producing mills. In Madhya Pradesh, major artificial thread cloth producing centres are at Indore, Gwalior, Nagda, Ujjain and Dewas.

Hydrogenated Oil: Oilseeds and soyabean are cultivated in the state on a mass scale. Hence, the production of hydrogenated oil is quite easy and popular here. Most of the factories are situated in the oil producing belts of the state like Malwa Plateau, Betul-Chhindwara Plateau, Central Narmada Valley and Chambal Valley area. Major oil mills in the state are in Ganj Bsauda, Jabalpur, Khandwa, Gwalior, Indore and Morena.

China Clay Industry: Due to the easy availability of China clay in the state, at Gwalior, Jabalpur and Ratlam some major China clay factories have been developed. In the state the fire clay bricks, pice and basins are also built at Katni and Jabalpur.

Heavy Electric Appliances: In Bhopal, with the help of Britain, in 1960 this industry was developed. It is known by the name of Bharat Heavy Electricals. In such factories transformers, capacitors, switchgears, electric fraction and industrial motors etc. are produced.

Beedi Industry: Since Madhya Pradesh is first in the procurement of tendu-leaves in the country. A fully established Beedi industry has been developed at Jabalpur, Sagar, Katni, Damoh and Satna.

Timber Industry: In Chhindwara and Mandla Timber Industry is majorly established.

Kattha Industry: Due to the abundance of Kattha trees in the state, the Kattha industry is very well flourished here. It is majorly run by the tribals of Khairwar tribe. Also there are a few units in Shivpuri and Banmor.

Chemical Industries: At Ujjain, Pithampur, Mandideep, Baidhan, Maksi, Sehore, Ratlam, Panna, Neemuch and other places chemicals, fertilizers and pesticides manufacturing units have been developed. Till 2008, 70 such units were already working. Detergent producing factories are at Pithampur, Chhindwara, Malanpur, Mandideep and at Singrauli the explosives manufacturing factories have been established.

Central Public Sector Industries

Industry	Place
Cotton Clothes and Yarn Industry	Indore, Bhopal, Burhanpur, Ujjain
Government Ordnance Factory	Khamaria (Jabalpur)
Gun Carriage Factory	Jabalpur
Heavy Vehicle Factory	Jabalpur
Government Telegraph and Post Workshop	Jabalpur
Hindustan Copper Project	Malanjkhand (Balaghat)
Northern Coal-field Project	Singrauli
Grey Iron Foundry	Bhopal
National News Print Mill	Nepanagar
Security Paper Limited	Hoshangabad
Currency Printing Press	Dewas
Alkaloid Factory (morphine and narcotic refinery)	Neemuch (Mandsaur)
Rail Coach Factory	Bhopal
Diesel Engine (rail)	Indore
Slate Factory	Mandsaur
Cotton Seed Solvent Extraction Plant	Ujjain
Pipe and Foundry Limited	Ujjain
Indian Heavy Electrical	Bhopal

Small Scale Industries

Industry	Place
Tungsten	Indore
Bakery	Indore
Plastic	Indore
Drugs and Pharmaceuticals	Indore, Ratlam
Glue and Gelatin	Indore, Bhopal, Jabalpur
Silk Industry	Indore, Ujjain, Dewas
Caustic Soda	Nepanagar, Amlai, Nagda
Moped Industry	Gwalior
Alcohol Industry	Ratlam
Dry Battery	Bhopal
Diamond Carving and Polishing Industry	Panna
Handloom Clothes	Jabalpur, Burhanpur, Chanderi
Graphite Electrode	Mandideep
Valve Engine	Bhopal
Fire Bricks	Katni, Jabalpur
Biscuit Factory	Gwalior

Industrial Growth Centres

There are 26 Industrial Growth Centres established in the state with a view to attract medium and large industries and the Non Resident Indians (NRIs) to the State and to provide various facilities and concessions to them. These Industrial Growth Centres have been set up under the five Audhyogik Kendra Vikas Nigams (AVKN), established by the Audhyogik Vikas Nigam.

List of industrial growth centres comes under different AKVN's

MP AKVN, Gwalior

Name	Nearest Town	Distance (Kms)
Malanpur	Gwalior	18
Ghirongi	Gwalior	18
Banmore	Gwalior	18
Pratappura	Jhansi	09
Sidgunwa	Sagar	12
Chainpura	Guna	32

MP AKVN, Jabalpur

Name	Nearest Town	Distance (Kms)
Bore Gaon	Nagpur	60
Maneri	Jabalpur	35
Puraina	Katni	22

MP AKVN, Bhopal

Name	Nearest Town	Distance (Kms)
Mandideep	Bhopal	22
Satlapur	Bhopal	25
Pilukhedi	Bhopal	50

MP AKVN, Indore

Name	Nearest Town	Distance (Kms)
Pithampur	Indore	30
Kheda	Indore	35
Maksi	Ujjain	37
Meghnagar	Jhabua	15

MP AKVN, Rewa

Name	Nearest Town	Distance (Kms)
Sidhi		
Waidhan	Singrauli	
Rewa	Udhyog Vihar	

SEZ in Madhya Pradesh

Madhya Pradesh : Special Economic Zone (SEZ)

SEZ	Development Agency	Location	Present Status
Multi-product SEZ, Indore	Industrial Centre Development Authority, Indore	Dhaar	First working greenfield SEZ of the state
Crystal IT Park, Indore	Industrial Centre Development Authority, Indore	Indore	Board of Approval, Commerce Ministry, Government of India notified for ITSEZ
Multi-product, SEZ Gwalior	Industrial Centre Development Authority, Gwalior	Gwalior	Board of Approval, Commerce Ministry, Government of India recognised for ITSEZ
IT/ITE SEZ Indore	Medicaps Limited, Indore	Indore	Board of Approval, Commerce Ministry, Government of India recognised for ITSEZ
IT/ITE SEZ Indore	Parshvanath Developers Ltd. New Delhi	Indore	Board of Approval, Commerce Ministry, Government of India recognised for ITSEZ
Product specific (Aluminum) SEZ, Sidhi	Ms. Hindalco	Indore	Board of Approval, Commerce Ministry, Government of India recognised for ITSEZ

Salient Feature & Facility in SEZ

- A new Special Economic Zone (SEZ) Scheme has been introduced in the Export & Import Policy with a view to provide an internationally competitive and hassle-free environment for export production.
- A designated duty free enclave to be treated as a foreign territory for trade operations and duties and tariffs.
- No license required for import.
- Exemption from Customs duty on import of capital goods, raw materials, consumables, spares, etc.
- Exemption from Central Excise duty on procurement of capital goods, raw materials, consumable spares, etc. from the domestic market.
- 100% Foreign Direct Investment in manufacturing sector allowed through automatic route except few sectors.

- Profits allowed to be repatriated freely without any dividend balancing requirement.
- Domestic sales on full duty subject to import policy in force.
- Full freedom for subcontracting.
- Sub contracting facility available to jewellery units.
- Duty free goods to be utilized in 5 years.
- Job work on behalf of domestic exporters for direct expose allowed.
- No routine examination by Customs of exports and import cargo.
- No separate documentation required for customs and Exim Policy.
- In house customs clearance.

Crystal IT-Park

Location : Bhawarkua, Indore

Total Area : 21.04 acres

Basic Available Infrastructure

- Wide well-lit roads, cheap transport, hospitals, schools, fire stations, power grid, banks and financial institution make Indore one of the best developed cities.
- Cheap Land Acquisition Cost
- Considering the way Indore is developed, land acquisition costs are much cheaper than other growing cities
- Low Manpower Acquisition Cost
- Being well connected with small towns like Dewas, Pithampur, Rau, Mhow etc. Indore has a regular stream of cheap labour. Indore being home to leading Management, Engineering and Medical Colleges specialized manpower like Engineers, IT Professionals, and Management Executives is made accessible.

Salient Features

- Centrally Air-conditioned
- Fire Fighting System
- Uninterrupted Power Supply with DG backup
- Good Primary and Secondary Road Network
- Most Advanced Optical Fibre Network
- Excellent Telecom Connectivity
- Professional Property Maintenance System
- Fast Track Clearance Mechanism for setting up Operations

Stone Park

Location : Salimnabad, Tah-Bahoriband, Distt. Katni

Total Area : 39.920 hectares

Concession Available to the Industries in Stone Park

- For First five units 50% rebate on land premium, next five units 25% rebate on land premium and for subsequent units payment of land premium in installment basis.
- Concessions will be provided for backward category "A" district.
- Adequate power and water supply
- Slurry disposal facility
- Developed infrastructure
- Italian quality marble is available
- Mortgageable mining lease available.

Integrated Infrastructure Development Centres

Pursuant to Policy Measures for promoting and strengthening small, tiny and village enterprises announced on 6th August 1991, the scheme of Integrated Infrastructure Development (IID) (including technological back up services) for small scale industries in rural/backward area has been prepared. The said Scheme has since been approved by the Government of India.

Objectives of the Scheme

1. To set up about 50 IID Centres in backward districts/rural areas in the country excluding those districts covered under the scheme of Growth Centres.
2. To Promote clusters of small scale and tiny units with a view to create employment opportunities and develop exports.
3. To promote stronger linkages between agriculture and industry.
4. To provide common service facilities and technological back-up services in the Selected Centres.
5. Creation/upgradation of infrastructure facilities like power, water communication etc. in the new/existing centres/industrial areas.

Activities & Work Items Admissible

1. Development of land/plots
2. Construction of roads within the project area and to nearest main road/ rail head.
3. Drainage facilities
4. Provision of water supply
5. Power distribution network within the industrial area
6. Influent Treatment and disposal system

7. Telecommunication facilities like telephone etc.
8. Common facilities/amenities such as built up accommodation for administrative office, bank, post office, conference hall and first-aid centre.
9. Raw material depot and marketing outlets
10. Built-up structure for setting up common services centre including technological back up services
11. Improving/upgrading the deficient infrastructural facilities to increase the productivity and optimum utilization of capacity in the existing centres/ clusters in backward/rural areas.

Madhya Pradesh Financial Corporation (MPFC)

Madhya Pradesh Financial Corporation is premier institution of the state, engaged in providing financial assistance and related services to small and medium sized industries. Also, it is registered as category-1 Merchant Banker with SEBI and has set up a separate merchant banking division in the name of MPFC Capital Markets.

Incorporated in the year 1955, under the State Financial Corporation Act, 1951, it works under the control of the Board of Directors, consisting of representatives from State Government, Small Industries Development Bank of India, Reserve Bank of India, Scheduled Banks, Insurance Companies, Cooperative Banks and other shareholders.

MPFC is a well knit organisation with its headquarters at Indore-the industrial hub of Madhya Pradesh and 20 offices at different places.

Madhya Pradesh State Industrial Development Corporation Ltd. (MPSIDC)

MPSIDC formerly known as MP Audhyogik Vikas Nigam (MPAVN) started its operations in 1965 primarily to augment industrial growth in Madhya Pradesh by providing financial assistance and subsequently in 1981, the State Government assigned infrastructure development work to it.

For balanced and sustained industrial development in Madhya Pradesh, MPSIDC has set up five subsidiary companies known as MP Audhyogik Kendra Vikas Nigam (MPAKVN) located in Bhopal, Indore, Gwalior, Jabalpur & Rewa. It has established many growth centres in Madhya Pradesh.

Since 1994, the focus of MPSIDC has been on infrastructure development to attract and promote industries, both domestic and foreign, in Madhya Pradesh. It has plans to develop and implement infrastructure projects like air cargo complexes, dry ports, express highway, power plants and industrial water supply projects.

MPSIDC is the central point and hub, which coordinates, activates and ensures implementation of mega projects to strengthen and upgrade infrastructure in Madhya Pradesh.

Madhya Pradesh Hastashilp Vikas Nigam (MPHSVN)

Madhya Pradesh Hastashilp Vikas Nigam was incorporated in 1981 under Indian Companies Act; 1956 for the development and promotion of handicrafts, handloom textiles, and carpet, manufacturing unit, (MPHSVN) imparts basic and advance training to unemployed, underemployed and traditional craftspersons, provides advanced tools on subsidised rates, technical and design guidance through 31 development centres and marketing support through its network of 24 emporia. MPHSVN's head office is situated in Bhopal, the capital of Madhya Pradesh.

The main of MPHSVN is preserving the rich crafts heritage of the people of the State. The corporation motivates craftspersons and assists them in marketing their products through a countrywide chain of emporiums under the well, known Mrignayanee banner.

TEST YOUR SELF

1. The Madhya Pradesh State Industrial Corporation was founded on
A. April, 1965 B. September, 1965
C. October, 1965 D. December, 1965

2. The railway sleepers in Madhya Pradesh are manufactured at
A. Bhopal B. Budhani C. Indore D. Dindori

3. Maheshwar is famous for
A. Silk Saree Industry B. Ahilya Ghat
C. Ahilya Museum D. All of the above

4. The note printing press in Madhya Pradesh is located at
A. Hoshangabad B. Nepanagar
C. Dewas D. Ujjain

5. Leather complex in Madhya Pradesh is located at
A. Dewas B. Ujjain C. Chhindwara D. Shajapur

6. Which chemical fertilizer is mostly used in Madhya Pradesh?
A. Nitrogen B. Potash C. Phosphate D. Sulphur

7. The biggest undertaking of Madhya Pradesh Government is
A. Madhya Pradesh Finance Corporation
B. Madhya Pradesh Electricity Corporation
C. Madhya Pradesh Transportation Corporation
D. Madhya Pradesh Small Industries Corporation

8. The air cargo complex, Indo-German tool room and dry sea-port in Madhya Pradesh are located at ....
A. Mandideep B. Pithampur C. Ujjain D. Korba

9. Malanpur Industrial Centre is located in
A. Bhind B. Morena C. Gwalior D. Shivpuri

10. A new oil processing unit in Madhya Pradesh is proposed at
A. Malanpur B. Pithampur C. Aagasaud D. Mandideep

11. Software Technology Park is located at
A. Ratlam B. Gwalior C. Indore D. All of these

12. The Cement Corporation of India is in which district of Madhya Pradesh?
A. Jabalpur B. Durg C. Katni D. Raisen

13. The first gem purifying centre in Madhya Pradesh is established at
A. Jabalpur B. Sidhi C. Shivni D. Indore

14. The largest cotton textile producing district of Madhya Pradesh is
A. Indore B. Jabalpur C. Raigarh D. Shivpuri

15. The HMT factory in Madhya Pradesh is established at
A. Bhopal B. Dewas C. Betul D. Datia

ANSWERS

1	2	3	4	5	6	7	8	9	10
B	A	D	C	A	A	B	B	C	C
11	**12**	**13**	**14**	**15**					
A	C	A	A	C					

❑❑❑

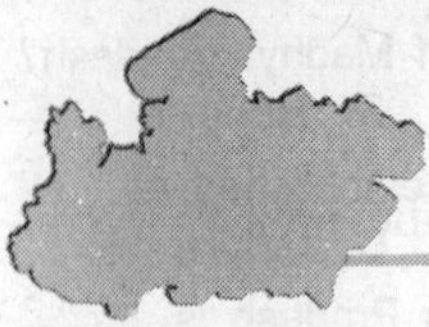

Sources of Energy

Energy is the vital infrastructural input for sustained economic development. It sets the basic foundation for economic development of a country. The stage of economic development attained by the state of a region can be identified by its pattern of generation and consumption of energy. There is close correlationship between the per capita GNP of a country and the per capita energy it consumes.

Demand for electricity grows very rapidly because of its versatility and efficiency in end-use; for some purposes, electricity is the only usable source of energy.

Conventional Energy Resources

The conventional energy resources are non-renewable and exhaustive nature. Majorly coal and water are conventional replenishable sources of energy. Conventional sources of energy produce electricity which can be divided as thermal and hydroelectricity.

Thermal Sector

Satpura Thermal Power Station: It is located on the northern slopes of the Satpura ranges. At present there are six units in operation with a total installed capacity of 1330 megawatts. The first power house of Satpura Thermal chain possesses 187.5 megawatts capacity, Satpura II units possesses 410 megawatts capacity whereas the Satpura III units has the capacity of 420 megawatts of electrical power. With the advent of Korba West bank of Satpura III power houses, Madhya Pradesh entered the 400 K.V. category. Some of the electrical power from this power station is shared by Rajasthan too, which is 545.00 megawatts. The Satpura generation units of 200/210 megawatts are indigenously manufactured and have been suffering from various equipment problems since their commissioning.

Amarkantak Thermal Power Station: The Amarkantak power station which has a total installed capacity of 450 megawatts is situated in the north eastern region of Madhya Pradesh. The power station has two groups of generation units: the Amarkantak II, and Amarkantak extension. The Amarkantak II station has installed capacity of 240 megawatts whereas the Amarkantak extension has an installed capacity of 210 megawatts. It has achieved best performance awards several times. Due to this power station the district of Shahdol has reached a high level of economic development.

Hydroelectric Power Stations

The kinetic energy of mighty rivers flowing through the state is very important for the production of hydroelectricity. The first hydroelectricity power station in the state was established under Chambal Valley Project. Today there are 14 Hydro Electric Power Stations in the state.

Installed Capacity

Sl. No.	Power Station	Installed Capacity (MW)	MP Share (MW)
1.	Amarkantak Extn (210 MW)	210	210
2.	Satpura II (200+210 MW)	410	410
3.	Satpura III (2x210 MW)	420	420
4.	Satpura IV (2x250 MW)	500	500
5.	Sanjay Gandhi, Birsinghpur -I (2x210 MW)	420	420
6.	Sanjay Gandhi Birsinghpur -II (2x210 MW)	420	420
7.	Sanjay Gandhi Birsinghpur -Extn (1x500 MW)	500	500
8.	Shri Singaji TPS Dongalia (2x600 MW)	1200	1200
9.	Shri Singaji TPS Dongalia Phase II (2x660 MW)	1320	1320
	Total Thermal Power Station Generation	**5400**	**5400**
1.	Gandhi Sagar (5x23 MW)	115	57.5
2.	Pench,Totladoh (2x80 MW)	160	107
3.	Rani Awanti Bai Bargi (2x45 MW)	90	90
4.	Ban Sagar-I Tons (3x105 MW)	315	315
5.	Birsinghpur (1x20 MW)	20	20
6.	Rajghat (3x15 MW)	45	22.5
7.	Ban Sagar-II Silpara (2x15 MW)	30	30
8.	Bansagar-III Deolond (3x20 MW)	60	60
9.	Bansagar-IV Jhinna (2x10 MW)	20	20
10.	Madhikheda (3x20 MW)	60	60
	Jawaharsagar & Ranapratapsagar Station of Rajasthan (99 MW & 172 MW), 50% of 271MW	**----**	**135.5**
	Total Hydro Power Station Generation	**915**	**917.5**
	Total	**6315**	**6317.5**

Hydel Sector

Gandhisagar Hydel Project: Situated in the Mandsaur district of Madhya Pradesh, in the north-western region, the Gandhisagar hydel project is owned by Madhya Pradesh Electricity Board. This accounts for 115 megawatts of electricity. The project has five generation units, each with an installed capacity of 23 megawatts. The first three units were commissioned in November 1960, wherreas the fourth and the fifth units were installed in August 1963, and November 1966 respectively.

Ranapratap Sagar Hydel Project: The Ranapratap Sagar Hydel project is a joint venture, owned both by Madhya Pradesh Electricity Board (MPEB) and Rajasthan State Electricity Board (RSEB), situated in south Rajasthan. It has a total installed capacity of 172 megawatts, with four generation units each with an installed capacity of 43 megawatts. Commissioned between February 1968 and May 1969, the project is shared in 60 per cent by Madhya Pradesh Electricity Board and another 40 per cent by the Rajasthan Electricity Board.

Jawahar Sagar Hydel Project: The Jawahar Sagar Hydel Project, situated in southern tip of Rajasthan, near the MP border accounts for 99 megawatts of electrical energy. It has in all three generation units each with an installed capacity of 33 megawatts. The first unit was commissioned in March 1972, after which the next two units were commissioned in March 1973.

Non-conventional Power Resources

These power resources are renewable and replenishable. Under these the commonly available resources are wind energy, solar energy, bio gas. In Madhya Pradesh the various projects for these resources are:

- **Solar Photo and Voltaic Cell:** These cell are used to convert the solar energy into electrical energy. These cells can be used for lighting purposes even during nights and for providing electricity for irrigational purposes. In Madhya Pradesh, such cells are being deployed at Betul, Jhabua, Hoshangabad etc. These cells could provide electricity upto 300 MW.
- **Solar Distilled Water Plant:** These plants are being implemented in educational institutions. In these plants the solar energy is used to evaporate water and convert it in the form of electricity.
- **Wind Energy:** Although, Madhya Pradesh lies in the normal latitudes and thus has no special sources for wind energy but still Madhya Pradesh is numero uno among other states in the establishment of wind energy power plants. Maximum wind mills have been installed in Indore and the power thus generated is majorly used for electricity production and irrigation purpose.
- **Bio-gas Plant:** First biogas plant in Madhya Padesh was established in 1984 in Bhopal in Bhadra Animal Husbandry Department. Its capacity was 85 metre cube and was capable of working for 46 families. At present 17 such plants are established in the state.
- **Biomass:** The energy creation from the decomposition of plants, live-waste and biodegradable waste is known as biomass. Today the state is capable of producing 13.50 MW of electricity from Biomass.

MP Urja Vikas Nigam

MP Urja Vikas Nigam (MPUVN) was constituted by the Government of Madhya Pradesh in August 1982. The main activities of the Urja Vikas Nigam are as under:

1. Establishment of various power projects based on the non-conventional energy sources in private sector.
2. Implementation of various non-conventional energy based projects in the state.
3. Promotion and popularisation of use of non-conventional energy sources.
4. Promotion of research and development activities in the field of non-conventional energy sources.
5. With a view to encourage energy conservation, arranging energy audits in selected industrial units and other institutions, offices etc.
6. Co-ordination among the Central, State government and investors for setting up power plants based on non-conventional energy sources.
7. Electrification of unelectrified villages through non-conventional energy sources under Integrated Rural Energy Programme (IREP).

Various efforts undertaken under these include, IREP, biogas, solar energy, energy conservation and management, rural electrification, biomass and solar photovoltaic, biofuel and energy parks.

TEST YOUR SELF

1. Which among the following thermal power stations is located in Umaria district of Madhya Pradesh?

A. Satpura B. Sanjay Gandhi
C. Chandani D. Vindhyachal

2. Which thermal station is a joint venture of Madhya Pradesh and Rajasthan?

A. Birsinghpur-II B. Pench
C. Malwa D. Satpura

3. Nepanagar is getting electricity from

A. Chandani Thermal B. Vindhyachal
C. Amarkantak D. Birsinghpur

4. How many hydroelectric power stations are there in Madhya Pradesh?

A. Nine B. Eleven C. Three D. Eight

5. Jawaharsagar hydropower project is on river

A. Pench B. Baansagar C. Chambal D. Sone

6. Gandhi Sagar hydel power project has an installed capacity of ....

A. 280 MW B. 310 MW C. 115 MW D. 210 MW

7. In Madhya Pradesh electricity is first produced in
A. Sohagpur B. Gwalior C. Umaria D. Jabalpur

8. The energy capital of Madhya Pradesh is
A. Shivni B. Korba C. Rajgarh D. Singrauli

9. The first solar village (district) of Madhya Pradesh is
A. Itarasi B. Sehore C. Indore D. Panchmarhi

10. Which of the districts is known as energy district of Madhya Pradesh?
A. Datia B. Singrauli C. Chhindwara D. Panchmarhi

11. Gandhi Sagar Power Station is located in
A. Mandsaur district B. Ujjain
C. Jhabua D. Umaria

12. When was the first bio gas plant established in Bhopal?
A. 1980 B. 1983 C. 1984 D. 1985

13. Indira Sagar Vidyut Kendra is located at
A. Punasa B. Khandwa
C. Omkareshwar D. Maheshwar

14. Which of the following cities is not covered under JNURM?
A. Indore B. Jabalpur C. Gwalior D. Ujjain

15. MP Urja Vikas Nigam was established in—
A. 1982 B. 1984 C. 1972 D. 1965

ANSWERS

1	2	3	4	5	6	7	8	9	10
B	D	A	B	C	C	B	D	A	B
11	12	13	14	15					
A	C	A	C	A					

❑❑❑

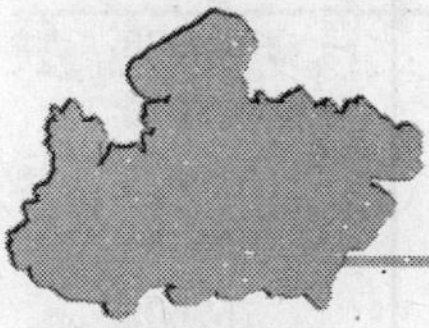

Population and Health

Population

Among the different states of India, Madhya Pradesh ranks 6th in terms of population and it has almost 6% share of the population in India. As per the Census 2011, data the total population of the state is about 72.62 million, of which 37.61 million are males and 35.01 million are female. Also, around 27.63% population is urban as against 72.37% of the rural population.

District-wise Population

District	Total	Male	Female
Sheopur	687861	361784	326077
Morena	1965970	1068417	897553
Bhind	1703005	926843	776162
Gwalior	2032036	1090327	941709
Datia	786754	420157	366597
Shivpuri	1726050	919795	806255
Tikamgarh	1445166	760355	684811
Chhatarpur	1762375	936121	826254
Panna	1016520	533480	483040
Sagar	2378458	1256257	1122201
Damoh	1264219	661873	602346
Satna	2228935	1157495	1071440
Rewa	2365106	1225100	1140006
Umaria	644758	330674	314084
Neemuch	826067	422653	403414
Mandsaur	1340411	682851	657560
Ratlam	1455069	738241	716828
Ujjain	1986864	1016289	970575
Shajapur	1512681	780520	732161
Dewas	1563715	805359	758356

District	Total	Male	Female
Dhar	2185793	1112725	1073068
Indore	3276697	1699627	1577070
Khargone (West Nimarh)	1873046	953121	919925
Barwani	1385881	699340	686541
Rajgarh	1545814	790212	755602
Vidisha	1458875	769568	689307
Bhopal	2371061	1236130	1134931
Sehore	1311332	683743	627589
Raisen	1331597	700358	631239
Betul	1575362	799236	776126
Harda	570465	294838	275627
Hoshangabad	1241350	648725	592625
Katni	1292042	662013	630029
Jabalpur	2463289	1277278	1186011
Narsimhapur	1091854	568810	523044
Dindori	704524	351913	352611
Mandla	1054905	525272	529633
Chhindwara	2090922	1064468	1026454
Seoni	1379131	695879	683252
Balaghat	1701698	842178	859520
Guna	1241519	649362	592157
Ashoknagar	845071	443837	401234
Shahdol	1066063	540021	526042
Anuppur	749237	379114	370123
Sidhi	1127033	575912	551121
Singrauli	1178273	613637	564636
Jhabua	1025048	515023	510025
Alirajpur	728999	362542	366457
Khandwa (East Nimarh)	1310061	674329	635732
Burhanpur	757847	388504	369343

Growth Rate

As per the current census 2011 data, the decadal growth rate for 2001-2011 is 20.30% as against the national average of 17.7%. This decade added a population of 12.27 million to the state. The growth rate of urban population lies lower as 18.4% as compared to the growth rate of rural population as 25.7%. These statistics give a clear indication towards the trend of urbanisation in the state.

Top Five Districts of Madhya Pradesh (in terms of growth rate)

District	Growth Rate	District	Growth Rate
Indore	32.9	Jhabua	30.7
Bhopal	28.6	Singrauli	28.0
Barwani	27.6		

Birth and Death Rate

Birth rate or crude birth rate i.e., number of childbirths per 1000 people per year stood at 28 in Madhya Pradesh as against 22.8 of India. Also the death rate is higher than Indian average as 8.6 against 7.4 of India.

Madhya Pradesh still remains amongst one of the lowest scoring states in terms of infant mortality rate i.e., the average number of children dying on every thousand live birth. IMR for Madhya Pradesh is 70 for the year 2009, as against 53 for India.

Within MP, the districts like Tikamgarh, Panna, Chhatarpur and Satna are among the most backward districts of the state, based on its development index. Datia is little better than those above mentioned districts. Health data also proves the same. There are variations within the districts of MP but the districts of northern MP are always on the worst side. In terms of life expectancy, while the best rate is that of district Indore (58.0 yrs.), the worst three are of districts Tikamgarh (40.8), Panna (41.3) and Chhatarpur (41.6) respectively. Datia (44.3) and Satna (44.5) are little better.

In terms of crude birth rates, district Indore again has the minimum and the best rate with 29.6 while Chhatarpur (42.6), Panna (42.2) and Tikamgarh (42.1) respectively, have the third, fifth and sixth highest rates in the state. Satna (41.1) and Datia (39.5) are also high.

The fertility rate in MP is the best for the district Indore which shows the minimum and the best with 3.6 children per women. On the worst side Chhatarpur (6.6), Tikamgarh (6.1), Panna (5.9), Datia (5.8) and Satna (5.7), respectively have third, fifth, eighth, tenth and fifteenth highest rates in the state.

The case of infant mortality rate is no better for Bundelkhand districts. While the district Indore with rate being only 84, the highest and the worst is the case with district Tikamgarh (195), followed neck to neck by Panna (185), Chhatarpur (182) and Satna (181) districts Datia is little better with the figure of 156 infant deaths.

Sex Ratio

Sex ratio being the number of females per 1000 males in the population is an important social indicator to measure the extent of prevailing equity in the society between males and females at a given point of time. As per the figures of Census 2011, the sex ratio of Madhya Pradesh is 931 as against the sex ratio of 943 for India. It still remains lower than the sex ratio of India for the census 2001 of 933.

At an individual level of Madhya Pradesh, the sex ratio of the state has increased by 12 points since Census 2001 to reach 931 at Census 2011. This is the highest sex ratio recorded since Census 1971 and a shade lower than 1961.

Top Five Districts in Madhya Pradesh

District	Sex-Ratio	District	Sex-Ratio
Balaghat	1021	Alirajpur	1011
Mandla	1008	Dindori	1002
Jhabua	990		

Literacy

Madhya Pradesh ranks in one of the bottom most states of India in terms of education and literacy. But, an increased trend of urbanisation and awareness among the people have improved the picture in present time. As per the Census 2011, the literacy percentage for the state stands at 69.32% as against 73% of the nation. Thus, the state average is not very far from the national average. But when the percentage is compared between males and females for literacy, there is a huge divide. When the literacy percentage for males is 78.73% and for females it is just 59.2%.

Top Five Districts by Literacy Rate : 2011

Name of District	Literacy Rate	Name of District	Literacy Rate
Jabalpur	81.1%	Indore	80.9%
Bhopal	80.4%	Balaghat	77.1%
Gwalior	76.7%		

Missions for Health

Ayushmati Yojana

This programme has been started by the government to help the rural women of landless families. Under this programme ₹ 400 are given in the first week for the in-house-treatment in the medical college hospitals for medicines and supplementary meal. The amount can be upto ₹ 1000 for further hospitalisation. Attendant of the patient is given free meal two times in a day.

Vatsalya Yojana

This programme aims at the proper care of pregnant women and to provide antenatal and postnatal services. Under this programme 500 rupees are given to rural landless labourer women during their first and second pregnancy, provided there is a gap of three years in these pregnancies and the women will opt for permanent family planning measures.

National Fileria Control Programme

The districts of Bundelkhand are prone to the disease of Fileria. That is why, the govt. has taken efforts to establish medical centres for the control and treatment of this disease. Out of the total 9 Fileria Control Units in the state, one such unit is set up in each of these districts, Chhatarpur, Tikamgarh, Satna, Panna and Datia. Out of total 7 Fileria Treatment Centres, 4 are centred in the districts, Satna, Chhatarpur, Tikamgarh and Panna. Panna also has a treatment cum-survey centre.

Rajiv Gandhi Mission for Control of Diarrhoeal Diseases

The mission is set up with the long term objective of reducing infant mortality in the state. Twenty eight per cent child deaths in the state are attributed to diarrhoea. The Mission initiated a series of steps to prevent diarrhoeal deaths.

Rajiv Gandhi Mission on Elimination of Iodine Deficiency Disorders

The mission had the target to universalise use of iodised salt to eliminate iodine deficiency disorders by 1996. It achieved its target 11 months ahead of schedule and thus was closed and a new Rajiv Gandhi Sanitation Mission was started.

Rajiv Gandhi Sanitation Mission

The Mission was started in 1996 and aims to make sanitation a people's movement in the state. The effort is to create public awareness to motivate private household investment in sanitation. It also seek to promote action by elected local body leadership. The role of the govt. will be only as a facilitator and not as a provider.

TEST YOUR SELF

1. The sex ratio of Madhya Pradesh has been increased in

A. More than half of the districts

B. less than half of the districts

C. all the districts

D. None of the above

2. How many districts of Madhya Pradesh have reported sex ratio lesser than 930?

A. 23 B. 24 C. 22 D. 28

3. Which of the following districts has the highest female literacy rate?

A. Bhopal B. Indore C. Alirajpur D. Jhabua

4. Which of the following districts of Madhya Pradesh has lowest male and female literacy rate?

A. Alirajpur B. Indore C. Bhopal D. Jhabua

5. Which of the following districts has the highest gap between male and female literacy?
A. Neemuch B. Bhopal C. Jhabua D. Jabalpur

6. Consider the following statements:
1. The death rate is higher than Indian average as 8.6 against 7.4 for India.
2. It means that health services in Madhya Pradesh are very good.

Which of the statements given above is/are not correct?
A. Only 1 B. Only 2
C. Both 1 and 2 D. None of these

7. Which of the following statements is/are incorrect?
1. Madhya Pradesh ranks 6th in terms of population.
2. It has almost 6% share of the population in India.

A. Only 1 B. Only 2
C. Both 1 and 2 D. None of these

8. The decadal growth rate of Madhya Pradesh is
A. 20.3% B. 40% C. 16.3% D. 8%

9. Which of the following religions comes second in terms of followers?
A. Hindu B. Muslim C. Sikh D. Christian

10. Which of the following districts is the smallest in terms of population?
A. Bhopal B. Harda C. Singrauli D. Anuppur

11. Which district has the highest sex ratio?
A. Balaghat B. Alirajpur C. Dindori D. Jhabua

12. The rural Population in Madhya Pradesh is ....
A. 72.4% B. 78% C. 74% D. 42%

13. Which of the following districts of the state shows the highest growth rate?
A. Indore B. Bhopal C. Barwani D. Jhabua

14. Which of the following districts of the state shows the lowest growth rate?
A. Anuppur B. Chhindwara
C. Mandsaur D. Narmadapuram

15. Which of the following districts of the state has the sex ratio higher than the national ratio?
A. Mandla B. Balaghat C. Jhabua D. All of these

ANSWERS

1	2	3	4	5	6	7	8	9	10
A	A	A	A	A	A	D	A	B	B
11	12	13	14	15					
A	A	A	A	D					

❑❑❑

Education

Education is the pillar for the success of all the development activities and efforts undertaken by government and volunteers. MP has been educationally backward as its literacy rate (69.32%) and literacy among women confirm it. The situation among backward communities, scheduled castes and tribes is further alarming. The Bundelkhand region of MP is one of the most backward regions of the state and lag far behind on the development indicators. The concept of universalisation of education, even at the primary level is far beyond the reach in this region. The literacy percentage among the SC/ST, and particularly female literacy among them, shows a very dismal picture. The availability of educational facilities, schools and technical institutions are also not enough to cover the needs of the rural masses. Though each district has a District Institute of Education and Training (DIET), the technical and commercial institutions of learning are very few in the districts concerned. Educational scene is very pessimistic in the region. A very few students from Bundelkhand have been able to show any achievement in the field of science and technology and the competition of some repute. Government figures of the coverage of schools, educational facility, students enrollment and drop out rates always leave a concern about its validity when the actual situation in the villages of Bundelkhand is observed and surveyed by any independent agency.

School Education

The directive principle of the Constitution of India envisages provision of free and compulsory elementary education to all children until they complete the age of 14 years. In pursuance of the constitutional directive, the need for a literate population and provision of elementary education as a crucial input for nation building, the National Policy of Education 1986 as revised in 1992 stated that free and compulsory education of satisfactory quality should be provided to all children up to 14 years of age.

The State has universalized access to primary and upper primary education. Primary school facility is available within a distance of one km. radius of each habitation while the Upper Primary Schools are now available within a reach of 3 kms.

Successful implementation of Sarva Shiksha Abhiyan (SSA) has created an urge in society to have secondary education facilities near their habitation. As a result of increase in enrollment and pass out rate at the elementary level, there is now a need to expand secondary education facilities. Besides expansion of educational facilities, the emphasis will also have to be on providing quality education at the secondary level.

Higher Education

The main objectives of the Higher Education Department is to improve the standards of higher education in government and private institutions, universities, research institutes, and the colleges/ institutes established for special and specific purposes. The activities carried out by the higher education department are to run the Government colleges, give assistance for running of the private colleges, opening of new subjects in Government colleges, promotion of Yoga and sports activities, organising seminars, providing grants to universities.

Universities

Central Universities

Department of Higher Education under Ministry of Human Resource Development lists 81 centrally funded institutes and 48 central universities. Two central universities and eight centrally funded institutes are located in Madhya Pradesh.

Universities	Location	Established	Type
Dr. Hari Singh Gour University	Sagar	1946	Central University
Indira Gandhi National Tribal University	Amarkantak	2007	Central University

State Universities

UGC recognizes fifteen state universities in Madhya Pradesh, of which eleven universities receive financial assistance from central government and UGC in addition to Madhya Pradesh state government. Universities eligible for central assistance are marked within table below.

Universities	Location	Established
Awdhesh Pratap Singh University	Rewa	1969
Barkatullah University	Bhopal	1970
Devi Ahilya University	Indore	1964
Jawaharlal Nehru Agricultural University	Jabalpur	1964
Jiwaji University	Gwalior	1964
Madhya Pradesh Bhoj Open University	Bhopal	1991
Maharishi Mahesh Yogi Vedic Vishwavidyalaya	Katni	1995

Universities	Location	Established
Maharishi Panini Sanskrit University	Ujjain	2008
Mahatma Gandhi Chitrakoot Gramoday University	Chitrakoot	1991
Makhanlal Chaturvedi National University of Journalism	Bhopal	1991
National Law Institute University	Bhopal	1998
Rajiv Gandhi Technical University	Bhopal	1998
Rajmata Vijayaraje Scindia Krishi Vishwa Vidyalaya	Gwalior	2008
Rani Durgavati University	Jabalpur	1956
Madhya Pradesh Pashu Chikitsa Vigyan Vishwa Vidyalaya	Jabalpur	2009
Vikram University	Ujjain	1957

Private Universities

Universities	Location	Established
Jaypee University of Engineering & Technology	Guna	2003
Amity University Madhya Pradesh	Gwalior	2010
ITM University	Gwalior	2011

Deemed Universities

Universities	Location	Established
Indian Institute of Information Technology, Design and Manufacturing	Jabalpur	2005
Indian Institute of Information Technology and Management	Gwalior	1997
Lakshmibai National University of Physical Education	Gwalior	1957

Autonomous Institutions

Institutes	Location	Established
Indian Institute of Forest Management	Bhopal	1982
Indian Institute of Tourism and Travel Management	Gwalior	1983
Indian Institute of Management	Indore	1998
Indian Institute of Science Education and Research	Bhopal	2008
Indian Institute of Technology	Indore	2009
Maulana Azad National Institute of Technology	Bhopal	1960
National Institute of Technical Teachers' Training and Research	Bhopal	—
School of Planning and Architecture	Bhopal	2008

Technical Education

Technical Education provides a strong base for harnessing qualitative, efficient and structured institutional training for the technological development of the society as a whole.

Infrastructure for Technical Education as it exists today; needs further strengthening to take care of the requirements of the state. With increased globalization and privatization, the private sector too has come up in a big way to provide technical education. Hence, the private sector is being encouraged to supplement and support the expansion of Technical Education. What is needed now in the government sector is consolidation, strengthening of the existing facilities, bringing about qualitative improvement in the delivery system, and also new initiatives to meet upcoming challenges thrown open by newer technologies.

Technical Institute

Central Govt.-aided Institutions

- Indian Institute of Technology, Indore
- Maulana Azad National Institute of Technology, Bhopal
- Indian Institute of Information Technology and Management, Gwalior
- Indian Institute of Information Technology, Design and Manufacturing, Jabalpur

Govt. Autonomous and State Govt.-aided Institutions

- Jabalpur Engineering College, Jabalpur (1947)
- Sri Govind Ram Saksariya Institute of Technology Indore (1952)
- Madhav Institute of Technology and Science (MITS), Gwalior (1957)
- Vidisha S.A. Institute of Technology (1960)
- Rewa Engineering College (1964)
- Ujjain Engineering College, Ujjain (1966)
- Indira Gandhi Engineering College, Sagar (1981)

Self Financing Institutions

- Barkatullah University Institute of Technology, Bhopal (1997)
- Institute of Engineering, Jiwaji University, Gwalior (1996)
- Institute of Engineering and Technology, DAVV, Indore
- IPST, Mahatma Gandhi Chitrakoot Gramoday University, Chitrakoot, Madhya Pradesh
- Rustamji Institute of Technology, Tekanpur, Gwalior (1999)
- University Institute of Technology, RGPV, Bhopal (1986)
- School of Engineering and Technology, Vikram University, Ujjain (2011)
- College of Agricultural Engineering, Jawaharlal Nehru Krishi Vishwa

Vidyalaya, Jabalpur, but this institute does not admit students from the counselling conducted by the Directorate of Technical Education.

Rajiv Gandhi Shiksha Mission

This is a mission to universalise primary education and promote literacy. Rajiv Gandhi Shiksha Mission (RGSM) is conceived of as a convergence modality that brings together the two programmes of universalising primary education through externally aided District Primary Education Programme (DPEP) and Total Literacy Campaigns of the National Literacy Mission.

The programme (DPEP) quite unlike previous centrally sponsored initiatives, has evolved an integrated approach to primary education with programme assistance being channeled through state projects office to district level implementing agencies. A special attempt has been made to target educationally backward districts (defined especially by low female literacy) with strategies to ensure educational needs of women, SC and STs and other weaker sections of the population.

State Sponsored Schemes

- **Education Guarantee Scheme (EGS):** Under Rajiv Gandhi Mission, Govt. of M.P. took a pioneering initiative in the country to provide an educational centre on demand by people. Under the scheme whenever there is a demand from a tribal area from 25 children for a facility to learn and from 40 children for non-tribal area and there is no school within one km., the govt. guarantees to provide a trained teacher within 90 days. The space for learning is provided by the community. Since the launching of the scheme on 1 January, 97, over 11579 centres have come up in the state.
- **Alternative Schools (AS):** For those children who are unable to participate in formal schooling, special schooling facilities designated as Alternative Schools have been opened. These schools have flexibility of time and space using an innovative learning method adapted to learner pace.
- **Shishu Shiksha Kendra (SSK):** A nursery service was introduced as pre-school education to rural schools through which attention is given to 3-5 age group of children to inculcate in them appropriate habits of learning. It provides the opportunity to girls engaged in sibling care to attend regular primary school.

Centrally Sponsored Schemes

- **Non-formal Education:** This is a centrally sponsored scheme which is implemented in the state and looks into the fundamental rights and directive principles of education for all. Non-formal education centres are operated for the free and compulsory education of dropout children, working children and children of weaker sections of villages in deprived geographical areas.

- **Professional Education:** Kothari Commission (1964-66) recommended for professional education at 10+2 level to provide employment oriented examination and to avoid crowding from college education.

  Professional education means training for such subjects/areas where sufficient possibility for employment is available. The main objective of this education is to meet the necessity of man power for the development of the nation and to end the unemployment from the society.
- **Operation Black Board:** Operation Black Board scheme was introduced in Madhya Pradesh in 1989-90. The funds were primarily utilized for teaching aids, sports articles/items and apparatus.
- **Mid Day Meal Scheme:** In the year 1995-96 Mid Day Meal Scheme was introduced in the government and aided primary schools of 297 blocks in the state. The school provides food to children. In the year 1997-98, the scheme was implemented in all the blocks of the state. In tribal regions the scheme provides prepared food and in non-tribal regions from September 1997 onwards the scheme of providing prepared food is stopped and now 3 kg. food is distributed for every child every month.
- **Class Project:** Information related to computers and its utility is crucial for students. Looking into this aspect class project was started in Higher Secondary Schools from the year 1996-97. Under this project basic training of computers is imparted to class IX students. In addition to this, computer training for XI to XII class has been started in 300 Higher Secondary Schools.
- **Shankhanaad Scheme:** This scheme was started in Jhabua on 26 January 1997. The aim of this scheme is to educate the tribal population.
- **Learn and Grow Programme:** The Learn and grow programme has been implemented in the district of Narsimhapur. Due to this programme the education status of the women in these districts has improved.
- **Padna Badna Andolan (2001):** Under this scheme a group of 20-30 illiterate people of the village was empowered to select a Guruji, who later on was trained by the govt., provided books, and he was assured to get assistance of Rs 100/- per successful neoliterate from the government.

Schemes for Middle Level Education

- **Head Start Programme:** Rajiv Gandhi Shiksha Mission supervises this scheme which aims to enable education through computers. It provides computer education to the children of middle school.
- **Kasturba Gandhi School Yojana:** It was launched to promote women education. It provides free hostel and Education facilities to the girl of more than 10 year age and above throughout their education career. Under this scheme 75 per cent of the seats are reserved for the SC/ST/OBC/Minority class women students.

Schemes for Higher Education

- **Abhinav Yojana:** It was launched by the state govt. to bring about some structural changes in the higher education system of the state, in order to make it of global standard. Some of the major ingredients of this schemes are as follows:
  - (a) To use Information Technology in education.
  - (b) To interconnect all the Universities and colleges through Internet.
  - (c) To provide job oriented education.
  - (d) To prepare qualified personnel to fillup the vacant positions.

  The establishment of **National Law Institute** at Bhopal was an outcome of this Yojana. This is a right step in the right direction to create a pool of able human resource who could tale us to the higher level of development and prosperity.

TEST YOUR SELF

1. National Policy of Education was formulated in
   A 1986 B. 1981 C. 1993 D. 1964
2. The number of central universities in Madhya Pradesh is
   A four B. three C. two D. five
3. Indira Gandhi National Tribal University is located at
   A Sagar B. Amarkantak C. Rewa D. Bhopal
4. Devi Ahilya University Indore was established in
   A 1961 B. 1970 C. 1964 D. 1980
5. Which among the following is not a private University located in Madhya Pradesh?
   A Amity University B. ITM University
   C. Jaypee University D. Vikram University
6. In Madhya Pradesh, Indian Institute of Technology is located at
   A Bhopal B. Jabalpur C. Indore D. Gwalior
7. The School of Planning and Architecture was established at Bhopal in
   A 1985 B. 1983 C. 1995 D. 2008
8. Shankhanad Scheme aimed to educate the tribal population was started in
   A Jhabua B. Gwalior C. Bhopal D. Indore
9. The Learn and Grow Programme has been implemented in the district of
   A Bhopal B. Shivni C. Jhabua D. Narsimhapur
10. Operation Black Board Scheme was introduced in Madhya Pradesh in
    A 1989-90 B. 1985-86 C. 1999-2000 D. 1980-81

11. Which of the following statements are not correct regarding Madhya Pradesh Jan Shiksha Adhiniyam, 2002?

A. This is the first act of the kind in the country

B. The act ensures availability of quality education for all children of Madhya Pradesh

C. It is a collective endeavour of government and society

D. For ensuring improvement of quality in elementary education in all the schools of Madhya Pradesh, civil society will regulate the Act

12. Which of the following schemes creates a three way partnership to ensure the right to primary education?

A. Education Guarantee Scheme

B. Education and Bank Initiative Venture

C. Sarv Shiksha Abhiyan

D. Skill and Vocation Training Programme

13. The first Tribal Research Communication Centre in the state is located at ....

A. Indore B. Bhopal C. Jhabua D. Jabalpur

14. Where is the first state sports college located?

A. Jhabua B. Sehore C. Macha D. Hoshangabad

15. Mahatma Gandhi Chitrakoot Gramodaya University was established in—

A. 1991 B. 1985 C. 1983 D. 1989

ANSWERS

1	2	3	4	5	6	7	8	9	10
A	C	B	C	D	C	D	A	D	A
11	12	13	14	15					
D	A	C	B	A					

❑❑❑

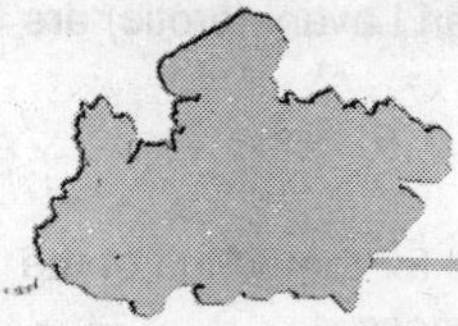

Fairs and Festivals

India is a land of festivals and so is the Madhya Pradesh. Our festivals are often related with the seasons and climate. Many festivals are based on the mythological beliefs and a few are often related with the crops and their harvesting. Madhya Pradesh is a state of diverse cultures and traditions and so it enjoys many festivals throughout the year. Major festivals of the state are:

Sanja Festival

Unmarried girls of Madhya Pradesh annually worship a legendary girl called Sanja. In the month of Asvina, the festivities of Sanja run consecutively for sixteen days.

Shivaratri Mela

Thousands of pilgrims flock to the fair grounds near the Mahakaleshwar temple and worship throught out the night. This festival is celebrated with great fervor among devotees of Lord Shiva.

Gobardhan Festival

Gobardhan festival is celebrated on the sixteenth day in the month of Kartika i.e. just on the day following Diwali. Gobardhan means 'prosperity for cows' and seems to have its source in the Krishna cult.

Karma Festival

The festival of Karma, a religious festival, calls for a huge celebration every year among the Korba tribals of MP. On the day of worship, devotees fast from morning till the next day—a good 24 hours. A branch from the Karma tree is planted in the middle of an open ground and the night is spent singing and dancing around it.

Lavani Festival

The Lavni came to Malwa along with the Marathas in the opening of the eighteenth century. The Nirguni Lavani (philosophical) and the Shringari Lavani (erotic) are the two types which is well-liked in the south of Nimad.

Rang Panchami

On the fifth day after Holi, an yearly music festival was held for the period of the Holkar reign. Even people celebrate this festival with eagerness.

Suwata Festival

The Suwata of Bundelkhand relates to the Ghadlya of Malwa, Girls, in this form of celebration prepare a tiny platform along the wall with clay. The three sides of this platform are provided with steps. On the platform an image of a devil is made to stand. The sun and the moon are drawn on the wall to give an idea of two brothers.

Chethiyagiri Vihara Festival

A Buddhist festival held at Sanchi at the end of November, Chethiyagiri Vihara Festival is attended by thousands of Buddhists monks and pilgrims.

Gana-Gour Festival

The Gana Gour festival is celebrated with much gaiety in Madhya Pradesh. The people believe that Gour, wife of Shiva, was married to Shiva and they stayed in Rajasthan. She could come home only once a year. This coming back is celebrated by these people here. They make small idols of the Gour and worship her along with her husband.

Ghadlya

Girls have their own feature in this festival. They gather in the evening in groups and visit every house of the village carrying earthen pots with holes for he light to come out, made by a wich oil lamp kept inside.

Kajri Navami

On the ninth day of the waxing-moon fortnight of the month of Sravana, falls the Kajri festival. In the Bundelkhandi-speaking area only those women, who are blessed with sons, observe this festival.

Malwa Festival

A festival of music, dance and gaiety, held for the period of the month of September at Mandu is a riot of color, melody and song.

Apart from the seasonal Hindu festivals, a monthly fair is held on each amavasya.

Navanna Festival

In Bundelkhand, it is performed on the eleventh day after Diwali. On this day cows are fed with cakes organised out of new corn. No one takes his food until this rite is done.

Ras-Nawa Festival

Ras-Nawa is a particular festival of the Baigas of Mandla district. Ras-Nawa means ceremonial eating of honey. The festival falls once in every nine years. The Baigas associate this festival to their legendary ancestor Nanga Baiga.

Bhagoria Festival

Held in the Jhabua district the Bhagoria is to the Bhils what the Madai is to the Gonds—a festival of fun and joy. It is held a week before the Hindu festival of colours, Holi. Men and women celebrate it with ritual dancing to the beat of drums and thalis and the sweet melody of shehnai and bansuri (flutes).

Hareli or Hariri

Harelı or Hariri falls on the day of **Sravana Amavasya**. In **Mandla**, it is celebrated on the new-moon day of the same month. The festival is major for the agriculturists of central India.

Laru Kaj Festival

Laru Kaj is the festival of Gonds which is related with the pig sacrifice. The ceremony is considered the pig's wedding in honour of Narayan Dev.

Other Prominent Festivals of the State

Festival	Place	Description
Alauddin Khan Sangeet Samaroh	Maihar, Satna	Indian Classical Music.
Ameer Khan Festival	Indore	Indian Classical art performances.
Rashtriya Hindi Natya Samaroh	Bhopal	Staging of Hindi's Best Drama's performances.
Pachmarhi Utsav	Pachmarhi	Indian Folk Art's performances.
Mandu Utsav	Mandu	—
Orchha Utsav	Orchha	—
Keshav Jayanti Samaroh	Orchha	Literary Presenatation.
Muktibodh Samaroh	Bhind	Literary Programmes.
Bhavbhuti Samaroh	Gwalior	Sanskrit's Literary Programmes.
Malwa Utsav	Ujjain & Indore	Folk Arts and Indian Classical Music related.
Festival of Dances	Khajuraho	Indian Classical Dance Performance
Akhil Bhartiya Kalidas Samaroh	Ujjain	Literary Presentations along with dramas and Indian Classical programmes.

Festival	Place	Description
Tansen Sangeet Samaroh	Gwalior	Indian Classical and Vocal Musical performances.
Dhrupad Samaroh	Bhopal	Vocal performances of Dhrupad style of Indian Classical Music.
Makhanlal Chaturvedi Samaroh	Jabalpur	Literary Programmes.
Lokrang Samaroh	Bhopal	Indian Folk Art's Presentations and performances.
Pt. Kumar Gandharva Samaroh	Dewas	Indian Classical Music performances
Bhoj Samaroh	Dhar	Sanskrit Literary Programmes.
Kabir Samaroh	Statewide	Folk Arts, Music, Dances and Literary Programmes.
Rashtriya Alankaran Samaroh	Bhopal	Distribution of Cultural Awards
Krishna Rao Shankar Pandit Samaroh	Gwalior	Indian Classical Music performance
Nimarh Utsava	Maheshwar	Indian folk and classical performance
Bharat Bhawan	Bhopal	Various Folk arts exhibitions and performances throughout the year.
Lata Mangeshkar Samaroh and Award Ceremony	Indore	National level light musical performance

Traditional Fairs

Chaitra Fair: The Chaitra fair includes various local fairs held in Chaitra month across the MP. These are—Chaitra fair of Biaora (Malwa), Dhup Devi Ka Mela of Hirapur (Rewa), Ram Navmi fair of Nayagaon, Bhilat Baba ka Mela of Seoni etc.

Tejaji Fair: It is celebrated in the month of Bhadra, to mark the birth of local deity Tejaji. Tejaji is a local deity of snake charmers and tribals. In his fairs rituals are done to cure snake-bite.

Somnath Sankarji ka Mela: In the month of Asadha and Bhadra at Deotalab (Rewa).

Other Fairs

- The Kumbha Mela (after every twelve years at Ujjain)
- Lachhandas Baba's Fair (Laljit ka Pura-Morena)
- The Fairs of Hira Bhumia (Gird-Gwalior)
- Kaluji Maharaj (Piptya Khurd-West Nimarh)
- Singaji (Rajpur Tehsil-Nimarh)
- Bhilat Baba ka Mela (Malapur and Seoni Malwa-Hoshangabad)
- Garibnath Baba ka Mela (Awantipur Barodia-Shajapur district)
- Kana Baba ka Mela (Harda Tehsil)
- Ramlila Mela of Bhander (oldest fair)
- The Bhaya Sokar Devi Fair of Rewa
- The Unao or Baramju Fair of Datia

TEST YOUR SELF

1. Tansen Samaroh is organised at
   A. Maihar   B. Gwalior   C. Khajuraho   D. Ujjain
2. All India Kalidas Samaroh is organised at
   A. Ujjain   B. Satna   C. Khandwa   D. Jabalpur
3. Find the correct one
   A. Tansen Samaroh : Gwalior
   B. Kalidas Samaroh : Ujjain
   C. Dhrupad Samaroh : Bhopal
   D. All of the above are true
4. Madhya Pradesh Utsav is organised at
   A. Bhopal   B. Indore   C. Khajuraho   D. Delhi
5. Bhagoria is a tribals festival of which district?
   A. Jhabua   B. Bastar   C. Mandla   D. Sarguja
6. 'Goal Gadhera' festival is celebrated by which tribe?
   A. Bhil   B. Gond   C. Madiya   D. Kol
7. 'Mahamrityunjay fair' is organised at
   A. Rewa   B. Chhatarpur   C. Sagar   D. Khargone
8. Gangour festival is related to ....
   A. Ram-Sita   B. Radha-Krishna
   C. Shankar-Parvati   D. None of the above
9. Which of the following is a festival of farmers only?
   A. Hareli   B. Neerta   C. Sangya   D. Dharalya
10. Meghnad festival is celebrated by the tribe ....
    A. Gond   B. Bhil   C. Korku   D. All of these

ANSWERS

1	2	3	4	5	6	7	8	9	10
B	A	D	D	A	D	A	C	A	A

❑❑❑

Art and Culture

Folk Music

Relo: The folk musical map of Madhya Pradesh comes from the tribal areas. The Relo is a remarkable type of the maria song. Every young man must respond to its call it is an everlasting favourite song of the maria boys and girls. They may sing the Relo on any occasion.

Leza: In the surrounding village of Jagdalpur the Leza song has a significant place. The leza has its origin with the 'send off ritual' to some dear one literally the leza means 'Take it'. Many of the leza songs are lengthy. The rhyming line serves as an epic and could be recited to unfold any song. The recitative line seldom has any affinity with the actual song. It merely helps to enhance the form of the song. Any subject could be the theme of the leza songs. The Bhatra and the panha classes of the Adivasi population sing numerous leza songs.

Dadoria: The marriage songs of the Kumars are generally short many of them are addressed to the trumpeter Moharia. The Dadoria of this region has a pattern of rhyming lines. They are also called Ban Bhajans or Salho. The Dadoria has a style of question answer rendering.

Chaukaria Phag: The songs of the poet Isuri come into prominence among the people of Baghelkhand region. His four lined compositions (Chaukaria Phag) have become part and parcel of the folk musical tradition of the region stretching down to Bhopal. In Nimarh songs attributed to Singa and Dalaji are very much alive. The ballads about Chhatrasal and the Rani of Jhansi have also becomes one with the existing folk music. As compared to the seasonal songs and the children's songs the music of Bundelkhand is not of much antiquity.

Pai: There are romantic led and the pai songs. The pai is associated with the saira dance of the rainy season.

Bambalia: The Bambalia of Bundelkhand has religious fervour and is always sung by the people who go for ceremonial bath to distant rivers. The song corresponds to the Batgamni of mithila.

Alha: The Alha of Jagnik nearest the account of fifty two battles fought by both Alha and Udal against Prithviraj or Delhi. The Alha receiters are known us Alhets.

Dirges: The dirges (songs sang for a dead person) of Nimarh are full of pathos and the sati songs of Malwa are haunted by sadness while the Jagiras and the songs about Raja Bhartrihari and the folk devotional type of sakhis of kabir sing of the transient nature of the world.

Garbi: The Garbi of the Narmada valley has a softer melody than the Garba songs of Nimarh. It has three variations like The Rewar Garbi, the simple Garbi and the Gujarati Garbi.

Daharia: The marriage songs of the kamars are usually short. Many of them are addressed to the trumpeter moharia. The daharia of this region has a pattern of rhyming lines. They are also called Ban Bhajans or Salho. The Dhadaria has a style of question answer rendering.

Musical Instruments

Wind Instruments

Flats and Trumpets: The flats and trumpets used by the tribal of Madhya Pradesh are of the simplest kind, played as part of religious ceremonies or for the sheer pleasured of it.

Singha: The Singha could well be the first aero-phonic instrument invented by man. It is simply the horn of a dead animal, the tip of which has been sawn off.

Pangi or Been: It is synonymous all over India with the community or Jogis or snake charmers. It has two parallel bamboo pipes fitted into a gaura, one of which gives the drone while the other has the finger holes. Even Margot fountain can't beat the grace of a cobra dancing to a Jogis Pangi.

Mohari: It is a cylindrical bamboo flute with seven holes that produces shrill, piercing notes. Almost all the commonalities in the region play it.

Bansuri: The modern flute is called bansuri. Usually with six finger holes it is an integral part of every music and dance performance. An older cousin of the modern flute, the bansuri is a cylindrical bamboo take with four finger holes used by the folk singers.

Percussion Instruments

Dholki: Almost every self-respecting north Indian can claim to play the dholki (a kind of drum). During marriages the women of the house gather together and sing songs to the lively beats of the dholki. But you can find innumerable variation of the drum.

Khanjari: It a small hand drum used by the folk musicians of Madhya Pradesh. Using the thumb, fingers, Knuckle and palm the drummers produce the most amazing number of sounds.

Mathal: It is belongs to the coos tail shape of drums (called gaspersavdya). The conical clay shell is stretched over with monkey skin and is struck with have hands used by the tribal, it gives a lively rhythm and linear beauty to their dances.

Dholak: It is a cylindrical wooden drum stretched with animal skin and beaten with sticks. It is especially common among the Pradhans and Achalpurs.

Autophonic Instruments

Clappers: Clappers of various kinds strict to maintain the rhythm of the songs are extremely popular all over India. The tribal of Madhya Pradesh have devised ingenious ways of clapping two pieces of wood to produce the most complex beats. The most primitive of the wooden clappers is the tabri, a hollow disc with two wooden clappers used by the tribal. The tapri was actually hang around the necks of cattle to help the herders locate runway cows.

Chat Kula: The saila dancers and Korku tribal have mastered the art of jangling the chat Kula, an oval clapper of wood or bell metal. Tiny bells attached to the two ends add a tinkling melody to the clang of the chat Kula.

Khirki: It is a bamboo rattle that the Gonds in the tribal district of Mandla play dexterously.

Stringed Instruments

Chikara: No performance is ever complete without the twang of the Chikara, seven stringed instrument played with a curved wooden bow attached with little bells. The pradhans are especially adept at playing the Chikara.

Ektara: The mendicant singers all over India use the single stringed ektara. The string is plucked with the forefinger a hollowed pumpkin or ground acting as the resonator.

Tanpoora: It is essentially a classical instrument in India. It is played by Goddess Saraswati the Hindu goddess of learning and the consort of lord Brahma.

Dances of Madhya Pradesh

- **Karma:** This indigenous folk dance belongs to the Gond and Oraon tribes of the State. Considered to be the oldest of all tribal dances in the State, the Karma is performed at the onset of spring when gaily dressed tribal men and women dance around the trees scattered in the village. Musical instruments like thumki, payri, challa and jhumki accompany the various tribal songs.

- **Tertali:** Tertali is a folk dance of the Kamar tribe of the State. Normally, two or three women of the tribe sit on the ground and initiate the dance performance. Small metal cymbals called Manjiras are tied to different parts of their body. They also carry a cymbal in each hand and strike them in rhythm. The head remains covered with a veil. Gnashing a small sword between their teeth and balancing a pot on their heads, they vigorously follow the beat of the Manjiras.

- **Jawara:** Performed by the people of the Bundelkhand region, as part of the celebrations of prosperity. Originally, a peasant dance, the Jawara follows the reaping of a good harvest. Colourfully dressed men and women dance and revel together, synchronising their movements to a variety of musical instruments. While dancing, the women also balance baskets, full of Jowar (A kind of grain), on their heads. The dance presents a wonderful picture as it is nothing short of a pleasure to notice the poise of the women, as they maintain the pace of the dance and keep up with the movements of the Jowar.

- **Lehangi:** Lehangi is a popular folk dance of the Banjara and Kanjar tribes of the Bhopal region and is performed during the blossoming monsoon period. The Banjara tribe also performs this dance during the festival of Rakhi. Young men hold sticks in their hands and rhythmically beat them while dancing. Various acrobatic tricks, incorporated into the dance, lend a dramatic touch to the performances.
- **Ahiri Dance:** Ahiri Dance is a trademark of the cattle herders of Gwalior. The dance also has religious overtones, as the various communities of Gwalior who perform this dance, are considered to be the descendants of Lord Krishna. People belonging to the Ahir, Gwala, Rawat, Raut and Baredi communities generally perform Ahiri. The Ahir community is the most avid follower of this dance form, as Ahiri performances mark all the major cultural and religious occasions.
- **Baredi or Yadav Dance:** Baredi is an important folk dance of the Gwalior region. Staring from Diwali, the dance is performed till the day of Karthik Purnima. A host of musical instruments like dholak, jhanz, manjira, mridang and daphli impart the tribal beat as the dancers perform and move around in circles. Folk songs, following a question and answer format, also accompany these performances that feature Dhoti clad dancers who are accessorised with peacock feathers.
- **Matki Dance:** The land of Malwa has comparatively very few dances. On wedding occasions, the countryside women in this region perform the 'Matki' dance with an earthen pot balanced on their heads, the Matki is almost always a solo performance. But sometimes just for merriment a couple of women join the main dancer who usually dances with a veil covering her face. The two other variations of the Matki are the Aada and Khada Nach.

- **Phulpati Dance:** The Phulpati is another dance, exclusively for unmarried girls. It is a dance of the semi-rural womenfolk. The agriculturist class of Malwa is not very inclined to dance by nature. But during the Holi festival the revelers cannot restrain themselves from coming out with some sort of dance movements to the uneven manipulation of drums.

- **Grida Dance:** When Rabi crops sway in the fields in full bloom, the parties from different villages come together and perform the Grida dance. It continues from morning till evening. The host village returns the visit next year by going to the village of their guests of the preceding year. The dance has three distinct phases: (1) Sela— the feet movements are slow and comparatively rigid. —(2) Selalarki —The feet movements become brisker and faster. —(3) Selabhadoni— With the acceleration of the beat, every limb of the body begins to sway to reflect the euphoria, they experience in anticipation of the crop and reaping season.
- **Gaur Dance:** The most popular among the Madhya Pradesh dances, is the Gaur dance of the Sing Marias or Tallaguda Marias (bison-horn Marias). This spectacular dance symbolizes the hunting spirit of the tribe.
- **Har Endanna:** On marriage celebrations, the Muria boys and girls perform a dance called Har Endanna. The dance commences with a group of boys carrying ritualistic offerings and gifts and conducting the bridegroom to the ceremonial place. In this light and happy dance, there are a variety of movements with the boy and the girl dancers and drummers participating to move in patterns with running steps and circles then changing directions, kneeling, bending and jumping. The movements of the drummers as they dance and manipulate their drums is fascinating.
- **Saila Dance:** Young boys of the plains of Chhattisgarh bring life to the post-harvest time by the Saila dance. Saila is a stick-dance and is popular among the people of Surguja, Chhindwara and Baitul districts. Sometimes the dancers form a circle, each standing on one leg and supporting himself by holding on to the man in front.
- **Kaksar Dance:** Kaksar is a festival dance, performed by the Abhujmaria. Prior to the rains, the Maria cultivators in every village worship the deity for reaping a rich harvest. To invoke the blessing of the deity, Kaksar, a group dance, in which young boys and girls take part, is performed. Boys put on a peculiar costume of a long white robe while girls are clad in all their finery. The dance presents to both girls and boys, a unique opportunity to choose their life partners, and marriage is enthusiastically celebrated afterwards.
- **Chaitra Festival Dance:** The Chaitra festival dance is another famous dance of the Gonds; it is performed after the harvest to thank goddess Annapurna for the harvest already gathered and to seek her blessings for the next crop. Men and women dance in a circle, in semi-circles or in rows; all dancers hold each other's waist.

Folk Dance

Folk dance is the dance of common man. It is simple entertaining, easy to perform, artistic, energetic and most important it is spontaneous i.e., it comes out automatically. The most important part of the folk dance is the music, dance and the instruments. The folk dances of Madhya Pradesh are very colourful and full of joy. As soon as the musician starts the music and the dancers begin to dance, the spectators automatically start capping and rejoicing the dance. The different types of folk dances are as follows:

- **Badhai Dance:** Badhai is one of the oldest traditional folk dances of the Bundelkhand region, it is considered as a ritual dance. Badhai is primary performed on the birth of a child. Through this dance the new born child is showered by blessings.
- **Rai Dance:** Rai dance is the famous dance of Bundelkhandis. It is basically the traditional dance of the Beria tribes. This dance is performed in a group with a single female dancer in the centre of all. The dance moves around the beauty of the woman hood. The expressions of the dance in the centre are very sweet and naughty. This centre dancer is called the "Berni".
- **Dhimrai Dance:** This dance is mainly performed by the Dhimar (Fisherman) tribes of Bundelkhand so it is called as the Dhimrai dance. This dance is performed on the occasion on weddings. The songs of the dance are full of love and on Dashera it is full of bravery and leadership. The foot work in this dance with proper balance and with the rhythm of musical instruments is very important.
- **Kanra Dance:** The Kanra dance is also called the Kanariyayi. It is basically the washer man's dance. The dance is performed on special occasions like on weddings, birthdays etc. The dance starts with the Guru Vandana. Then the story of lord Ganesh is narrated.
- **Saira Dance:** The saira dance is a famous tribal dance of Bundelkhand. This dance is performed either on weddings or in Dushera. The expressions of the songs in the dance are either shringar or veer depending on the occasion. On Deshera the expressions are of veer or of victory and an weddings the expressions are shringar.
- **Dadra Dance:** It is a famous dance of Baghelkhand which is mainly performed on some festivals. It is a male dominated dance with male artists performing the female roles. It is most prevalent in Kol, Kahar Kotwar castes of the region. 'Dhol Nagade' and 'Shalmail' are the main musical instruments of the dance.
- **Bagheli Rai:** This dance is different from the Bundelkhand Rai. This is performed by a group of boys. The musical instrument used in this dance is dholak and nagada. The dancers are dressed in dhoti kurta and turban on the fore head.

- **Ahir or Birhavi:** The Birhavi dance is a common folk dance of Baghelkhand. Birha is basically a folk song of Baghelkhand also performed as dance. It is performed by all the tribes of Baghelkhand specially Bari Godaria, Teeli and Ahir. When birha is performed by the Ahir's it is called the Ahiraji, the Birha dance is mainly performed on the occasion of Diwali or wedding by a group of male dancers or female dancers.
- **Kemalia Dance:** Kemalia is performed on the weddings it is also called sajan-sajan dance (husband wife dance). Both men and women take part in this dance. The song of this dance is in the form of question and answer.
- **Kahera Dance:** Kahera is another form of folk dance. Either males or Females perform the dance. They both have a different style of performing the Kahera dance. Kahera dance is most popular in the Baari tribes.
- **Kalsa Dance:** The Kalsa dance is performed on the weddings on the arrival of the bride and his relatives and friends; males perform this dance. The most important part of this dance is the balancing of 7 pots on the heads.
- **Gangaur Dance:** The Gangaur dance is the traditional dance of Nimarh region. Gangaur is festival which is celebrated in the spring season. It is basically the traditional festival of Rajasthan but it is celebrated in the Nimarh region also with the same dignity and respect. On this occasion the married women dressed in beautiful saris and ornaments collect together and go to the temple where they sing the Gangaur song and dance along with it. The Dhol is the main musical instrument played in this dance.
- **Aara Khara Dance:** The dance performed on the occasions of weddings birthdays and other auspicious ceremonies in the Nimarh region are called the Aara Khara dance. Usually 2 or 3 ladies of Nimarh perform this dance. The musical instruments used in this dance are dhol and bronze plates.
- **Danda Dance:** The dancers in the danda dance hold a stick in one hand so the dance is called the danda dance. 20-25 males perform the dance by making sound from the sticks. The musical instrument used are Dhol and bronze plates.
- **Phephariya Dance:** The phephariya dance is performed on the weddings. It is a traditional dance performed in group by both male and female, forming alternative pair. Phephariya is a piece of pipe (used like a musical instrument) sounds like the cymabal or the Shahnai.
- **Kathi Dance:** Kathi dance is the traditional dance of Nimarh performed in the honour of deity parvati. During the Matha Shivratri times, the kathi dance is performed whole day. The musical instrument used in this dance is the Dhaak. Both male and female perform this dance.
- **Mandalya Dance:** This is a group dance performed on festivals and other auspicious occasions. In the group only the girls dance and the boys play the Dhol.

- **Ara Khara Rajwadi Dance:** It is traditional dance of Malwa region performed on weddings. This is a women oriented dance. It is danced on the tune of Kimri, Drums and sticks.
- **Patang (kite) Dance:** It is performed on the music of Qadra and Kasherva. Patang dance is a beautiful representation of the act of flying kites. It is a very popular dance.

Folk Theatres of Madhya Pradesh

- **Bundeli Swang:** 'Swang' is a traditional art form, which means to change the get-up to play some other character. In Madhya Pradesh, it is majorly done in Bundelkhand and is an integral part of the famous **Rai folk dance**.
- **Chahur:** It is the folk drama of Baghelkhand filled with songs and dance depicting mass grievances of 'Ahir' Bamer who rose against the discrimination of his caste by the feudal cords.
- **Gammat:** It is a famous folk art of Nimarh region, which carries entertainment along with a social message. It is mostly celebrated in festive season of Holi, Navratri and Gangaur. Its themes are generally traditional and the language used is generally Nimarhi.
- **Khamb Swang:** It is folk drama prevalent in the Korka tribe of Madhya Pradesh. It is a dance drama devoted to lord 'Megnad' and in his name a pillar (Khamb) is erected in the village of tribals and the swang is performed around this pillar.
- **Manch:** It is a traditional art form of folk theatre of Malwa region. It is the only complete drama of Malwa as well as Madhya Pradesh. It was originated in Ujjain and got its name from the Hindi term 'Manch', which means stage. It is based on various religious, mythological and social themes and is preceded by various traditional rituals.
- **Ragini:** It is drama art form of 'Saharia' tribe of Gwalior region. It is mostly performed during Navratri festival. The drama starts with folk songs and prayers of Lord Ganesha and Goddess Saraswati. It is an affective method to entertain and create awareness among the masses for social issues.

Art and Crafts

- **Bamboo and Cane:** Bamboo and Cane occupy an important place in rural life: utility articles such as agricultural implements, fishing traps, hunting tools and baskets are made of bamboo. In Madhya Pradesh these are generally made by a community called Basor or Basod, who sell them in weekly markets. Shahdol, Balaghat, Mandla and Seoni regions of Madhya Pradesh are main bamboo producing centres.
- **Dolls:** Cute little dolls made out of small cloth pieces are produced in Gwalior, Bhopal and Jhabua. The work of Battobai, a craftswoman from Gwalior has achieved international fame.
- **Floor Covering Durries:** The floor coverings of Madhya Pradesh consist mainly of durries and carpets in a rich variety of designs. A durrie essentially

a thick cotton woven fabric, is meant for spreading on the floor, and is made all over Madhya Pradesh, especially near Sironj. Apart of Sironj, Jhabua, Jabalpur and Shahdol are leading centres of durrie weaving in Madhya Pradesh.

- **Carpets:** Since the mughal times, Gwalior in Madhya Pradesh has carved a niche for its self in the wearing of carpets. Later on; weaving also began in the Shahdol & Mandla belt.
- **Iron Craft:** In the interiors of Madhya Pradesh villages, the craftspersons practise traditional skills and techniques to craft iron in myriad inimitable forms. Iron Grafting begins with obtaining iron ore from local mines which the ironsmiths mould into various shapes and forms. Gond, Muria, Bhatra, Dhruva tribals, practise the tradition of offering horses, swings, trishuls etc. made out of iron.
- **Jute Handicraft:** Jute handicrafts are available at Bhopal, Indore and Gwalior. The items include hanging lamps, baskets, flower vases, swings, hammocks, purses, table mats and footwear etc.
- **Metal Craft:** Metal ornaments, boxes, lamps, rice measure bowls, animal figurines are a few examples of the ingenuity of craftspersons of Madhya Pradesh.
- **Papier Mache:** Papier Mache, a craft practised since time immemorial, finds expression in varied forms. In Madhya Pradesh, the main centre for papier mache is Ujjain, but it is also practised in Gwalior, Bhopal and Ratlam. The Nagvanshi community, which makes mud toys and dolls, is also engaged in making of papier mache articles.
- **Stone Carvings:** India's stone carving tradition is perhaps one of the richest in the world. The famous rock cut temples of Vidisha, the sculptured stone temples of Khajuraho, the monuments of Orchha and Gwalior, all stand testimony to the excellence and originality of the stone carvers of Madhya Pradesh. Each region has a distinct style. Gwalior specialises in jalii (lattice) work, Jabalpur and Tikamgarh in decorative items such as statues of animals and human figures.
- **Terracotta:** The terracotta products of each region in Madhya Pradesh have their own identity and distinctiveness. The art of moulding terracotta in Madhya Pradesh shows a mature ability, the pantheon being even more varied and localised. In the rural areas, it is common to see terracotta animal figures placed under trees and in shrines made by potters.
- **Hand Block Printing:** Hand block printing is among the important crafts of Madhya Pradesh. The popular colours used in this process are vegetable and natural dyes like Indigo, turmeric roots, pomegranate skin, lac, iron, and other substances that create an effect that is rich yet subtle. Bherongarh near Ujjain, has large printer communities who specialise in lugda, jajarns, oudhnis and quilts.

- **Batik:** Batik is a resist process in which the fabric is painted with molten wax and then dyed in cold dyes. Batik is done on a large scale in Indore and Bherongarh. Multi coloured and variously designed Batik sarees are popular and attractive for their contrast colour schemes.
- **Weaving:** Madhya Pradesh is famous for its delicate weaves in Chanderi and Maheshwari sarees. In Chanderi, traditional craftspersons used silk as warp and fine cotton as weft. The Chanderi cotton sarees are ideal summer wear.
- **Wood Craft:** The wood carvers of Madhya Pradesh, with great sensitivity and skill transform different varieties of wood such as shisham, teak, dhudi, sal and kikar into works of art. Besides the famous wooden memorials, the craftspersons of Malwa, Nimarh and Bundelkhand, Sheopur-Kalan, and Rewa also make pipes, masks, doors, window frames and sculptures.
- **Zari Work:** The craft of Zari work is concentrated in Bhopal, which is famous for its exquisite craftsmanship. Also practised in Gwalior and Indore, its origin can be traced back to 300 years.

Folk Paintings

- **Bundelkhand Folk Paintings:** These paintings are drawn on floor with the flour of rice, wheat and jowar. It is a kind of dry painting also known as 'Rangoli'. Chowk Chitra is the most famous style of this floor painting. Another, important folk art of Bundelkhand is 'Surath', which is drawn on the occasion of Laxmi Puja. It is a grid pattern painting. 'Morte' is another style of Bundelkhand paintings drawn on the occasion of marriage. Naurata is a type of wall paintings drawn on the occasion of weddings as well as during the Navratra festival.
- **Baghelkhand Art:** In Baghelkhand art along with the floor and wall paintings, engraved wall paintings are also done. Kohbar is drawn on marriage ceremony, which is worshipped by the newly wedded couple. Neuran is drawn on the birth of a baby for its protection.
- **Malwa Art:** The most popular art form of Malwa region is **Madra** which is mostly drawn on Deepawali festival or some other occasions. It is drawn on floor with white chalk and geru (brown powdered earth). The floor is Kuccha polished with cow dung and yellow mud.
- **Nimarh Art:** The paintings of this region are pre-historic in nature as the worship of eye shaped figures 'Jirauti' on Hariyali Amavasya, 'Navrat' on Navratri, 'Mordhan' on Deepawali, 'Nagchitra' on Nagpanchmi, etc.

Language and Literatures

The cultural variations and regional diversities in the state have many different languages and dialects in Madhya Pradesh. As the region and culture changes, the language also changes. The various traditional languages of the state are:

- **Bundelkhandi:** Bundelkhandi is evolved out of the Shourseni and is a major local dialect (boli) of Western Madhya Pradesh. This boli is more popular as compared to the other bolis of the state. This boli is spoken from Maharashtra's Chanda, Nagpur, Buldhana, Bhandara, Akola districts and Jhansi, Jalaun, Lalitpur, Agra, Hamirpur, Itawah, Banda districts and Chhatarpur, Tikamgarh, Damoh, Sagar, Panna, Jabalpur, Narsimhapur, Shivni and Hoshangabad districts of Madhya Pradesh. This language is important for literature writing. The major poets in this dialect are Jaganik, Keshav, Padmakar, Lal, Esuri etc.

- **Nimarhi:** This boli is majorly spoken in Khandwa, Khargone, Dhar, Dewas, Badwani, Jhabua and Indore. It has also evolved out of Shourseni and is often called as Dakshin Rajasthani.
- **Baghelkhandi:** Baghelkhandi or Bagheli has evolved out of the Ardha-Magadhi. It is a major language of Eastern-Hindi. In Madhya Pradesh, Bagheli in purest form is spoken in Rewa, Shahdol, Satna and Sidhi districts. In this boli, lokgeet and lok katha i.e., the folk songs and stories have also been written.
- **Malwi:** It is a type of Hindi spoken in Rajasthan. It is majorly spoken in Sehore, Neemuch, Ratlam, Mandsaur, Shajapur, Jhabua, Ujjain, Dewas and Indore districts.
- **Brijbhasha:** It is a type of straight Hindi majorly spoken in Bhind, Morena and Gwalior. The major poets and writers of the literature written in this boli are Surdas, Meera, Raskhan etc.
- **Korku:** This is a tribal boli spoken in Betul, Hoshangabad, Chhindwara, Khargone districts.

Cultural Institutions

- **Srijan Peeth:** By creating suitable environment for established and senior literary persons of the country an opportunity and guidance is given to young leading persons for promotion of literary activities. For this purpose following Srijan Peeth are constituted under the control of Sahitya Academy. Mukti Bodh—Srijan Peeth at Sagar, Prem Chand Srijan Peeth at Ujjain, Nirala Srijan Peeth at Bhopal.
- **Ravindra Bhawan:** For performing various cultural and social activities Ravindra Bhawan is the only Air-conditional fully equipped Auditorium is available in the capital city Bhopal. This Auditorium has seating capacity to accommodate 700 spectators. In this Auditorium complex there is an open-air stage and ample space for holding exhibition is also available.
- **Aadivasi Lok Kala Academy:** Aadivasi Lok Kala Academy was established in 1980 under the aegis of Madhya Pradesh. The main objectives are to encourage, preserve and develop the tribal arts. To fulfil these objectives, the academy conducts surveys, organises programs and publishes texts and materials centreed on the various aspects of tribal folk arts.
- **Kalidas Academy:** The department of culture of the Government of Madhya Pradesh established the Kalidas Academy in the year 1978 at Ujjain. The

basic idea of establishing Kalidas Academy in Ujjain is two fold. One is to keep the memory of the great poet-dramatist Kalidas constantly refreshed. The other is to establish a multi-disciplinary institution, which would project the totality of classical tradition with Kalidas as its centre; provide facilities for research and study in Sanskrit classical and traditional literary thought, tradition of fine as well as performing arts and their adaptation for contemporary times in different cultural an linguistic Milieu.

- **Sahitya Academy (Madhya Pradesh Cultural Council):** To fulfil the objective of patronage, encouragement and development of literature and writers of the state, the state government constituted Madhya Pradesh Sahitya Parishad in the form of Sahitya Academy in the year 1954, in the erstwhile capital of state, Nagpur. In the year 1956, the council shifted to the capital city of Bhopal as soon as the state of Madhya Pradesh was formed. Since then the council has been able to mark its dedicated presence on the literary and cultural scenario of the state through distance activities.
- **Kala Parishad:** 'Kala Parishad' was established in 1952 under the aegis of Madhya Pradesh. The main objectives are to Protect and conserve the Music, Dance, for art and Theatre art of the State and to promot and motivate the young budding artists of the state.
- **Tulsi Academy:** It was founded in the year of 1987 at Bhopal. The main objectives are to search all the writing of Tulsi Das and to copile, publish and propagate the same.
- **Sanskrit Academy:** Madhya Pradesh 'Sanskrit Academy' was founded in the year 1985 at Bhopal. The main objective are conservation, development and enrichment of Sanskrit Literature in Madhya Pradesh. It also aims to promote new Sanskrit Literature.
- **Urdu Academy:** Urdu academy was founded in the year 1976 at Bhopal. The main objectives; are to conduct various activities for the upliftment, development and promotion of the Urdu Literature.
- **Hindi Granth Academy:** 'Hindi Granth' Academy was founded in the year 1969 at Bhopal. The main Activities are to publishes books and related subjects matter with the help of respective masters of the subject for University. It is also involved in translation of books in other Language to Hindi. It publishes a bimonthly magazine called 'Rachna'.
- **Kul Hind Alama Iqbal Adabi Margaz:** Alama Iqbal Adabi Margaz was constituted on September 27, 1984 by the cultural division of Madhya Pradesh government to disseminate Iqbal literature. On January 2, 1988 this unit was formed by the name of All India Alama Iqbal Adabi Margaz. Presently, it is functioning as a section of Sahitya Academy.
- **Sindh Sahitya Academy:** The objective of Sindhi literature section of Madhya Pradesh Cultural Council, Sahitya Academy, is to encourage and develop Sindhi language, literature, culture and art, to publish new creative and critical literature, to organise literature, gathering, meeting, assembly, national seminar etc.

- **Ustad Alauddin Khan Sangeet Evam Kala Academy:** Ustad Alauddin Khan Sangeet Evam Kala Academi, Bhopal was established by Madhya Pradesh government in 1952, academy of MP government is working as a state academy of culture department, now with the formation of Madhya Pradesh Art Council its name has changed to Ustad Alauddin Khan Music and Art Academy. While its name at the time of establishment was "Madhya Pradesh Kala Parishad". The Academy was established to in order to protect, preserve and develop Indian Classical music, dance, drama, other metaphorical arts and creative cinema.
- **Bharat Bhawan:** Inaugurated by the Prime Minister of India, Shrimati Indira Gandhi on 13th February 1982, Bharat Bhavan is multi art centre set up to create an interactive proximity between the verbal, visual and performing arts. It provides space for contemporary expression, thought, quest and innovation. Bharat Bhavan seek to provide a creative and thought provoking milieu to those who wish to contribute something new and meaningful, in contemporary scene in the fine arts, literature, theatre, cinema, dance and music.

TEST YOUR SELF

1. Madhya Pradesh Kala Parishad was established in ....
   A. 1952 B. 1956 C. 1942 D. 1941
2. Tulsi Academy was founded in 1987 at
   A. Jhabua B. Bhopal C. Ujjain D. Nagpur
3. Which of the following dialects is known as Dakshin Rajasthani?
   A. Malwi B. Nimarhi
   C. Bundelkhandi D. Baghelkhandi
4. 'Korku' is a dialect of
   A. Tribal language B. Baghelkhandi
   C. Bundelkhandi D. Brijbhasha
5. Consider the following statements
   1. Balkrishna Sharma 'Naveen' Samaroh has been organised since 1982.
   2. Its main concern is for national society, poets and literature.

   Which of the statements given above is/are correct?
   A. Only 1 B. Only 2
   C. Both 1 and 2 D. None of these
6. Consider the following statements
   1. Amir Khan festival is celebrated in Indore.
   2. Indian classical music is performed in this festival.

   Which of the statements given above is/are correct?
   A. Only 1 B. Only 2 C. Both 1 and 2 D. None of these

7. What is the star attraction of Khajuraho festival of dance ....
   A. Classical dance
   B. Folk dance
   C. Dances performed by international reputed dances
   D. Dances of Madhya Pradesh

8. Tejaji is a local deity of snake charmers and tribals. In Tejaji fair rituals are done to
   A. worship snakes
   B. catch snake
   C. kill snakes
   D. cure snake bite

9. Consider the following statements
   1. Baba Dike founded a theatre called 'Little Theatre'.
   2. He was also an active freedom fighter and participated in the Quit India Movement.

   Which of the statements given above is/are correct?
   A. Only 1
   B. Only 2
   C. Both 1 and 2
   D. None of these

10. 'Khamb Swang' is a
   A. folk festival
   B. folk drama
   C. song
   D. folk music

11. Which art drama is performed during Navratri festival?
   A. Gammat
   B. Ragini
   C. Khamb Swang
   D. Chahur

12. Gammat is a famous folk art of Nimarh region. It carries entertainment along with
   A. art and craft
   B. culture and tradition
   C. employment
   D. social message

13. Which dance drama is devoted to Lord Megnad?
   A. Khamb Swang
   B. Manch
   C. Gammat
   D. Chahur

14. Consider the following statements
   1. Ragini is a dance drama of 'Saharia' tribe of Gwalior region.
   2. It is mostly performed during Navratri festival.

   Which of the statements given above is/are correct?
   A. Only 1
   B. Only 2
   C. Both 1 and 2
   D. None of these

15. 'Saira Dance' is a famous dance of Bundelkhand. It is performed either on weddings or on
   A. Diwali
   B. Holi
   C. Dusshera
   D. Harvest season

16. 'Devani Gayan' is a song of which festival?
A. Diwali
B. Holi
C. Dusshera
D. Harvest season

17. Which Phaag is sung by girls for boys?
A. Thakur Phaag
B. Devani
C. Rai
D. Isuri

18. Which of the songs is based on Lord Shiva?
A. Bambulia
B. Jagdeb ka Puwara
C. Berayta Gayan
D. Devani Gayan

19. Which dance is also known as 'Sajan Sajni' dance?
A. Kalash
B. Kemalia
C. Ahir
D. Birhavi

20. Which dance form is similar to the Bhavai of Gujarat?
A. Dadra dance
B. Kalash dance
C. Kemalia dance
D. Ahir

ANSWERS

1	2	3	4	5	6	7	8	9	10
A	B	B	A	C	C	A	D	C	B
11	**12**	**13**	**14**	**15**	**16**	**17**	**18**	**19**	**20**
B	D	A	C	C	A	A	A	B	B

❑❑❑

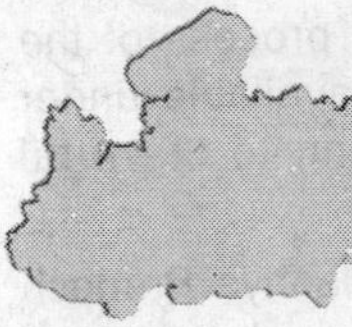

Transport & Communication

Transport

There are four modes of transport, railways, roadways, airways and the waterways. The modes of transport are the lifeline of any country. M.P. is a land locked state so there are three main modes of transport in the State, the roadways, airways and the railways. These different modes of transport are as follows:

Roads

Roads are one of the very fundamental instruments of connectivity. Good roads are essential for the development of the country; not only economic but also equally necessary for social development and reducing regional disparity by providing access to the remotest part of the country. Roads are important as they connect people and places through the means of travel and trade and keep the economy running.

Road Length in Madhya Pradesh

Till 2020 total length of the roads in the state is 70,961 km. in which National Highway is 8,858 km. and State Highway is 11,389 km. long.

Length of Roads in Madhya Pradesh (2020)

S. No.	Particulars	Length of Roads (in Kms)
1.	National Highways	8,858
2.	State Highways	11,389
3.	Major District roads	22,091
4.	Other District/Rural Roads	28,623
5.	**Total**	**70,961**

State Government has established a State Highway Development Fund to cater the requirements of development and maintenance of State Highways.

Rural connectivity has also been given the utmost priority. The phased development of rural roads has acquired urgency due to commitment of the State Government. For this purpose, a Kisan Road Fund from part process of the Mandi Tax has been constituted. In addition, the resources available under the Pradhanmantri Gramin Sadak Yojna are also contributing to the rural connectivity.

The Golden Quadrilateral (GQ) comprehensively misses Madhya Pradesh with just 621 km of North-South-East-West corridors passing through the state. Again, it may be noted that the East West corridor has only a fleeting presence in the northern fringe of the state while much of the 621 kms of road comes under the North South corridor. Of the total length of GQ, only 4.68 per cent passes through the state. Though the state covers 10 per cent of the nation's area, it has only 8 per cent of the national highways passing through them.

Madhya Pradesh has 46 national highways, with total length of 8,858 km. These highways are: NH-3, NH-7, NH-12, NH-12A, NH-25, NH-26, NH-27, NH-59, NH-59A, NH-69, NH-75, NH-75Ext., NH-76, NH-78, NH-79, NH-86, NH-86Ext, NH-92.

Major NHs Passing Through the State

NH No.	Route	Length (in kms)
3	Rajasthan/Madhya Pradesh Border-Morena-Gwalior-Ghatigaon-Shivpuri-Luckwara-Sarangpur-Badarwas-Bhadaura-Guna-Binaganj-Penchi-Biaora-Karaswar-Sarangpur-Shajapur-Dewas-Indore-Mhow-Thikri-Julwania-Sendhwo-MP/Maharashtra Border	712
7	Uttar Pradesh/Madhya Pradesh Border-Mauganj-Mangawan-Rewa-Amarpatan-Murwara-Katni-Sihora-Jabalpur-Bargi-Hulki-Dhuma-Laknadon-Seoni-Gopalganj-Khawara	504
12	Jabalpur-Shahpura-Deori-Bareli-Bari-Obaidullaganj-Bhopal-Doraha-Sharnpur-Narsinghgarh-Biaora-Raigarh-Khilchipur-MP/Rajasthan Border	486
12A	Madhya Pradesh/Uttar Pradesh Border-Orchha-Pithipur-Tikamgarh-Shahgarh-Hirapur-Batigarh-Damoh-Tendukheda-Jabalpur-Mandala-Motinala-MP/Chhattisgarh Border	482
25	Shivpuri-Karera-Madhya Pradesh/Uttar Pradesh Border	82
26	Uttar Pradesh/Madhya Pradesh Border-Barodh-Bandra-Sagar-Gaurjhama-Deori-Maharajpur-Kareli-Narsimha	268

NH No.	Route	Length (in kms)
26A	The highway starting from its junction with NH-86 near Sagar-connecting Jeruwakhera-Khurai and terminating at Bina	75
27	Uttar Pradesh/Madhya Pradesh Border-Sohagi-Katra-Mangawan	50
59	Gujarat/Madhya Pradesh Border-Rama-Raigarh-Bhandheri-Dhar-Ghat-Bilod-Betma-Indore	139
59A	Indore-Chapra-Kannod-Khategaon-Nemawar-Handia-Harda-Timurni Muafi-Sodalpur-Bori-Chirapatla-Chicholi-Betul	264
69	Obaidullaganj-Bakhera-Hoshangabad-Itarsi-Kesla-Chaukipura-Shahpur-Nimpani-Betul-Mulitai-Tigaon-Pandhurna Chicholi-MP/Maharashtra Border	295
75	Uttar Pradesh/Madhya Pradesh Border-Alipura-Nowgaon-Chhatarpur-Panna-Baroura-Nagod-Satna-Madhogarh-Connecting on NH-7 near Rewa	600
76	Rajasthan/Madhya Pradesh Border-Kota-Shivpuri	60
78	Katni-Umaria-Pali-Shahdol-Burhar-Anuppur-MP/Chhattisgarh	178
86	Madhya Pradesh/Uttar Pradesh Border-Malhara-Chhatarpur-Gulganj-86-A, Shahgarh-Rurawan	379
86A	Dalopatpur-Banda-Sagar-Rahatgarh-Vidisha-Sanchi-Raisen-Bhopal	-
92	Madhya Pradesh/Uttar Pradesh Border-Phup Kolan-Bhind-Mahgawan-Gwalior	96

NH 76-Smallest National Highway in the State.

MPRRDA

The Madhya Pradesh Rural Road Development Authority (MPRRDA) is the implementing agency (IA) for central flagship programme Pradhan Mantri Gram Sadak Yojana (PMGSY). The MPRRDA is a registered society under the Societies Registration Act of 1860.

It was registered on the 25th of December 2000. The Authority has a general body that is headed by the chief minister, an executive council headed by the rural development minister and an empowered committee that is headed by the chief secretary.

Central Road Fund (CRF): The scheme is in implementation since 2000-01, wherein, certain proportion of tax collected by imposing a cess of ₹ 1.00 on each litre of petrol and diesel is distributed among state governments for improving the state highways and major district roads in the state. Out of CRF, MP is getting more than ₹ 100 crore annually on 100 per cent funding basis.

The state government has developed some roads in past few years by issuing of bonds and taking loan from Housing and Urban Development Corporation Limited (HUDCO). The state government is currently developing many roads by taking loan from Asian Development Bank (ADB). Also it is negotiating a loan from ADB for upgradation of 1768.16 km roads. The approach roads to villages are being undertaken by the state government under National Bank for Agriculture and Rural Development (NABARD). Currently, rural connectivity is being provided under the PMGSY in a big way. Besides the road construction being undertaken through the state plan, significant quanta of roads and bridges/culverts are being constructed under PMGSY.

Public-Private Partnership

MPRDC is executing the projects both through contract scheme and by providing grant/subsidy to the concessionaire on competitive bidding basis. While the former route is being adopted in projects that are funded through loans (from ADB and HUDCO), the latter route leads to public-private partnership (PPP) that results in roads being built on built-operate-transfer (BOT) basis. The story of PPP in MP is a successful one as it is attracting private partners for building the state highways in MP. This has been achieved by the state through creating an enabling environment that has been nurturing PPP since its inception.

Eleven roads covering a length of 1,664 kms, have already been undertaken under PPP of which two are already under construction.

Six road projects covering a length of 652.64 kms costing Rs. 1,519.12 crore were recently bid out and will be developed with GoI assistance under Viability Gap Funding.

Rural Road Connectivity

The broad objective of MPRRDA is to provide rural road connectivity to human habitations in the state under PMGSY. It aims at providing connectivity to all unconnected habitations with 500 and above general population and population of 250 in tribal areas with all weather roads and construction and upgradation of connecting rural roads. Currently, MPRRDA has been entrusted with the task of constructing 36636.46 kms of village roads in MP, expected to benefit 9571 villages worth Rs. 7751.69 crore in different phases. This is nearly 66 per cent of the total rural roads of Madhya Pradesh. This works out to nearly 49 per cent of the total road length in the state and makes it one of the most important road-constructing agencies in the state.

Railways

Railways are a unique provider of transport, a connector and a lifeline for this nation. The railways perhaps is the most pro-poor of all mass transport systems—they offer relatively cheap, affordable and safe travel for all economic levels, and transport basic goods, food grains, minerals, manufactured goods, even essential commodities such as medicines and perishable commodities such as fruits, fish and milk from one place to another—offering better markets to farmers and providing essential commodities to commodity scarce areas. Access to railways opens up a world of opportunities to labourers, especially during times of distress or to prospective and current migrants. Railways enable long distance migration as well as a lifeline linking back home.

As a centrally located state, the major north-south rail lines and some east to west rail lines pass through the state. Main junctions in the state are Bhopal, Bina, Gwalior, Indore, Itarsi, Jabalpur, Katni, Ratlam and Ujjain.

The first rail route made in the state was from Allahabad to Jabalpur in 1867. There are 20 big and 13 small junctions in the state out of which Itarsi is the largest junction of the state.

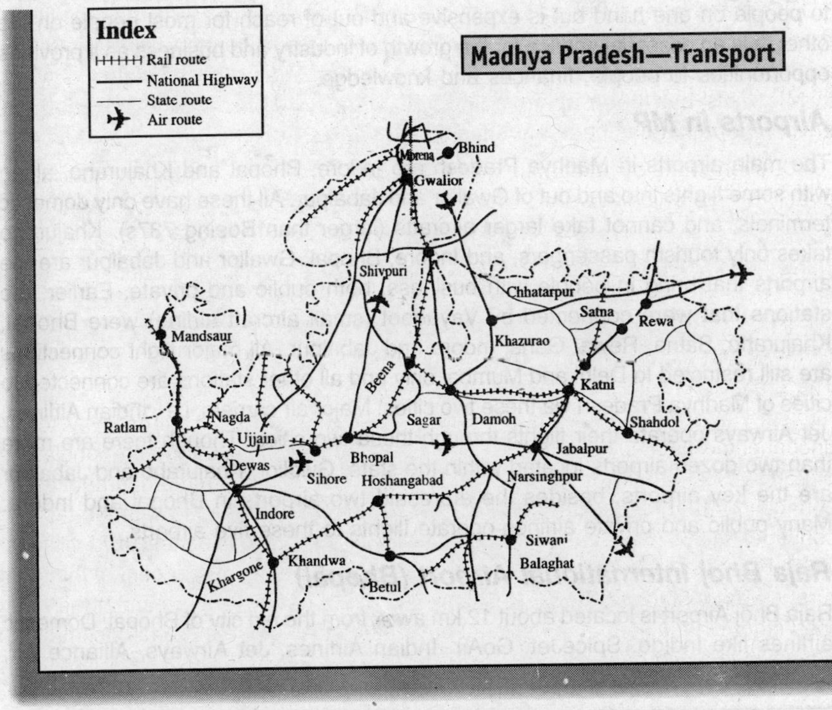

The railway administration in Madhya Pradesh has been divided into three categories as

- South-Eastern Railways
- Western Railways
- Central Railways

Railway Divisions in Madhya Pradesh

Railway Divisions	Districts Under these Divisions
South-Eastern Railways	Chhindwara, Umaria, Shahdol, Balaghat, Seoni
Western Railways	Indore, Mandsaur, Ujjain, Ratlam, Sehore, Dewas
Central Railways	Jabalpur, Gwalior, Rewa Bhopal

Aviation Sector in MP

As a means of transport, aviation is faster, comfortable and provides quality travel to people on one hand but is expensive and out of reach for most people on the other. It is an essential service for the growth of industry and business as it provides opportunities to people, finances and knowledge.

Airports in MP

The main airports in Madhya Pradesh are Indore, Bhopal and Khajuraho, along with some flights into and out of Gwalior and Jabalpur. All these have only domestic terminals, and cannot take larger aircrafts (larger than Boeing 737s). Khajuraho takes only tourism passengers, and Indore, Bhopal, Gwalior and Jabalpur are the airports that bring in people with business, both public and private. Earlier, the stations that were connected by Vayudoot (small aircraft airline) were Bhopal, Khajuraho, Satna, Rewa, Guna, Indore and Jabalpur. All major flight connections are still restricted to Delhi and Mumbai only and all other stations are connected to cities of Madhya Pradesh via these two cities. Major air carriers, i.e., Indian Airlines, Jet Airways operate their flights through these two cities. Though there are more than two dozen airports located within the state, Gwalior, Khajuraho and Jabalpur are the key airports, besides the aforesaid two airports in Bhopal and Indore. Many public and private airlines operate flights to these five airports.

Raja Bhoj International Airport (Bhopal)

Raja Bhoj Airport is located about 12 km away from the old city of Bhopal. Domestic airlines like Indigo, SpiceJet, GoAir, Indian Airlines, Jet Airways, Alliance Air,

Paramount Airways and Air Deccan, connect the terminus to the places in and around the state. International flights of Indian Airlines and Air India also operate from here, to places like Dubai, Singapore, Sharjah and Bangkok. Keeping in mind the convenience of the travellers, the airport is well equipped with facilities like comfortable lounge, facilities for refreshments, clean washrooms and car hire.

Devi Ahilyabai Holkar International Airport (Indore)

Named after the legendary Holkar Queen, Devi Ahilyabai, Indore airport is located 8 km to the southeast of the city centre and caters to the air traffic needs of people travelling to/from Indore.

Domestic airlines (like Jet Airways and Indian Airlines) and private airlines (like SpiceJet and Indigo) shuttle regular flights to different parts of India. Silk Air, Air Arabia, Indian Airlines and Air-India Express are international airlines that fly from this airport. Facilities include parking, restaurant, coffee shop, luggage keeping, information desk, medical facilities, pre-paid taxi booth, baggage wrapping and gift shop.

Communications

A separate Post and Telegraph deptt. was established in Madhya Pradesh on 1st April, 1962, it was a step in the beginning of communication services in the state initially the head office of Post and Telegraph division was established at Nagpur which was shifted to Bhopal on 1st July, 1965.

There are fifteen Akashwani Centres in Madhya Pradesh, (1) Indore, (2) Bhopal, (3) Gwalior, (4) Jabalpur, (5) Rewa, (6) Chhatarpur, (7) Shivpuri, (8) Guna, (9) Betul, (10) Khandwa, (11) Chhindwara, (12) Balaghat, (13) Sagar, (14) Shahdol, (15) Rajgarh. Beside Akashwani Centre is under construction at Mandla.

Broadcasting of Akashwani programmes in Madhya Pradesh started in 1955, when the first Akashwani Centre was established at Indore. It was inaugurated on 22nd May, 1955.

On 31st October, 1956 second Akashwani Centre of Madhya Pradesh started at Bhopal. Akashwani Centres on 15th August, 1964 at Gwalior, 6th November, 1964 at Jabalpur, 7th August, 1976 at Chhatarpur, and 2nd October, 1977 at Rewa were also established.

Doordarshan in Madhya Pradesh entered in 1975 through Raipur. In 1982, a low power transmeter at Bhopal and in 1984 a high power transmeter at Indore was established. At Gwalior and Jabalpur high power broadcasting centres are established.

First T.V. Studio was established in Bhopal.

TEST YOUR SELF

1. Consider the following statements
   1. Roadways for any state are very essential as they are the views of economy being the cheapest mode of transport.
   2. State roadways are not very well developed.

   Which of the statements given above is/are correct?
   A. Only 1 B. Only 2
   C. Both 1 and 2 D. None of these

2. How many National Highways pass through the state?
   A. 49 B. 38 C. 40 D. 46

3. The longest national highway is NH-3 with a length of 712 km. The second longest is NH-75 with a length of
   A. 603 km B. 659 km C. 600 km D. 400 km

4. What per cent does the National Highway of Madhya Pradesh constitute in total road length in MP?
   A. 10% B. 12% C. 7% D. 6%

5. Which is the smallest highway of Madhya Pradesh?
   A. 16 B. 76 C. 15 D. 83

6. Consider the following statements
   1. The total length of the railway network in India till 31 March, 2020 is 67,956 km.
   2. Only 9.5% of this is in Madhya Pradesh.

   Which of the statements given above is/are correct?
   A. Only 1 B. Only 2
   C. Both 1 and 2 D. None of these

7. When was the first rail route made in the state?
   A. 1832 B. 1857 C. 1852 D. 1867

8. Which of the following is the largest junction of the state?
   A. Gondia B. Itarasi C. Ujjain D. Chilpi

9. How many State Highways are there in the Madhya Pradesh?
   A. 54 B. 48 C. 49 D. 50

10. Which of the following is the International airport of Madhya Pradesh?
   A. Malanpur B. Khajuraho C. Ujjain D. Indore

11. Rani Ahilyabai International Airport is located at ....
   A. Gwalior B. Indore C. Ujjain D. Bhopal

12. Which of the following is the first newspaper of Madhya Pradesh?
   A. Jyoti B. Gwalior Akhbar
   C. Navjeevan D. Jeevan Bharti

13. When was the first radio station of Madhya Pradesh established?

A. 1952 B. 1955 C. 1961 D. 1960

14. When was the department of post and telecommunications started in Madhya Pradesh?

A. 1961 B. 1948 C. 1962 D. 1960

15. 'Navjeevan' started in 1939 from Indore. It was

A. first Hindi newspaper

B. first newspaper of Madhya Pradesh

C. first weekly newspaper

D. first daily newspaper

ANSWERS

1	2	3	4	5	6	7	8	9	10
C	D	C	D	B	C	D	B	B	D
11	**12**	**13**	**14**	**15**					
B	B	B	C	D					

❑❑❑

Tourism

Madhya Pradesh has an inherent charm and a place of its own because of its interior location, unmatched beauty and primitiveness. It is a giant state with rich endowments of land, people, history and culture. It also has its own share of negative aspects, especially the size and distances that have, in a way, hampered the growth of communication. Even a methodological appraisal of its resources would compare it more favourably with any other region in the country.

Wildlife

- **Kanha National Park:** Located in the Kipling country, it was one of the 9 parks initially selected for Project Tiger Scheme. This park is known for Central Indian Swamp Deer, the Barasingha, a rare species. Tiger Safari is a high point of the visit to this park.
- **Bandhavgarh:** An old forest preserve of Rewa rulers, it is a veritable tiger land. The other wild-life species to be found are bison, sambhar, barking deer, nilgai and a large variety of avifauna.
- **Shivpuri:** This place was the summer capital and tiger hunting area of rulers of Gwalior. The national park is surrounded on one side with a huge lake with a sailing club. The cenotaphs of the former ruler in marble with inlay work, similar to Taj Mahal, is very attractive.

Scenic Beauty

- **Panchmarhi:** A hill-girdled plateau located on the Satpura Hills, it is 1067 metres high. It has a bracing climate all the year round and has 45 attractive points for nature based tourist activities.
- **Marble Rocks (Bhedaghat):** A place of extraordinary beauty. It has the river Narmada passing through a gorge with towering rocks of marble on either side. These rocks are of various colours and hues, which reflect on the water. Boating in the moonlit nights is a pleasant experience.

Pilgrim Centres

- **Ujjain:** The city of Mahakal Temple with one of the twelve Jyotirlingas of Shiva. It is a temple town on the banks of river Kshipra. It is also the land of poet laureate Kalidas who wrote the immortal Meghdootam.
- **Omkareshwar:** Another religious town having Jyotirlinga, it is located in the confluence of Narmada and Kaveri. It is an Om shaped island having the famous temple of Omkar Mandhata.
- **Maheshwar:** A town located on the bank of river Narmada, it was the seat of Devi Ahilyabai of Holkar Dynasty. It has a number of temples and sprawling ghats and is also known for the handloom sarees.
- **Amarkantak:** It is the place of origin of Narmada and Sone rivers, it is a holy city and a hill retreat. It has more than dozen beautiful falls and viewpoints.
- **Chitrakoot:** The land hallowed by the name of Lord Rama, who spent a part of his 14 years exile at Chitrakoot. All the scenic places are associated with Rama, Sita and Laxmana. Saint Tulsidas is supposed to have written a major part of Ramayana here.

Madhya Pradesh—Tourist Map

Other Places

- **Gwalior:** Gwalior is a historic town having one of the impregnable forts of India. It was also called "the pearl in the necklace of castles of Hind" by the Mughal chroniclers. It is also associated with the romantic episode of Raja Mansingh and Gujari, a village belle. The fort precincts have Manmandir Palace, Gujari Mahal, Sas-Bahu temple, Teli temple and the colossal statues of Jain Tirthankaras. The other attractions are the royal heritage of Jaivilas Palace, a Durbar hall having two of the biggest chandeliers, dining hall with crystal mini train for service and the Palace museum.
- **Shivpuri:** Shivpuri was the summer capital and shikar preserve of Scindias, the rulers of Gwalior. Madhav National Park has a variety of wildlife and avifauna. It is surrounded on one side by Sakhya Sagar lake with a stately sailing club. The cenotaphs of Scindia rulers in marble with inlay work, on the pattern of Taj Mahal, are the other attractions. Some of the excursions near about Shivpuri are Narwar Fort, Kuno Lion Safari park and the ruins of ancient temples of Surwaya.
- **Orchha:** Located 100 kms from Shivpuri, it is a medieval laid back town on the banks of river Betwa. It was the seat of warrior Bundela king Bir Singdeo. It is probably the only place, which represents the best of Bundela architecture and paintings. Jehangir Mahal, Laxmi Mandir, Rai Praveen Mahal, Chaturbhuj temple, Ram Raja Mandir and Chhatris (Cenatophs) of Bundela kings on the banks of the river are a few of the monuments. The star attraction of Orchha is Ram Raja Mandir where the idol of Rama was brought from Ayodhya for installation by one of the queens. This palace is located 20 kms away from Jhansi, which is an important railway station and also the alighting point for Khajuraho.
- **Khajuraho:** Khajuraho is a famous medieval temple town of Central India. It has 22 temples divided in western, eastern, and southern groups built by the kings of Chandella Dynasty. The western group has the largest number of temples, which include the towering Kandaria Mahadev temple, Laxman temple and Devi Jagadamba temple. The plastic art and finesse of the medieval temple architecture are at their pinnacle in these temples. The eastern group has the Jain temples, named because of the Thirthankara statues installed in the sanctum sanctorum. The southern group, which is at a little distance, has two temples, Dulahdeo and Chaturbhuj. Though both eastern and southern groups of temples are later constructions, yet the architectural lines are superb. The ancillary attractions around Khajuraho are Panna Tiger Reserve, the sanctuary for tiger and crocodiles and the Gharial (of alligator family) sanctuary at Raneh falls.
- **Indore:** Indore is a bustling commercial town, which was the seat of Holkar rulers. It is well connected by air, rail and road from Delhi and Mumbai. It has a few interesting features, the Rajwada Palace and the cenotaphs of Holkar rulers. It is called the "Mini Mumbai" because of its importance of commercial activities.

- **Mandu:** A small town bordering the plains of Nimarh has the massive Afghan monuments of various shapes and sizes, e.g. the Jahaz Mahal (the Ship Palace). The romantic tales of Bazbahadur, the last Afghan king, and Roopmati, a Rajput princess, are still sung by balladeers of Mandu. The Mughal monarch Jehangir was fascinated by this place and named it the "City of Joy".
- **Jabalpur:** Situated on the Howrah-Mumbai line (via Allahabad) of Central Railways. Jabalpur has the palace of Gond kings, the Madan Mahal and a museum of archaeological finds in the vicinity.
- **Bhopal:** The capital of Madhya Pradesh, is well connected by air, rail and road. It has tremendous scenic wealth with lakes and hillocks. It has one of the biggest mosques in Asia, the Tajul Masajid, Van Vihar National Park, the museum of Man, multiart centre of Bharat Bhawan and archaeological museums. Boating and water sports in the Upper Lake are a pleasant evening activities.
- **Sanchi:** The Buddhist Stupas at Sanchi, dates back to 3rd century B.C. The gateways around the stupas have stone carvings of Jataka Kathas. The relics of two of the disciples of Buddha were found in one of the stupas. From here Emperor Ashoka deputed his son to Srilanka to propagate Buddhism. The archaeological museum houses the finds collected from the area around. The ancient town of Vidisha is only 10 kms where the 5th Century caves with rock cut sculptures can be seen in Udaigiri caves.
- **Bhojpur:** Raja Bhoja, the king and architect, built a colossal temple dedicated to Lord Shiva. Due to onslaughts in other parts of his kingdom, the temple was left half built but the design, drawings and stone sections are still visible around the temple. It has a massive shiva linga at the centre.

Caves

Madhya Pradesh has some historical caves in its various mountain ranges significant of early civilisations, ancient history and mythology. Most significant of them all are Bhimbetka caves situated 46 km away from Bhopal and even enlisted as UNESCO world heritage site. Some other important caves are Bagh caves, Bhartrihari caves, Udaigiri and Pandav caves.

- **Bhimbetka Caves:** These rock shelters situated in the Raisen district of MP, have a number of interesting paintings which depict the lives and times of our predecessors, who lived in these caves including scenes of child birth, communal dancing and drinking and religious ceremonies and rituals.

- **Bhartrihari Caves:** These caves are situated on the bank of river Kshipra, near Gadkalika Temple of Ujjain. These are named after the famous sage 'Bhartrihari' believed to be the step brother of Vikramaditya, who lived and meditated here.
- **Bagh Caves:** These are located 50 km West of Mandu, these caves are the finest example of Buddhist art and architecture in India.
- **Pandav Caves:** A famous tourist destination of Panchmarhi, these caves have a mythological significance. As per the Mahabharata, the five Pandav brothers spent a part of their exile here alongwith their wife, Draupadi.
- **Udaygiri Caves:** These caves are situated near Bhopal are a magnificent example of Guptas architectural expertise and finesse.

Forts

The staggering forts of Madhya Pradesh are live proofs of the rich cultural and historical saga of various dynasties ruled here. Also, these forts are examples of their rich architectural knowledge and taste for art and culture.

- **Asirgarh Fort:** The fort of Asirgarh is situated in the Satpura Range, 20 km North of Burhanpur in Burhanpur district of Madhya Pradesh. This fort is believed to be built by the 'Asiagah' jats. But during the history, it was conquested and possessed by various Hindu and Muslim rulers. Raja Ali Khan (1576-1596) also known as Adil Shah who ruled here constructed many buildings in and around it like Jama Masjid in upper portion of Asir, Jama Masjid at Burhanpur, Idgah at Asir, Mausoleums and Serai at Burhanpur and Serai, and a mosque at Zainabad.
- **Bandhavgarh Fort:** It is situated in Bandhavgarh in Umaria district of Madhya Pradesh. It is believed to be some 2000 years old with no specific records of its constructors. Various dynasties ruled the fort and the last inhabitants deserted in 1935.
- **Chanderi Fort:** It is located at Chanderi in Ashoknagar district of Madhya Pradesh. It has a strategic location on the borders of Malwa and Bundelkhand. Chanderi, an excellent Mughal Fort was once used to dominated by the trade routes of central India.

Asirgarh Fort

Bandhavgarh Fort

Chanderi Fort

- **Deogarh Fort:** It is also known as Devgarh, is in Chhindwara district of Madhya Pradesh. It used to be Kingdom of Gonds in late 17th century and hence believed to be built by them.
- **Gwalior Fort:** The fort of Gwalior or Gwalior Qila situated on an isolated rock and has a number of historic structures. It has several remarkable temples like Saas Bahu Ka Mandir, Teli Ka Mandir etc. An Indian stamp has also been issued of this fort on 3 August, 1984.
- **Gohad Fort:** It is situated at Gohad city in Bhind district of Madhya Pradesh. According to some British historians, it was settled by the Jats of Bamrauli village in 1505. Later on it became the power centre of Jat rulers. The fort has 7 gates named after the villages they face. These are Itayali (South), Barthara (West), Gohadi (North-West), Birkhari (North-East), Kathwan (East), Kanava (in South-East) and Saraswati.
- **Hinglajgarh Fort:** It is an ancient fort situated near Navali village in Bhanpura of Mandsaur district. It is believed to be built by the Parmara rulers. It has been a centre of excellence in craftsmanship of sculptures.
- **Mandsaur Fort:** The fort of Mandsaur also known as Dashpur Fort, situated in Mandsaur district of Madhya Pradesh. It has also witnessed the various chapters of medieval history of India. It is believed to be built by the successor of Dilawar Khan Gauri, the Hushang Shah Gauri to strengthen his North-West boundary.

  This fort has twelve gates and the fort premises are now-a-days used by the District Collector as his office.
- **Narwar Fort:** It is situated on a hill about 500 ft above ground, it is situated at Narwar in Madhya Pradesh. It is believed to have been built by Kachwaha Rajputs in 10th century. Then it was occupied by various rulers like Parihara, Tomara till it was captured by Mughals in the 16th century. Later on, it was conquered by the Maratha Chief Scindia in the early 19th century.

Museums

The museums are the best showcases to reflect the richness of vivid culture and traditions of any place. Madhya Pradesh being a witness of many dynasties and rulers in its historical past has a rich heritage of artifacts, statues and pieces to be preserved and displayed for the generations. To do the same, several museums have been developed here and even some are built on the excavation sites itself.

- **Archaeological Museum, Khajuraho:** In 1910, at the initiative of a local officer of British Government in Bundelkhand, the loose sculptures and ruins of temples of Khajuraho were collected and preserved. Successively, the first excavation was done in 1938-39 by Garde. A large miscellany of coins, terracottas, beads, pottery etc. were unearthed and hence, the site was subjected to extensive excavations again from 1955 to 1958 by NR Bannerjee and KM Srivastava in 1964 respectively.

- **Archaeological Museum, Sanchi:** This small museum was established on the hill top in 1919 by Sir John Marshall, then Director of ASI. Later on the ASI acquired, a college building at the foot hill of Sanchi Stupa and it got shifted there. The museum comprises of a main hall and four galleries. The colossal image of Nagaraja, a Torana depicting Buddha's enlightenment etc are its major attractions.
- **Birla Museum, Bhopal:** This museum is a collection of entire history of Madhya Padesh. It even has tools and instruments of Paleolithic and Neolithic age. The major attraction of this museum is the scale model of Bhimbetka caves.
- **Archaeological Museum, Gwalior:** The open air collection of Jardine museum was changed to Archaeological museum in 1952. Now, it is being used for reserve collection and the public entry is prohibited. The present museum was established in 1967 out of the open air museum.
- **Maharaja Jivajirao Scindia Museum, Gwalior:** It is established in 1964, the museum is situated in the famous Jai Vilas Palace in Gwalior. It has on display various objects like sculptures, bronze statues, miniature paintings and coins etc.

Eco & Adventure Tourism

The State has also identified areas suitable for promotion of eco and adventure tourism. The activities included in these forms of tourism and the areas identified are:-

Camping & Trekking and Elephant Safari

Areas adjacent to

1. Satpura National Park — Panchmarhi
2. Panna National Park — Panna
3. Pench National Park — Seoni

Water Sports:- Sailing, Kayaking, Water Skiing, Regatta

1. Tawa Project, District Hoshangabad
2. Kaliasot Project, District Bhopal
3. Halali Project, District Raisen
4. Barna Project, District Raisen
5. Gandhi Sagar Project, District Mandsaur
6. Tigra Project, District Gwalior
7. Harsi Project, District Gwalior
8. Mohini Sagar Project, District Shivpuri
9. Kolar Project, District Sehore
10. Avanti Bai Project, District Jabalpur

Canoeing Safari / White Water Rafting

1. River Narmada
2. River Chambal
3. River Ken
4. River Sone

Rock Climbing & Mountaineering

1. Panchmarhi Escarpment, District Hoshangabad
2. Raisen Fort
3. Gwalior Fort
4. Narwar Fort
5. Asirgarh Fort

Para Sailing / Para Gliding / Hot Air Ballooning

1. Panchmarhi Escarpment, District Hoshangabad
2. Tamia to Patalkot, District Chhindwara
3. Mandu, District Dhar
4. Wanchu Point, District Indore
5. Raisen Fort, District Raisen

These areas would be open for private sector to take on long lease and build necessary infrastructure and facilities.

Tourist Festivals

The rich cultural heritage and the variety of folk and performing arts are displayed in a series of Tourist Festivals organised annually at Khajuraho, Orchha, Panchmarhi, Indore-Ujjain (Malwa) and Bhopal. Among these Khajuraho and Bhopal have made a mark in the tourist markets and have become important supplements to the tourists resource.

Madhya Pradesh has all the resources, except snow and surf, to ensure its place as a major tourist region in the country. Its product profile is mainly heritage oriented with pilgrim and wildlife tourism as important ad-ons. It also has more than adequate potential for development of sports, adventure, youth and eco tourism.

Recreation Centres

With the twin objectives of providing evening entertainment to the visitor and boosting foreign exchange earnings, the Government of Madhya Pradesh proposes to license Recreation Centres with games of skill and slot machines, at prime tourist locations in the State.

Such centres shall be set up in areas notified by the State Government, and private sector investment shall be invited for operating them.

It will be ensured that such establishments do not in any way spoil or endanger the cultural ethos and traditions of India or pose a threat to the social fabric of the area. It is expected that substantial local employment opportunities shall be forthcoming. Revenue earned by the Government through taxes and license fees shall be fully utilized in developmental activities.

Joint Venture Companies

The Government of Madhya Pradesh has decided to set up Joint Venture Companies for the development of tourism-related projects in Madhya Pradesh by way of five-star and other reasonably priced hotels at locations of tourist interest. The Government approves in principle the formation of Joint Venture Department/ MPSTDC and private sector hotel chains and their associates. Essentially, the Government will be willing to offer land and built-up facilities, wherever they are available, as equity participation on its behalf.

The State Government will confine its efforts to infrastructural development, ensuring uninterrupted electricity, water supply, and provision of basic medical facilities. It will also be responsible for dissemination of information, organisation of festivals and inter-departmental coordination to create conditions for attracting private sector investment in the tourism sector. For this, it will provide fiscal incentives, assist in providing suitable sites and remove bottlenecks, especially those connected with infrastructural development.

Eco and Adventure Tourism Policy, 2001

The tourism policy of Madhya Pradesh, 1995 had as one of its major objectives, the promotion of eco and adventure tourism. This was keeping in view the demand for such tourism and the potential for the same in the state.

Instead of depending upon its limited resources, the state government has decided to open up this sector for private participation for optimum utilisation of these resources.

While on one hand, with these efforts, the government hopes to attract tourists in large numbers, on the other hand, it is expected that it would help in generating a greater demand for local products and in creating new employment avenues for the local communities.

Heritage Tourism Policy, 2002

One of the objectives of the tourism policy of Madhya Pradesh, 1995 was to convert the heritage wealth of the state i.e., forts, palaces, *havelis* and *kothis* into heritage hotels. The efforts made in this direction in Rajasthan and Gujarat have been highly successful both in conservation of heritage wealth and generating economic benefits.

The state is committed to promote and support private investment and community effort for the conversion of these historic buildings into heritage hotels and development of heritage buildings.

Special Area Development Authority (SADA)

SADA was created to look after special areas and it administered full control, initially even overriding local self-governments in their designated areas. But now *nagarpalikas* and *nagar panchayats* have been put incharge of the operations. Some of the major tourism sites in the state are under the administrative control of SADA—Mandu and Khajuraho. SADA has been able to prevent to a large extent illegal construction and encroachments, and keep these sites relatively safe and secure from urban growth and environmental damages.

Adivasi Lok Kala Parishad

The state's Adivasi Lok Kala Parishad has been an active agency managing, planning and implementing a large number of tribal folk performances, including national and international level festivals across Madhya Pradesh. Further, this agency has also been promoting local events. Its role in initiating events of tourist interest in major tourism locations and in building a momentum around tribal and folk culture is a strength for the state to explore further.

Madhya Pradesh Ecotourism Development Board (MPEDB)

The state government through its forest department constituted the MPEDB in July 2005 to act as the nodal agency for development and promotion of ecotourism in the state. It shall be the board's mandate to ensure the attainment of the objectives and adherence to the guiding principles set forth in the policy for ecotourism development. For this, the board shall develop the necessary systems, standards and institutions. The board shall be equipped with required technical and financial resources to implement this policy. It shall liaise with local, national and international stakeholders for planning, developing and implementing projects compatible with this policy.

TEST YOUR SELF

1. When was the Adivasi Lok Kala Academy established?
A. 1957 B. 1980 C. 1965 D. 1985

2. Which national park is famous for Indian swamp deer in Madhya Pradesh?
A. Kanha National Park B. Bandhavgarh National Park
C. Shivpuri National Park D. All of these

3. Bhedaghat, famous for its marble rocks is situated near
A. Jabalpur B. Panchmarhi C. Ujjain D. Chitrakoot

4. Which is famous for handloom sarees in Madhya Pradesh?
A. Maheshwar B. Omkareshwar
C. Ujjain D. Chitrakoot

5. Manmandir Palace, Gujari Mahal and Sas-Bahu Temple are located in
A. Shivpuri B. Gwalior C. Shivni D. Jhabua

6. Shivpuri was the summer capital of
A. Chandellas B. Scindias
C. Gonds D. Nawab of Bhopal

7. Jehangir Mahal is located at
A. Khajuraho B. Indore C. Orchha D. Mandu

8. Which city in Madhya Pradesh is called mini Mumbai?
A. Jabalpur B. Indore C. Bhopal D. None of these

9. Which rock shelters have prehistoric paintings on the walls?
A. Bhimbetka B. Bhojpur C. Sanchi D. Bhopal

10. Udayagiri caves situated near Bhopal are a magnificent example of
A. Maurya Architecture B. Chandella Architecture
C. Gupta Architecture D. Parmara Architecture

11. Which among the following is enlisted as UNESCO world heritage site?
A. Bhartrihari caves B. Bagh caves
C. Pandav caves D. Bhimbetka caves

12. Birla Museum in Madhya Pradesh was established in
A. Bhopal B. Gwalior C. Sanchi D. Khajuraho

13. Archaeological Museum Khajuraho was established in
A. 1920 B. 1930 C. 1910 D. 1915

14. Which National Park is not a part of elephant safari?
A. Satpura National Park B. Tawa National Park
C. Pench National Park D. Panna National Park

15. Which among the following is famous for rock climbing and mountaineering in Madhya Pradesh?
A. Panchmarhi Escarpment B. Raisen Fort
C. Gwalior Fort D. All of these

ANSWERS

1	2	3	4	5	6	7	8	9	10
B	A	A	A	B	B	C	B	A	C
11	12	13	14	15					
D	A	C	B	D					

❑❑❑

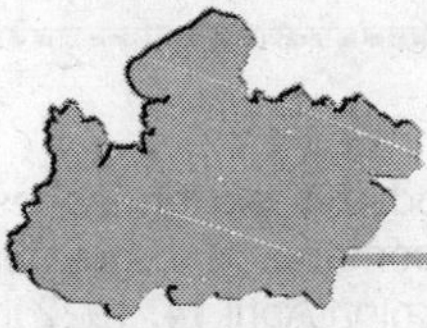

Personalities

Abhinav Kashyap

Abhinav Singh Kashyap is an Indian film director and screenwriter. His directorial debut film, Dabangg was the biggest hit of 2010 and is currently the fourth biggest grossing Bollywood film in history. Abhinav Kashyap was born in Obra, Uttar Pradesh where his father worked for the state electricity board. He is an alumnus of The Scindia School, Gwalior and completed his graduation in English Hons from Hansraj College, University of Delhi in 1995. He is the younger brother of acclaimed director Anurag Kashyap.

Akashaditya Lama

Akashaditya Lama is an Indian Film Director and scriptwriter based in Bollywood. Born in Ranchi, Jharkhand and brought up in Kolkata (West Bengal) Bhilai (Chhattisgarh) Gwalior (Madhya Pradesh) and Faridkot (Punjab). Lama got his diploma in Mechanical Engineering in 1996-97. He got his first break in the business of films and television in 1998 by assisting in Ad films Pillsbury Wheat Flour, Camelin and more.

Alauddin Khan

Alauddin Khan (1862-1972) was a Bengali sarod player and multi-instrumentalist and one of the greatest music teachers of the 20th Century, father of Ali Akbar Khan and Annapurna Devi and guru to Ravi Shankar, Nikhil Banerjee, Vasant Rai, Pannalal Ghosh, and other influential musicians. He himself was a disciple of many great musicians, most importantly the legendary Wazir Khan. Alauddin Khan was born in Shibpur village in Brahmanbaria, in Bangladesh.

Alla Rakha Khan

Ustad Alla Rakha (1919-2000) was a master of the tabla, a classical Hindustani percussion instrument. He is considered one of the greatest tabla players of the

20th century. He was born as *Allarakha Qureshi* on April 29, 1919 at Phagwal village, near Jammu.

Ali Akbar Khan

Ustad Ali Akbar Khan (Bengali) was a master of the sarod, His performances worldwide have established the modern sarod idiom and contributed to greater awareness of Indian classical music. Ali Akbar Khan was born on April 14, 1922 in the village of Shivpur, Comilla, in present day Bangladesh (then East Bengal).

Amjad Ali Khan

Ustad Amjad Ali Khan is a highly acclaimed Indian Sarod player and composer. Khan was born in Gwalior, Madhya Pradesh in 1945. Khan was taught by his father Hafiz Ali Khan, a musician to the royal family of Gwalior. Amjad Ali Khan has developed a unique style of playing the sarod. The key innovations in his style are compositions based on vocal music, the technical ability to play highly complex phrases (ekhara taans).

Asgari Bai

Asgari Bai (1918-2006) was a renowned Dhrupad singer from Chhatarpur district in Madhya Pradesh. She was a recipient of Padma Shri, Tansen Samman, Academy Samman and Shikhar Samman. She has also been felicitated with Nari Shakti Samman. Crowned with many awards, the artiste enthralled music lovers not only in Madhya Pradesh but also across the country with her unique style and talent for decades.

Abida Sultan

Princess Abida Sultan (1913-2002) was the eldest daughter of Hamidullah Khan, the last nawab of the Bhopal state. Abida Sultan was the presumptive heiress of the Bhopal throne. However, she gave up her right to the throne and migrated to the newly formed Pakistan in 1950. In Pakistan, she joined the foreign service. Therefore, the Government of India excluded her from the succession and her younger sister Sajida succeeded her instead.

Ahilyabai Holkar

Punyaslok Rajmata Ahilyadevi Holkar, called "Catherine the Great, Elizabeth, Margaret of India" (1725-1795, ruled 1767-1795) was a Holkar dynasty ruler. Rani

Bihari Lal

Bihari Lal Chaube or Bihari (1595-1663) was a Hindi poet, who is famous for writing the *Satasai* (a collection of approximately Seven Hundred Verses) in Brajbhasha, which is perhaps the most celebrated Hindi work of poetic art, as distinguished from narrative and simpler styles.

Baiju Bawra

Baiju Bawra or Baijnath Prasad or Baijnath Mishra (1542-1613) was a legendary Indian Dhrupad singer. He was the court musician of Raja Mansingh of Gwalior. Baiju Bawra was born in Chanderi in Gwalior on Sharad Purnima in the month of Ashwin. He got the name "Bawra" (crazy) because he was crazily in love with a dancer in Chanderi.

Bahadur Khan

Ustad Bahadur Khan was a sarod player. Ustad Bahadur Khan, a Bengali, was born in January 19, 1931 in Shibpur, Comilla, Bangladesh, (then British India), and died in October 3, 1989 in Calcutta. He was the son of famous Indian classical musician Ustad Ayet Ali Khan nephew of the Sarod legend Ustad Alauddin Khan. His special contribution to Indian classical music, that he could wonderfully combine folk music elements with that of the classical music, made a unique niche for himself among fellow musicians.

Balkrishna Sharma 'Naveen'

'Naveen' was born in 1897 at Shajapur (MP). He was greatly influenced with the works of Pt. Makhanlak Chaturvedi and Shri Ganesh Shankar Vidyarthi. He was editor of "Prabha" and "Pratap" news papers. He participated in Indian freedom struggle under the leadership of Gandhiji, 'Urmila', Pranarpan, Kumkum Apalak, Rashmi Rekha etc. were his famous writings.

Bhoja

Bhoja was philosopher, king and polymath of medieval India. He ruled the kingdom of Malwa in Central India from 1010 to 1060. The name means "bountiful, liberal" and appears as the name of a tribe, the descendants of Mahabhoja in the Mahabharata.

Baz Bahadur

Miyan Bayezid Baz Bahadur was a sultan of Malwa from 1555 to 1562. He is known for his romantic liaison with Roopmati, a singer of Rajput birth. His capital was Mandu (now in Madhya Pradesh). Mandu was an important city for the Mughal emperors too. Akbar, Jehangir and Noor Jahan have visited Mandu. The Jahaj Mahal is in Mandu.

C.K. Nayudu

C.K. Nayudu (born 31 October 1895 in Nagpur, India; died 14 November 1967, Indore) was the first captain of India in Test cricket. C.K. Nayudu was tall, right handed batsman, and a useful change bowler. He was a batsman who could hit the ball tremendously hard, and as a leader that he became famous. He was the first cricketer to be honoured with the Padma Bhushan.

Dr. Shankar Dayal Sharma

Shankar Dayal Sharma (19 August 1918–26 December 1999) was the 9th President of republic of India, serving from 1992 to 1997. Prior to his presidency Dr. Sharma had been the 8th Vice President of India, under President Ramaswamy Venkataraman. He was also Chief Minister of the erstwhile Bhopal state (1952–1956), Cabinet Minister Government of Madhya Pradesh, holding the portfolios of Education, Law, Public Works, Industry and Commerce.

Digvijay Singh

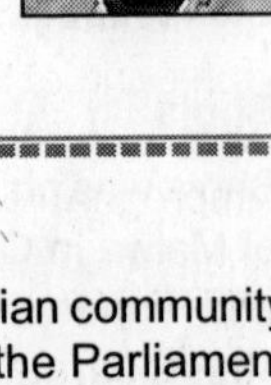

Digvijay Singh is a senior Congress (I) politician in India and has been the Chief Minister of Madhya Pradesh state for two five-year terms. He was born on February 28, 1947 in the royal family of Raghogarh principality, in Guna district of Madhya Pradesh. He first became Chief Minister of Madhya Pradesh on December 7, 1993 and continued to hold the post till congress was voted out of power in the November 2003 State Assembly elections in the state. He is popularly known as Diggi Raja.

Frank Anthony

Frank Anthony (1908–1993) was a prominent leader of the Anglo-Indian community in India, and was until his death their nominated representative in the Parliament of India. Frank Anthony was born in Jabalpur in 1908. In 1942, he was elected the president-in-chief of the Community of the All India Anglo-Indian Association.

Fatima Bano

Fatima Bano is a female wrestling coach from Bhopal, Madhya Pradesh. Born in a Muslim family, Fatima Bano started her career in sports by playing Kabaddi, in which she won three national medals.

Gurbaksh Singh Dhillon

Gurbaksh Singh Dhillon (18 March 1914–6 February 2006), popularly known as Col. G.S. Dhillon was one of those (with Gen. Shah Nawaz Khan and Col. Prem Kumar Sahgal) from the Indian National Army charged with "waging war against His Majesty the King Emperor". They were tried by the British at the end of World War II in the historical trial that began on 5 November 1945 at Red Fort, and was important in the Indian independence negotiations. Gurbaksh Singh Dhillon was born at Algon on 18 March 1914. His father and mother were descendants of the Dhillon and Dhariwal Sikh Jat clans, respectively.

Hafiz Ali Khan

Hafiz Ali Khan (1888-1972) was an iconoclast figure in twentieth-century sarod music. A fifth-generation descendant of the famous Bangash Gharana of sarod players, Hafiz Ali was known for the lyrical beauty of his music and the crystal-clear tone of his strokes.

Hoshang Shah

Originally known as Alp Khan, he had taken the title of Hoshang Shah Gori when he was crowned the second King of Malwa. Alp Khan's father Khan Ghori had belonged to the court of Firozshah Tughlaq, the Sultan of Delhi. Hoshang Shah showed promise of being equally able and much bolder than his father. In fact, he was far more ambitious and did not care what steps he took to achieve his ambition. Hoshang Shah ruled Malwa for 27 years. Despite being a warrior, he had a sympathetic heart and was dearly loved by his subjects. He was also an impartial ruler and extended his patronage to other religions. He is also remembered for his wonderful taste in architecture. It was he who made Mandu one of the most impregnable forts of India.

Jaan Nisaar Akhtar

Jaan Nisaar Akhtar (February 14, 1914 – August 19, 1976) was a famous Indian poet of Urdu ghazals and nazms, and also a lyricist for Hollywood and father of lyricist and script-writer Javed Akhtar and psychiatrist and poet Salman Akhtar and grandfather of Farhan Akhtar and Zoya Akhtar.

Javed Akhtar

Javed Akhtar (born 17 January 1945) is a poet, lyricist and scriptwriter from India. Some of his most successful work was done in the late 1970s and 1980s with Salim Khan as half of the script-writing duo credited as Salim-Javed. Akhtar continues to be a prominent figure in Bollywood and is one of the most popular and sought-after lyricists.

Janaki Devi Bajaj

Janaki Devi Bajaj (1893-1979) was an Indian independence activist who was jailed for participating in freedom movement. She was born in 1893 in Jaora in Madhya Pradesh in India and married to Jamnalal Bajaj who was a leading industrialist. After independence she worked with Vinoba Bhave on Bhoodan movement. She was conferred Padma Vibhushan the second highest civilian award in 1956. She died in 1979.

Kalidas

An Indian poet and dramatist, Kalidas lived sometime between the reign of Agnimitra the second Shunga king (170 BC) who was the hero of one of his dramas, and the Aihole inscription of AD 634 which praises Kalidas's poetic skills.

Keshavdas

He was a Sanskrit scholar and Hindi poet, best known for his Rasikpriya, a pioneering work of the riti kaal (Procedure period) of Literature. He was born in Orchha in a Sanadhya Brahmin family. His father Kashinath was Rajguru the rulers of Orchha.

Kumar Gandharva

Kumar Gandharva (April 8, 1924–January 12, 1992) was a famous Hindustani singer, famous for his unique vocal style, refusal to be bound by the tradition of any gharana, and his innovative genius. He was born in Sulebhavi near Dharwad (Karnataka). He was awarded the Padma Vibhushan award in 1990.

Kirat Singh

Rana Kirat Singh was the last Jat ruler of Gohad state (1803-1805) in Madhya Pradesh, India. He was the first Jat Rana ruler of Dholpur (princely state) (1806-1836). He was from Bamraulia gotra of Jats.

Kailash Nath Katju

Dr Kailash Nath Katju (1887-1968) was a prominent politician of India. He was also one of India's most prominent lawyers. He was part of some of the most riveting cases of his times, including the famous INA trials. Dr Katju joined the freedom struggle against the British rule in India early on and spent several years incarcerated with fellow freedom fighters. Following the independence of India, he held many high political positions. Initially he was the Governor of Odisha (1947–1948) and later the Governor of West Bengal (1948–1951). In 1951 he was elected to the Lok Sabha from the Mandsaur constituency, joining the cabinet of Jawaharlal Nehru as Law Minister in 1951.

Kamal Nath

Kamal Nath (born 18 November 1946) is an Indian politician and the former Chief Minister of Madhya Pradesh. He is also the former Union Cabinet Minister of Urban Development. He is a member of the Indian National Congress (INC) political party. He is an alumnus of The Doon School and a graduate of St. Xavier's College of the University of Kolkata.

Kavi Pradeep

Kavi Pradeep (6 February 1915 – 11 December 1998) was a popular Indian poet and film lyricist, most known for his patriotic song, *Aye Mere Watan Ke Logo* written as tribute to the soldiers who had died defending the country during the Sino-Indian War. In 1997, he was honoured by India's highest award in Cinema, the Dada Saheb Phalke Award for Life-time Achievement.

Kushabhau Thakre

Kushabhau Thakre (August 15, 1922 – December 28, 2003) was a political leader in India. In 1942, he was inducted as a Pracharak by the Rashtriya Swayamsevak Sangh. He moved up in the Jana Sangh, the political wing of the RSS at the time, and then in the Janata Party when the parties merged. During the 1977–1979 Emergency, he was jailed for 19 months alongside other opposition political leaders.

He was elected to Lok Sabha in 1979 in a by-election from Khandwa, Madhya Pradesh.

Mamta Sharma

Mamta Sharma is an Indian playback singer. She is particularly known for song *Munni Badnaam Hui* from *'Dabangg'*. The song was super hit and fetched her several awards and nominations, including a Filmfare award for Best Playback Singer (Female).

Madhavrao Scindia

Madhavrao Scindia (1945–2001) was a prominent Indian politician and minister from the Congress Party. He was born into the Scindia family, who formerly ruled Gwalior. Madhavrao Scindia was the son of the last ruling Maharaja of Gwalior, Jivajirao Scindia. He was educated at the Scindia School, endowed by his family, in Gwalior and then at Oxford University.

Mushtaq Ali

Syed Mushtaq Ali (December 17, 1914-June 18, 2005) was a former Indian cricketer, and an aggressive Test batsman. Ali holds the distinction of scoring the first test century by any Indian overseas, when he smashed a ton for the team in 1936 at Manchester in England.

Maharishi Mahesh Yogi

Maharishi Mahesh Yogi (January 12, 1917-February 5, 2008) founded and developed the Transcendental Meditation technique and related programs and initiatives, including schools and universities with campuses in India, the United States, Mexico, the United Kingdom, and China.

Nareshchandra Singh

Raja Nareshchandra Singh (21 November 1908–11 September 1987), former ruler of Sarangarh Princely State in Raigarh District, Chhattisgarh and Indian National Congress politician and a former Chief Minister of undivided Madhya Pradesh. An allumni of the Rajkumar College, Raipur in the footsteps of his father, Naresh Chandra Singh worked as an Honorary Magistrate in Raipur district before being inducted as the Education Minister in the administration of Sarangarh State.

Nasir Hussain

Nasir Hussain (1931–2002) was an Indian film producer and director. Nasir Hussain was born in Bhopal, Madhya Pradesh.

Narendra Hirwani

Narendra Deepchand Hirwani (born October 18, 1968 in Gorakhpur, Uttar Pradesh) is a leg spin bowler who played for India. He is mainly remembered for his outstanding success on his last debut.

Nirmala Srivastava

Nirmala Srivastava (more widely known as Shri Mataji Nirmala Devi) is the founder of Sahaja Yoga, a new religious movement. She has proclaimed that she is the complete incarnation of the Adi Shakti, and is worshiped as such. Nirmala Srivastava was born on March 21, 1923 in Chhindawara, to Christian parents, Prasad and Cornelia Salve.

Piyush Mishra

Piyush Mishra (born 1963) is an Indian film and theatre actor, music director, lyricist, singer, scriptwriter.

Padmakar

'Padmakar' was born in 1753 at Sagar (M.P.) in the intellectual Brahmin Family. He is one of the prominent writers of medieval period in Indian Literature. He presented a clear and vivid picture of the common man's life. His famous writings are 'Ganga Lehri' Rag Rasayan, Jay Vinod, Himmat Bahadur, Virudhawati Padmabharan, Prabodh Pachasa etc.

Pt. Makhanlal Chaturvedi

He was born in 1889 at Bawani in Khandwa District. He is considered to be a frontline nationalist poet of modern era. He created mass awakening through his baring words and became an icon in Indian Freedom struggle. He was influenced by Gandhiji and therefore took part in freedom struggle, his writings became more patrolling in the company of Shri Ganesh Shankar Vidyarthi.

Pandit Ravi Shankar

Pandit Ravi Shankar was born on April 7, 1920, in Benaras and died on Dec. 11, 2012. His family originates from Bangladesh. He was a disciple of Baba Alauddin Khan, the founder of the Maihar gharana of Hindustani classical music. In 1999, Ravi Shankar was awarded the Bharat Ratna Award, India's highest civilian honour.

Pannalal Ghosh

A virtuoso of Hindustani classical music on the transverse flute, Pt. Pannalal Ghosh was born on July 31, 1911. Born in Barisal, East Bengal now Bangladesh the family first lived in the village of Amarnathganj and later moved to the town of Fatehpur. As the music director of the dance troupe of the princely state of Seraikella, Pannalal Ghosh visited and performed in Europe in 1938, and was one of the first classical musicians to have crossed the boundaries of India.

Ramnath Goenka

Ramnath Goenka (April 3, 1904–October 5, 1991) was a newspaper baron of India. He launched The Indian Express and created the Indian Express Group with various English and regional language publications. In its 2000 millennium issue, India Today magazine, named him amongst "100 People Who Shaped India". Goenka was born in Darbhanga district of Bihar. He completed his primary education in Varanasi. At the age of 15, he came to Chennai to learn the ropes of the business by venturing into the trade of yarn and jute. He was married to Moongibai.

Rohit Sharma

Rohit Gurunath Sharma (born 30 April 1987) is an Indian cricketer. Sharma is a right-handed middle-order batsman and occasional right-arm off-break bowler. Having started his international playing career at the age of 20, Sharma quickly exhibited his athletic fielding and cool temperament to compliment his graceful stroke play. Currently he is captain of Indian Cricket team.

Rani Durgavati

Rani Durgavati (October 5, 1524-June 24, 1564) was born in the family of famous Chandel Emperor Keerat Rai. She was born at the fort of Kalanjar (Banda, Uttar Pradesh). Chandel Dynasty is famous in the Indian History for the defense of king

Vidyadhar who repulsed the attacks of Mahmud Ghaznavi. His love for sculptures is shown in the world famed temples of Khajuraho and Kalanjar fort. Rani Durgavati's achievements further enhanced the glory of her ancestral tradition of courage and patronage of arts.

Raja Birbal

Raja Birbal (1528-1586) (real name: Maheshdas Bhatt) was the Grand Vizier (Wazir-e-Azam) of the Mughal court in the administration of the Mughal emperor Akbar and one of his most trusted members along with being a part of Akbar's inner council of nine advisors, known as the navaratna, a Sanskrit word meaning nine jewels. He was only person other than Akbar who was a Din-i-Ilahi believer.

Rani Rupmati

Rani Rupmati, also spelt Roopmati, was a Hindu singer of Malwa. Sultan Baz Bahadur and Roopmati fell in love with each other and were married according to muslim and Hindu rites. Adham Khan was prompted to conquer Mandu partly due to Rupmati's beauty. When Adham Khan marched on the fort Baz Bahadur met him with his small force and was defeated, Roopmati poisoned herself.

Ranoji Scindia

Ranoji Scindia was Peshwa Bajirao's General during 1720 to 1745. He was the founder of princely Gwalior State of Scindias. Ranoji was a Patil of Kandherkheda (Kannerkhera) a small place in Satara district, Maharashtra, east of Satara. He started his career under the leadership of Peshwa Bajirao and later on established himself in Malwa.

Raghubir Yadav

He spent earlier years of his life in (Ranjhi), Jabalpur one of the prominent city in Madhya Pradesh. He joined the Parsi Theatre Company at the age of fifteen. Later he moved to Delhi, where he joined the National School of Drama (NSD), and graduated in 1977. He made his film debut with *Massey Sahib* (1985) in which he payed the title role of Massey. He also starred in the milestone films like Laagan (2000) and *Water* (2005).

Sneha Khanwalkar

Sneha Khanwalkar is a female Indian music director in Bollywood, the fourth ever in the industry after Jaddan Bai (mother of Nargis and grandmother of Sanjay

Dutt), Saraswati Devi and Usha Khanna. She is most known for her score for the film, Oye Lucky! Lucky Oye! (2008), which won the National Film Award for the Best Popular Film.

Sunil Mittal (Sunil Bharti Mittal)

Sunil Bharti Mittal is an Indian telecom mogul, philanthropist and the founder, chairman and Group CEO of Bharti Enterprises. The US$15 billion turnover company runs India's second largest GSM-based mobile phone service and world's fifth largest wireless company with over 400 million customers across 18 countries in Asia and Africa. He is the son of Sat Paul (former MP) and Lalita.

Subhadra Kumari Chauhan

Subhadra Kumari Chauhan (1904-February 15, 1948) was an Indian poetess famous for her emotionally charged Hindi songs. She was born in Nihalpur village in Allahabad District of present day Uttar Pradesh. Subhadra Kumari initially studied in the Crosthwaite Girls' School in Allahabad and passed the middle-school examination in 1919. After her marriage to Thakur Lakshman Singh Chauhan of Khandwa in the same year, she moved to Jabalpur. She joined the Non-Cooperation Movement in 1921 and was the first woman Satyagrahi to court arrest in Nagpur. She was jailed twice for her involvement in protests against the British rule in 1923 and 1942. She has authored a number of popular works in Hindi poetry. Her most famous composition is Jhansi ki Rani.

Sharad Joshi

Sharad Joshi was a noted Hindi poet, writer, satirist and a dialogue and scriptwriter in Hindi films and television. He was awarded the Padma Shri in 1990. Sharad Joshi was born on May 21, 1931 in Ujjain, Madhya Pradesh to Sriniwas and Santi Joshi, a second child in the family of two sons, and four daughters. Sharad was interested in writing right from his childhood. He did his B.A., from Holkar College, Indore.

Sunder Lal Patwa

Sunder Lal Patwa was Chief Minister of Madhya Pradesh and cabinet minister in Government of India. He twice became Chief Minister of Madhya Pradesh, from 20 January 1980 to 17 February 1980 and from 5 March 1990 to 15 December 1992. He died on Dec. 28, 2016.

Shivraj Singh Chouhan

Shivraj Singh Chouhan (born 5 March 1959) is the current Chief Minister of Madhya Pradesh. On March 23, 2020 be took oath as Chief Minister of Madhya Pradesh for the 4th time. He represents the Budhni constituency of Madhya Pradesh and is a member of the Bharatiya Janata Party (BJP) political party.

Sriniwas Tiwari

Sriniwas Tiwari (17 September 1926-19 January 2018) was a politician from Rewa. He had a long career in Madhya Pradesh state politics. He was a six-time member of the Madhya Pradesh Legislative Assembly. For most of his political career, he was a member of the Indian National Congress, and had stints in Socialist Party and Samyukta Socialist Party in his younger days. He also served as a member of the Vindhya Pradesh Legislative Assembly between 1952 and 1956, before it was merged into Madhya Pradesh. He was bitterly opposed to the merger and advocated the separation of Vindhya Pradesh region from Madhya Pradesh during his political career. He was known as the *White Tiger* of Madhya Pradesh

Shaan

He was a host for the popular show *Sa Re Ga Ma Pa* from 2000-2006 and also for *Sa Re Ga Ma Pa Little Champs*. Shaan was born into a Bengali family on 30th September 1972. He is the son of the late music director Manas Mukherjee and brother of singer Sagarika. He is married to Radhika and has two sons.

Shankar Lakshman

Shankar Lakshman (1933 – April 29, 2006) was an Indian hockey player. He was goalkeeper of the Indian team in the 1956, 1960 and 1964 Olympics, that won two gold medals and one silver medal. He was captain of the Indian team which won the gold in the 1966 Asian Games. He belonged to Mhow and lived his retired life there until his death in 2006.

Sandhya Agarwal

Sandhya Agarwal (born 9 May 1963) is a former captain of the Indian women's cricket team. She hails from Indore. She played in 13 test matches from 1984 to 1995, scoring 1110 runs at a batting average of 50.45, including 4 centuries.

Salim Khan

Salim Khan (born 1935) is an Indian actor and scriptwriter. He wrote numerous screenplays for Bollywood film in the 1970s. He frequently collaborated with writer Javed Akhtar; the duo is credited as Salim-Javed. He is the father of Bollywood actor Salman Khan.

S.H. Raza

Syed Haider Raza was an eminent Indian artist who had lived and worked in France since 1950, but maintained strong ties with India. His works are mainly abstracts in oil or acrylic, with a very rich use of colour, replete with icons from Indian cosmology. He was awarded the Padma Shri and Fellowship of the Lalit Kala Akademi in 1981 and Padma Bhushan in 2007. He died on July 23, 2016.

Tansen

Tansen is considered among the greatest composer-musicians in Hindustani classical music. He was an extraordinarily gifted vocalist, known for a large number of compositions, and also an instrumentalist who popularized and improved the rabab (of Central Asian origin). He was one of the Navaratnas (nine jewels) at the court of the Mughal Emperor Akbar. Akbar gave him the title Miyan (an honorific, meaning learned man).

Tatya Tope

Ram Chandra Pandurang Tope (1814-1859), also known as Tatya Tope, was an Indian leader in the Indian Mutiny of 1857. Born in village Yeola in Maharashtra, he was the only son of Pandurang Rao Tope and his wife Rukhmabai, an important noble at the court of the Maratha Peshwa Baji Rao II. His father shifted his family with the Peshwa to Bithur where his son became the most intimate friend of the Peshwa's adopted son, Nana Dhondu Pant (known as Nana Sahib) and Maharaja Madhav Singhji.

Uma Bharati

Uma Ragini Bharati (born 3 May 1959), is an Indian politician. She was born to a religious Lodhi Rajput family and from a very young age, started holding discourses on Indian Epics. Raised under the care of the late Rajmata Vijayaraje Scindia of Gwalior. Uma Bharati, along with Sadhvi Ritambhara played a prominent part in the Ayodhya Ram Janmabhoomi Movement. Her signature slogan during the movement was ("Ramlala Hum Aayenge, Mandir Wahin Banayenge") which translates to "Dear Ram we will come, and build temple at the place". In the Vajpayee Administration, she held various state-level portfolios of Human Resource Development, Tourism, Youth Affairs & Sports, and finally Coal & Mines. In the 2003 Assembly polls, she led the BJP to a three-fourth majority in Madhya Pradesh. She was drinking water and sanitation minister in Modi Government.

Vasundhara Raje

Vasundhara Raje is a senior BJP leader and has been the Chief Minister of Rajasthan state for two five year terms. She has honour to become the first woman Chief Minister of Rajasthan. Vasundhara Raje was born on 8 March 1953 in Mumbai. She is daughter of Vijayaraje Scindia and Jivajirao Scindia, Maharaja of Gwalior, members of the prominent Scindia royal Maratha family. She completed her school education from Presentation Convent, Kodaikanal, Tamil Nadu, and later graduated with Economics and Political Science degrees (Hons.) from Sophia College, affiliated to Mumbai University, Mumbai.

Walchand Hirachand Doshi

Walchand Hirachand Doshi (23 November 1882–8 April 1953) was an Indian industrialist. He established India's first modern shipyard, first aircraft factory and first car factory.

TEST YOUR SELF

1. Who was known as Sarod Samrat?
   A. Sheeraj Khan
   B. Amjad Ali Khan
   C. Baba Alauddin Khan
   D. Hafiz Mohammed Khan
2. Raja Bhoj ruled over
   A. Bustar
   B. Dhar
   C. Mahakaushal
   D. Ujjain
3. Which of the following scholars does not belong to Madhya Pradesh?
   A. Kalhan
   B. Bhavbhuti
   C. Padmakar
   D. Kalidas
4. The famous singer and music director Kishore Kumar was born in Madhya Pradesh at
   A. Indore
   B. Bhopal
   C. Khajuraho
   D. Khandwa

5. Kumar Gandharva is related to
   A. Hindustani Music
   B. Khayal Singing
   C. Folk Music
   D. Hindi Cinema
6. MF Hussain was related to
   A. Painting
   B. Music
   C. Stage and Drama
   D. Flute Playing
7. The masoleum of famous musician Tansen who was also a courtier of Akbar is at
   A. Agra
   B. Fatehpur Sikri
   C. Delhi
   D. Gwalior
8. Asgari Bai was famous for
   A. Dhrupad Singing
   B. Manipuri Dancing
   C. Painting
   D. Kathak Dancing
9. Teejan Bai is known for
   A. Painting
   B. Journalism
   C. Dancing
   D. Bhajan and Folk Singing
10. Ustad Amjad Ali Khan is a famous
   A. Sitar Player
   B. Tabla Player
   C. Flute Player
   D. Sarod Player

ANSWERS

1	2	3	4	5	6	7	8	9	10
C	B	A	D	B	A	D	A	D	D

❑❑❑

Administration and Governance

The formation of present Madhya Pradesh took place after India was set free. At the time of Britishers there was a Central Province and Berar State, but its boundaries were totally different from the boundaries of present Madhya Pradesh. Districts of Berar and Mahakaushal were included in this province. Beside this Bhagelkhand and Chhattisgarh were the small estates in between them and they were collectively known as Central India. In 1947 Bhagelkhand and Chhattisgarh estates were included in Central province and Berar and Madhya Pradesh state was formed which was the state of part A and Nagpur was its capital. At the same time estates situated in the north were merged and Vindhya Pradesh State was formed. Rewa was its Capital. By merging estates of Western Madhya Pradesh, Madhya Bharat State was formed which was a state of B Cadre, Gwalior and Indore were its Capitals. Bhopal estate was a separate state and was a part of C "Cadre State".

Following changes were made by the state reorganisation commission of 1956.

1. Buldhana, Akola, Amravati, Yavatmal, Wardha, Nagpur, Bhandara and Chanda district, were merged with Mumbai State which at present are the part of Maharashtra. Beside this the remaining part was merged with Madhya Pradesh.
2. Leaving the part of Sunol Tappa, Bhanpura Tehsil of Mandsaur district and Part C State were merged with Madhya Pradesh.
3. Bhopal state was also merged with Madhya Pradesh.
4. Shiraj Tehsil of Kota district of Rajasthan was merged with Vidisha district of Madhya Pradesh.

On 1st November, 1956 Bhopal became the Capital of New Madhya Pradesh State which was a Tehsil of Sihore district and its first Chief Minister was Ravi Shankar Shukla and Pattabhi Sitarammaihia was its Governor.

On the basis of State re-organisation Chhattisgarh State was separated from Madhya Pradesh on 1st November, 2000 and Madhya Pradesh was divided into nine divisions and 45 districts. But at present there are 52 districts (including Niwari the newly created district) and 10 divisions in Madhya Pradesh.

Government and Politics

Madhya Pradesh Legislative Assembly consists of (230 + 1) members. The State also sends 40 members to the Parliament of India: 29 are elected to the Lok Sabha and 11 to the Rajya Sabha.

The structure of the State legislature is Unicameral. The term of the Assembly is five years. By an Act of parliament, titled—the Madhya Pradesh Reorganisation Act, 2000, the State was bifurcated into two States, viz. Madhya Pradesh and Chhattisgarh on 1st November, 2000. Consequently, the strength of the State legislature has come down to 231, including a nominated member.

The Governor

A Governor in the State is analogous to the President in the Centre. He is the constitutional head and carries out his duties, in consultation with the Council of Ministers.

The Governor is appointed by the President on the advice of the Prime Minister for a five year term. He holds office during the pleasure of the President. His tenure can be extended by the President and he continues to be in the office till the appointment of his replacement. He can resign before the completion of his tenure. By convention, Governor is usually a non-resident of the State where he is appointed. The State Government may be consulted in the appointment of a Governor.

Any person, who is a citizen of India, has completed 35 years of age and does not hold any office of profit in the State or Central Government, can become Governor of a State. The executive powers of the State are vested in the Governor.

Council of Ministers

As in the Centre, there is a Council of Ministers at the State level. It is appointed by the Governor but is responsible to Vidhan Sabha, the lower house of State legislature. The leader of the majority party/group is appointed Chief Minister and other ministers are appointed on his recommendation. The Chief Minister allocates work among the ministers. He can recommend their dismissal, or can bring about changes in the portfolios of the ministers. All the ministers are individually as well as collectively responsible to Vidhan Sabha.

The Chief Minister is first among the equals. Besides appointing his other ministers and allocating work to them, he takes all the major policy decisions.

He presides over the Cabinet meetings and all the ministers consult him on important matters. The Chief Minister suggests names for the posts for which the Governor makes appointments in the State. He is the Chief spokesman of the Government and is the communication link between the Government and the Governor.

High Court

On 1st of November 1956, the States Reorganisation Act was enacted. Sub-section (1) of Section 49 of the States Reorganisation Act ordained that from the appointed day, i.e., 1st of November 1956, the High Court exercising jurisdiction, in relation to the existing State of Madhya Pradesh, i.e., Nagpur High Court, shall be deemed to be the High Court for the present State of Madhya Pradesh. Thus, Nagpur High Court was not abolished but by a legal fiction, it became High Court for the new State of Madhya Pradesh with its seat at Jabalpur.

Hon'ble the Chief Justice, vide order dated 1st of November 1956, constituted temporary benches of the High Court of Madhya Pradesh at Indore and Gwalior. Later, by a Presidential Notification Dated 28th of November 1968, issued in the exercise of the powers conferred by the sub-section (2) of section 51 of the States Reorganisation Act, 1956, permanent benches of the High Court of Madhya Pradesh at Indore and Gwalior were established.

High Courts have superintendence over all courts and tribunals throughout the territories in relation to which it exercises jurisdiction except military courts. This is a wide power because it includes all courts or tribunals whether an appeal against its decision lies to the High Court or not. High Courts can intervene and revise the decisions where it feels gross injustice or non-exercise or abuse of jurisdiction. High Courts have administrative control over the subordinate judiciary in the State which includes district judges, judges of city civil courts as well as Metropolitan magistrates and members of the judicial service of the State. This control is exercised in the manner of appointments, posting, promotion and administrative controls. They can make and issue general rules and prescribe forms for regulating the practice and proceedings of lower courts. They can transfer case from the court to the other.

Law and Order Institution

At least one statutory institution that came into inception in MP by 1982, consequent upon an enactment in 1981, was the institution of ombudsman *(Lokayukta)* and deputy ombudsman *(Uplokayukta)*. This institution is critical to the governance because it is the legitimate body of check and balance in the state's governance at all levels and especially at the level of ministries and the state secretariat.

Ombudsman (Lokayukta)

The office of MP state ombudsman works as an economic offence's wing of state government. It has exclusive jurisdiction to enquire into the complaints against chief minister, deputy chief minister, state ministers, leaders of opposition and all secretary level officers. *Uplokayukta* is empowered to look into the complaints against all those government, semi-government, quasi-government and autonomous institutions like the vice-chancellors and registrars of universities, officers that are not covered by the office of *lokayukta*. The lokayukta or the Uplokayukta cannot look into any complaint the subject matter of which is more than five years old. They cannot also enquire into any case which is the subject matter of an enquiry under the Public Servants Inquiries Act, 1850 or which has been referred for enquiry under the Commission of Inquiry Act, 1952. Meanwhile, the lokayukta's and Uplokayukta's office in MP, with the help of Special Police Establishment, under its aegis, has taken action against 483 government employees (in five years between 2001 and 2006) and 376 of them were gazetted officers. Moreover, there were 905 special cases that were tried by special court between April 2002 and March 2008, of which 494 or 54 per cent of the 905 tried were convicted.

Government Initiatives for Improving Governance

Maintaining Law and Order

Some of the steps which the state government has proposed to maintain law and order situation in the state are as follows:

- Constitution of a high-level committee headed by the chief minister for constant monitoring of law and order.
- All the police control rooms in the state to be strengthened.
- Necessary equipment will be provided to make the police communication system effective.
- Security will be beefed up at places of historical, religious and archaeological importance.
- Separate investigating agencies will be constituted for incidents related to underworld and terrorism. Act will be promulgated for giving information about tenants, house servants and customers and employees of hotels and Internet cafes compulsory.
- Anti-Terror Squad (ATS) has been constituted in the state. Constitution of a parallel force can also be contemplated if need be.

Establishment of School of Good Governance and Policy Analysis (SGPA)

SGPA has been set up by the government of Madhya Pradesh to work as a think tank in the context of prevailing trends in global and local governance and also to analyse government policies and their effects. The school works as an autonomous organisation of GoMP. The chief minister of the state is the chairman of the governing body. The school is working towards providing a platform for various organisations and welfare groups to make administration people-oriented. It will also provide technical guidance and services to local bodies and organisations of national and international standard for research in their programme and administrative reforms.

e-Governance

IT policy of the state government has ushered the following objectives to take the state into 21st century.

- Improve the life of the common man by leveraging the strengths of e-Governance.

- Attracting investment in the sector so that the educated youth is able to contribute to the development of the state.
- Create a pool of highly skilled professionals who are at par with the best in the country.
- Transforming resource-based economy to knowledge-based economy.

Madhya Pradesh in last few years has implemented several e-Governance projects. The state's IT policy emphasises induction of IT in all walks of government functioning with the focus on masses and aims to leverage IT for transparency and better governance.

PANCHLEKHA: A Panchayat Raj Institution Accounting System Software (PRIASoft), designed, developed and implemented in most of the districts of Madhya Pradesh since 2005. The system is aimed at efficient management and monitoring of funds at *janpad panchayat*, *zilla panchayat* and *state headquarters*, and is empowering the administrators to monitor the fund receipt, availability and expenditure at all four-tier administrative set-up of PRIs.

e-Gram Suvidha: Implemented in collectorates/zilla panchayats of five districts (Chhatarpur, Bhopal, Mandla, Dhar and Damoh) e-Gram Suvidha is a geomatics-based decision support system towards creation and management of facilities at village level in rural areas. It covers about 20 facilities organised under 10 major sectors like education, health, communication and roads etc.

PARAKH (Basic Services/Amenities Management System): Government of Madhya Pradesh, recognising the fact that access to minimum level of social infrastructure facilities must be an integral part of a strategy for improving the quality of life of the people and for eradicating poverty, has introduced the Basic Services/Amenities Management System called PARAKH for improving the delivery of the basic services/amenities in rural areas of the state. For this purpose, a computerised system for maintaining the basic services/ amenities is put into place.

Right to Information Act

The RTI Act was notified on June 15, 2005, and implemented in Madhya Pradesh from October 12, 2005. Samarthan, a Poorest Areas Civil Society (PACS) Programme partner, has prepared a status report on the RTI Act in Madhya Pradesh. The report highlights several implementation problems. Public information officers (PIOs), appointed in all departments to handle RTI queries, are often unaware of rules and guidelines such as the application of fees and what information is excluded from the Act.

Citizens complained that they were kept waiting for hours before their applications were accepted, did not get the information within the stipulated time-frame, and were provided irrelevant information.

Decentralisation

The main aim of decentralising the powers at the district level is to reduce the delay in securing sanctions and to empower the people's representatives in the districts to take decision at the district level itself.

Panchayati Raj Institutions

Three-tiered Panchayati Raj bodies are the vital democratic institutions of rural India. The institution of Panchayati Raj was brought into modern independent India's political set-up exactly five decades ago. Panchayati Raj institutions were born with the Nagaur Convention of 1958, but these remained at their level of infancy before 1993. 73rd Amendment to the Indian Constitution that was passed in 1992 and subsequently which was applied with effect from 1993 planted actual teeth to these institutions. With passing of this bill, the panchayats which used to linger in Directive Principles of the Constitution and hence were not mandatory, suddenly became a very powerful tool when many grassroot development programmes got implemented through them. Panchayats, block level panchayats and district level panchayats became the harbingers of development schemes to the villages. This churning process of participatory village-level democracy at one level heralded the golden phase of power devolution that hastened the process of development.

The District Planning Committee (DPC)

In pursuance of the Article 243 ZD of the Constitution, the Madhya Pradesh government enacted the Madhya Pradesh Zila Yojana Samiti Adhiniyam, 1995 that received the assent of the Governor on 19th May 1995. The Zila Yojana Samiti Act provides for the constitution of the district planning committee (DPC) in all the districts of the state. As a part of revitalisation of Panchayat Raj institution and urban local bodies, the DPC is constituted in every district. Further, the districts were categorised as comprising of 15, 20 or 25 members in the committee. The membership to DPC has been provided to the elected members of the *panchayats*, municipalities, *zila panchayats* and the *prabhari* minister of the state government and the district collector. The *prabhari* minister has been designated as the Chairperson of the committee. Apart from the Chairperson, other members of the DPC are elected from amongst members of panchayats and municipalities. As DPC, the committee has the powers of planning, raising resources for financing their plans, and to monitor and evaluate the programmes and schemes that are implemented under the system of decentralised planning, including the money to be allocated by the MP/MLA fund.

The guiding principles were a major breakthrough for the state in transferring the work, the staff and the budgets to panchayats. In pursuance of the principles, works of 19 departments and the budget under demand number 15, 80 and 82 of these departments was placed at the discretion of panchayats. All the functions indicated in Schedule II have been transferred to panchayats and all concerned departments (nearly 23) have issued circulars and orders that effectively transferred their work, as well as issued orders that transferred the staff under the purview and control of panchayats.

State Election Commission

The state government that is responsible to conduct elections for panchayats has also constituted the State Election Commission. In the past, the Election Commission has conducted two general elections and elections for seats and posts as and when they become vacant. Since 1994, there have been four rounds of elections for panchayats in the state—1994, 2000, 2004 and 2009. Presently, there are 3,44,424 panchayat representatives in the state, which includes 22,387 members as leaders of their respective panchayat bodies. Of the total representatives, 33.8 per cent are women. If the women were not given the reservation, they would not have found the chance to contest and win the election and prove their calibre as administrative leaders. In one of its commendable steps, the state government has increased the women quota in panchayat reservation from 33 per cent to 50 per cent, thus motivating women's participation in local government.

State Finance Commission

In pursuance of the mandatory provisions of the 73rd Constitutional Amendment, the state government had constituted four State Finance Commission to decide upon the principle of devolution of funds to the panchayats. Three Finance Commissions have submitted their reports and in response to that State Government has prepared action taken report.

Gram Nyayalaya

Madhya Pradesh had a unique concept of gram nyayalaya, where disputes regarding land encroachments were dealt with. The experience has been that the orders passed by gram nyayalayas are not implemented properly as no separate agency has been provided to them. The gram nyayalayas have to seek assistance of police and revenue officials for the purpose that leads to avoidable delay. The decision to restore the powers under Sections 248 and 250 of the Madhya Pradesh Land Revenue Code to tahsildar has been taken with a view to curb the tendency of encroaching upon government land and to ensure prompt removal of encroachments.

The state cabinet approved the draft Gram Nyayalaya Amendment Bill, 2005. The amendment bill seeks to withdraw the powers of hearing and disposing off the cases under Sections 248 and 250 of the Madhya Pradesh Land Revenue Code, 1959 from village courts (gram nyayalayas) and to place them under the exclusive jurisdiction of tahsildar again. The proposed amendment bill provides for restoring the powers to tahsildar for dispossessing such persons under Section 248 of the Madhya Pradesh Land Revenue Code who has encroached upon the land of somebody else or the land reserved for some special purpose or service or government land. Under Section 250, tahsildar would be authorised to restore the possession of land to the rightful owner who might have been dispossessed from it.

Gram Swarajya

The existing panchayat system was constantly being criticised for two major weaknesses or problems. One was the growing and almost over-bearing influence of *sarpanch* over the panchayat, and the second was the gram sabha not being able to establish its role, character and importance and there was dwindling interest in *gram sabhas* and therefore, declining attendance in its meetings. The gram sabha actually had considerable powers under the existing provisions of decisions and planning, but most of this had become redundant in practice.

Recognising both these problems, the idea of *gram swaraj* was evolved, inspired also by the ideals and thinking of Mahatma Gandhi. Empowering gram sabhas further and granting them a greater role, the idea is to tone down the unnecessary influence of the sarpanch and to give a comprehensive role to gram sabha so that people find it worthwhile to attend the meetings and thereby participate directly in their concerns—a change towards direct democracy.

The Madhya Pradesh government amended the Madhya Pradesh Panchayat Raj Act to give effect to *gram swaraj* in the state. The amendment has brought in substantive changes in the Act and in the nature of panchayat institutions, especially at the village level.

Divisions and Districts of Madhya Pradesh

Bhopal	
• Bhopal	• Sehore
• Raisen	• Rajgarh
• Vidisha	
Gwalior	
• Gwalior	• Shivpuri
• Guna	• Ashoknagar
• Datia	
Jabalpur	
• Jabalpur	• Katni
• Narsimhapur	• Chhindwara
• Seoni	• Mandla
• Balaghat	

Indore	
• Indore	• Dhar
• Alirajpur	• Jhabua
• Khargone	• Badwani
• Khandwa	• Burhanpur
Sagar	
• Sagar	• Damoh
• Panna	• Chhatarpur
• Tikamgarh	• Niwari
Ujjain	
• Ujjain	• Dewas
• Ratlam	• Shajapur
• Agar Malwa	• Mandsaur
• Neemuch	
Shahdol	
• Shahdol	• Umaria
• Dindori	• Anuppur
Chambal	
• Sheopur	• Morena
• Bhind	
Rewa	
• Rewa	• Singrauli
• Sidhi	• Satna
Narmadapuram/Hoshangabad	
• Hoshangabad	• Betul
• Harda	

Policing in MP

Anusuchit Janjati Kalyan

Madhya Pradesh has a sizeable population of Scheduled Tribes and scheduled castes, who have remained cut off from the mainstream for centuries. Most of them lived in abject poverty under sub-human conditions and were exploited by the society in general.

Consequently, it was enjoined on police to play a more decisive role in the implementation of social laws. The Government of Madhya Pradesh, recognizing: this change and realizing that normal police structure will not the sufficient to play the desired role, created specialized police set-up for this. Consequently, a separate Anusuchit Jati Janjati Kalyan Wing (AJK) was created in 1973 and special AJK police stations look into the complains of SC/ST persons and investigate cases registered on such complaints. The network of AJK police stations works under a separate ADG level officer and form a very important constituent of M.P. Police today.

Village Defence Society

The concept of Village Defence Society involving people in Community policing was first introduced in 1956 in M.P. in the docoity infested area with the express purpose of enlisting the corporation of the villages in the fight against the dreaded dacoits. At the out set such defence societies were first established in Gwalior, Bhind and Morena districts. Subsequently this was extended to Shivpuri, Datia, Rewa, and Sagar districts as well.

These societies have the primary responsibility in their respective villages of protection of people and their property as well as maintenance of peace and harmony.

The State Government is also considering a proposal to arm the members of the societies so as to enable the members to discharge their duties in a determined manner. The members would be entitled to use weapons as long as their membership lasts. In the meantime the district police authorities have been advised to help the eligible and willing members obtain valid arms licences.

Efforts are being made to form such Gram Raksha Samities in every village of the state and impart training to the members. Meetings at various level are also being organised to sensitise the members towards the role they are expected to play in maintenance of Law and Order in their respective juridiction.

Parivar Paramarsh Kendra

Family Counselling Centres (launched on 10th October 1995) aimed at alleviating the suffering of women in the family setup in our society. This effort has positively galvanised the functioning of the Police department hitherto not known to or associated with positive humanitarian endeavour. In Indore many centres are working to save the families from disintegrating. These centres are run by the active support and cooperation of volunteers from society, these include social workers, lawyers, medical professional's etc.

Nagar Suraksha Samiti

Town Defence Committee (launched in January 1996) originally aimed at creating a group of right thinking citizens without any criminal record or known political affiliations, this effort has acquired dimensions, which were not originally thought of. Apart from assisting the police in doing its normal duties like managing major processions, generating awareness about police working, assisting in management of traffic. These centres have proceeded beyond the original charter and organised social work such as blood donation grouping/HIV testing, tree plantations, charter drive etc. This has helped in improving Police-Community relations and insured coordination. There is a great enthusiasm amongst the citizens to join the societies.

Mobile Police Thana (Launched in October 1996)

This is a novel initiative towards providing social justice to villagers. Under this initiative officers of police station camp at a fixed place, date and time. Officers of revenue and forest department are also requested to be present depending on the need. These meetings are held to dispose off the minor incidents or problems of the village.

Bal Mitra Scheme

Under this scheme, school students of different age group are brought to Police Stations to acquaint them with the working of the Police station and give them the opportunity to interact with Police Officers. This is done with the help of the school administration. Besides the opportunity to exchange views with Policemen, this effort helps allay the fear of about the Police from the minds of these children. Thus their negative views and fears about the Police change favourably.

Community Policing Centres

The first such centre was started in the crime prone and sensitive areas of Indore called 'Rustam Ka Bagicha'. Under this scheme police personnels make contacts with the local residents by door visit and successfully solved the problems of the people. This led to considerable decrease in the crime about 25 percent especially on the front of Alcohol and women exploitation and other minor offense. This experiment is based on the famous "KOBAN" technique of Japan.

Development Programmes

Madhya Pradesh Government has launched two programmes for the girls of age group of 11 to 18 years. These programmes are implemented in 48 Blocks of 18 districts. By this programme only those families will be benefitted whose annual income is less than ₹ 6,400. In this programme girls are being educated through, Anganwadi workers, and they will be nourished also. For the girls ageing between 15 to 18 years formal education will be provided.

Stamp Vendor Programme has been started in Madhya Pradesh to provide employment to the educated unemployed people of scheduled caste & scheduled tribe. Under this programme the beneficiary will be given a loan of ₹ 35,000 through the Self-Employment Scheme in which ₹ 5000 as grant will also be given. In this programme, the beneficiary will get 3% commission on total sale of stamp paper and tickets.

- **Vasundhara Programme**—There is a programme to provide interest free loan to the landless agriculturists of scheduled caste and tribe for purchasing the land.
- **Jal Jeewan Programme**—Collective irrigation project for the agriculturists of scheduled caste and tribe.
- **Swavlamban Programme**—To announce the allocation of shops to the poor people of scheduled caste and scheduled tribe people.
- **Pawanputra Programme**—To provide the self-employment through the Auto Rickshwa and Tempo to the poor youth of scheduled caste and scheduled tribe.
- **Madhuvan Programme**—Under this programme Dairy farm and Pastoral development farms are being established under the modern technique, which will run on the basis of community by the beneficiaries of scheduled tribe.
- **Nirmit Programme (Shram Tektha Samiti)**—Under this programme the skilled labourers are trained for building construction.
- **Sahkar Programme**—Under this minerals and brick making co-operative societies will be formed to provide the direct benefit to skilled labourer.
- **Vanja Programme**—The aim of this programme to provide benefit in small scale industries to labourers of scheduled tribe near by their residence (Based on small forest products).
- **Dhanwantri Programme**—It is a programme to provide aid for private practice to the youth of scheduled caste and scheduled tribe.
- **Vatsalya Programme** is to provide safety and other conveniences at the time of delivery to the pregnant women families of landless labourers.
- **Ayushmati Programme** is related to ill women of the landless families admitting them in the hospital to provide facilities for treatment, under this programme women admitting to hospital attached to medical college will be provided by medicines and nourish food.
- **Kalpvrakash Programme** is being implemented with the aim of providing direct employment to the women of scheduled tribe. This programme started from Rajgarh.

- **Deen Dayal Samarth Yojana**—This Programme has been started by the Madhya Pradesh Government for mentally and physically weaker sections of the society to bring them into the main stream of the society as well as strengthen them from every point of view. The programme was sanctioned by the state cabinet on 2nd June, 2004.
- **Gokul Gram Prakalp Yojana 2004**—This programme was started on 25th September, 2004. Under this project the consolidated development based on "Panchaj" basis principles will be carried on integrated basis for selected villages within a year. All the infrastructure facilities will be provided to these villages.
- **Deen Dayal Antodaya Upchar Yojana 2004**—Started on 25th September, 2004, this programme was for the families of scheduled caste, scheduled tribe and for the families living below the poverty line. The treatment (diseases) of the people of these categories shall be born by the State Government, and under this about maximum ₹ 20 thousand will be the expenditure by the Govt. over each family of this class. For this blue and yellow colour cards will be provided by the govt. for the beneficiary families.
- **Deen-Dayal Rojgar Yojana 2004**—Educated unemployed will be helped through Yojana. The State Government will also provide necessary margin money to the unemployed for getting the loan from banks.
- **Ayodhya-Yojana 2004**—On the basis of adjustment of Gokul Gram Yojana for the villages of Madhya Pradesh Ayodhya Yojana was started for urban slums areas. The first foundation of Ayodhya settlement was laid down by Chief Minister on 4th October, 2004 at Rahul Nagar Pampapur in Bhopal.

  Under the Ayodhya Settlement Yojana, good Quality roads, Nallis (Sewage), electric, cleanliness and proper water supply arrangement will be done by the State government. People living in these places will be provided for basic amenities.
- **Rashtriya Gramin Rojgar Yojana 2005**—During its first phase among 200 districts in the country, 18 districts of Madhya Pradesh were selected, these are Jhabua, Mandla, Umaria, Shahdol Badwani, Khargone (West Nimarh), Shivpuri, Sidhi, Tikamgarh, Balaghat, Chhatarpur, Betul, Khandwa (East Nimarh) Sheopur, Siwani, Dindori and Satna.
- **Bal Shakti Yojana**—In a survey of October-November 2005 under the Bal Sanjeevani Programme, it was found that near about 33.48 lac children upto the age of 5 years are suffering from malnutrition. It is near about 50%

of the total children population of the state. Under the malnutrition 10,913 children are of category 4, and 67,352 children are of category 3. Most of the malnutritioned children belong to poor class and backward class.

The State Govt. has started Bal Shakti Yojana to eradicate the malnutrition among the children. The main aim of this programme which is running jointly with the co-operation of Public-health Department and Bal Vikas Department, to bring the no. of children upto one per cent to the category of Class-IV and Class-III Children.

- **Vijaya Raje Janani Welfare Insurance Yojana**—This programme is running in Madhya Pradesh to help the pregnant women of those families, which are living below the poverty line. Under the programme ₹1000 is paid to compensate the expenses made out by woman at the time of delivery and an amount of ₹50,000 is paid as an insurance money to the heirs on the death at the time of delivery. The benefit of this is given only when the three investigations would have taken place by the female and delivery would have taken place in the hospital. Even if the delivery has taken place in the recognised hospital the benefit of Yojana will be given, but the amount will be paid to hospital.

- **Ladli Laxmi Yojana**—A new Ladli Laxmi Yojana for girls has been started from 1st April, 2007 by Madhya Pradesh Govt. In this unique programme, started on 1st April, 2007, the necessities for marriage of girl is also considered. Started for the girls of all caste and religion the girls of those families who have two children born after 31st December, 2005 as well as non income tax payable shall also be benefitted. It is the necessary for them to get themselves registered to any Angan Badi Centre and to present there regulatory. The girls living in orphan and escorts house shall also be benefitted along with two daughters of every family.

  Under the programme, after getting registration ₹6000 each National Saving Certificates will be purchased for 5 years in the name of each girls thus an amount of ₹30,000 will be invested in girl's name with the interest of this investment.

- **Mukhya Mantri Annapurna Project**—Mukhya Mantri Annapurna Project was started on 26th April, 2008 for providing cereals at concessional rate to those population who is living below the poverty line in Madhya Pradesh. This was inaugurated in Bhopal by M. Venkta Naidu, the then Vice-President of B.J.P., in the presence of Chief Minister Shiv Raj Singh Chouhan. Under this project wheat at the cost of ₹3 per kg and rice at the cost of ₹4.50 per kg will be given to the families of B.P.L. Each B.P.L. family will get 20 kg food grain per month under this project.

TEST YOUR SELF

1. Who among the following was not the Chief Minister of Madhya Pradesh?
   A. Shri Prakash Chand Sethi
   B. Shri Govind Narayan Singh
   C. Shri V. C. Shukla
   D. Shri D. P. Mishra
2. Who was the first Chief Minister of Madhya Pradesh?
   A. Shyam Charan Shukla
   B. Kailash Nath Katju
   C. Pt Ravi Shankar Shukla
   D. Bhagwant Rao Mandloi
3. Which leader of Madhya Pradesh became the Defence Minister and later Home Minister in Nehru's cabinet?
   A. Prakash Chandra Sethi
   B. Ravi Shankar Shukla
   C. Kailash Nath Katju
   D. Dwarka Nath Mishra
4. Who amongst the following has served as longest Chief Minister?
   A. Pandit Ravishankar Shukla
   B. Arjun Singh
   C. Dr Kailash Nath Katju
   D. Shiv Raj Singh Chouhan
5. Which among the following division in Madhya Pradesh has least number of districts?
   A. Hoshangabad
   B. Indore
   C. Bhopal
   D. Rewa
6. Where was the first 'gram nyayalaya' inaugurated in Madhya Pradesh?
   A. Jhantla (Neemuch)
   B. Bhanpura
   C. Dhar
   D. Rampur
7. The Madhya Pradesh Secretariat is known as
   A. Vallabh Bhawan
   B. Jawahar Bhawan
   C. Satpura Bhawan
   D. Vindhyachal Bhawan
8. The number of Lok Sabha seats from Madhya Pradesh is
   A. 29 B. 30 C. 31 D. 32
9. The first Governor of Madhya Pradesh was
   A. RC Punacha
   B. Pt Ravi Shankar
   C. Pattabhi Sitaramaiya
   D. Naresh Chandra
10. The High Court of Madhya Pradesh is located at
    A. Bhopal B. Jabalpur C. Indore D. Gwalior
11. Chief Minister's 'Annapurna Yojana' was started on .... and at ....
    A. 5th April, 2008 at Sidhi
    B. 15th April, 2008 at Dewas
    C. 12th April, 2008 at Rewa
    D. 26th April, 2008 at Bhopal
12. Which of the following was the first Indian city to have a Municipal Corporation?
    A. Dewas
    B. Chennai
    C. Kolkata
    D. Katni

13. Under the Panchayati Raj Regulation 1993, how many subjects have been transferred to Panchayatas?
A. 18 B. 29 C. 49 D. 51

14. 'Gram Swaraj' was initiated in Madhya Pradesh in ....
A. 1996 B. 1998 C. 1999 D. 2001

15. When was the Panchayati Raj Regulation 1993 inacted in Madhya Pradesh?
A. 25 January, 1994 B. 31st July, 1995
C. 30th July, 1994 D. 31st June, 1994

ANSWERS

1	2	3	4	5	6	7	8	9	10
C	C	C	D	A	A	A	A	C	B
11	**12**	**13**	**14**	**15**					
D	B	B	D	A					

❑❑❑

Scheduled Tribes in MP

The State of Madhya Pradesh has been reorganised many times changing its boundaries. One phenomenon has, however, remained unchanged, i.e., it always has had the largest population of the Scheduled Tribes as compared to any other state in the country. Even after the present reorganisation carving out Chhattisgarh as a separate state, Madhya Pradesh comprises 153.16 lakhs Scheduled Tribe population.

Tribal population of Madhya Pradesh can be divided into many categories according to their area of habitat. As per Madhya Pradesh reorganisation Act of 18th September, 2000, tribes like Gonds and Bhils have large population whereas tribes like Andh, Birhor have a negligible population. After reorganisation, the tribal area of Madhya Pradesh can be divided into four main zones as follows:-

1. Western Cultural Zone: Districts of Ratlam, Jhabua, Dhar, Barwani, Khargone, Khandwa, Harda, Dewas and Indore fall under this zone. The main tribes residing in this zone are Bhil, Bhilala, Barela and Patelia.
2. Central Cultural Zone: This zone comprises of Mandla, Dindori, Balaghat, Seoni, Chhindwara, Jabalpur, Katni, Narsimhapur, Sagar, Damoh, Umaria, Sehore and Bhopal. The main tribes residing in this zone are Gond, Pardhan, Korku, Baiga, Bharia, Nagarachi and Ojha.
3. North-Eastern Cultural Zone: Districts of Shahdol, Sidhi, Rewa, Satna, Panna, Chhatarpur, Guna and Tikamgarh fall under this zone. Kol, Biar, Panika, Sour and Pav are the main tribes residing in this zone.
4. North-Western Cultural Zone: This zone consists of Morena, Shivpuri, Sheopur, Datia, Gwalior and Bhind districts. The main tribe residing in this zone is Seharia. Three Special Primitive Tribal Groups - Bharia (Patalkot, Chhindwara), Baiga (Umaria, Shahdol, Dindori, Balaghat and Mandla) and Seharia (Shivpuri, Sheopur, Guna, Gwalior, Morena) reside in Madhya Pradesh.

Gond

Gond is an important and the largest tribe of India. Madhya Pradesh and Chhattisgarh have their largest concentrations. Gond tribes heavily reside in the areas of Betul, Hoshangabad, Chhindwara, Balaghat, Shahdol, Mandla, Sagar and Damoh districts of Madhya Pradesh. Some branches of Gonds live in the forests of Vindhya and Satpura ranges right from Amarkantak.

The term Gond is considered a corrupt form of Kond. In Telugu Kond means a forest covered mountain. Some historical evidences of the Gonds are found in Madhya Pradesh. In ancient times a large area was called Gondwana. Their myths mention various Gond forts and kings. On the basis of archaeology an opinion is formed, that there was a time when Gond community ruled a considerable area. Opinions differ on origin of the Gonds. Some scholars have opinion that they had come from south whereas others believe that their origin place is Amarkantak or Narmada region. On the basis of Gondi dialect their arrival from the south is confirmed. Gondi is member of Dravidian language group.

The Gonds living in different regions are known by many sub-branches. Even if their names are the same, there is lot of difference in their lifestyle. In Mandla the Gonds are engaged in farming in a big way so they are called Rajgond. Most of the Gond artists who had worked at the Museum belong to Mandla-Dindori area. Pardhan Gonds, the singers of Gond rulers and Badadev, the Agarias who keep moving from one place to antoher, Bhimma, Dhoba, Koila Bhuta, iron melter Agaria also are found in this area.

The Gond houses have a courtyard in the middle, surrounded by a corridor or Parchhi and Kurai or rooms are adjacent to them. The kitchen, which they call Mudhat, also has a place dedicated to the family god. The main entrance to the house is east-facing and the first room is meant for the guests, which is called Paitha Bangla.

The walls of Gond houses are decorated by women with clay and colours which are called Noh Dora. A Dhig is painted with indigo, ochre, chalk and black colour along the lower portion of the walls, which is called Dhigana. In fact, the main source of this style of painting is the murals painted by the women on the walls of their houses.

The Gonds are also very fond of stories, sayings, riddles, dancing and singing. Karma, Saila, Rina, Dadaria and Sua are their main dance forms, which are called Swang, Gammat or Tamasha. Festivals associated with weather cycle like Bidari Puja, Hardhili, Navakhani, Jawara, Madai, Chherata Bakbad etc are celebrated with great enthusiasm by dancing and singing.

Bhil

Bhil is the third largest tribe of India. They are spread in Madhya Pradesh, Gujarat, Rajasthan and Maharashtra. In Madhya Pradesh they mainly live in Jhabua, Thandla, Petalawad, Alirajpur, Jobat, Narkundi, Bag, Chhota Udaipur, Dhar, Barwani, Khargone, Talod, Shahada, Sirpur, Amjhera and Ratlam areas.

The term Bhil is probably derived from "Bil", a Dravidian term used for a bow. There is a saying in Sanskrit- Bhidanti Iti Bhillah", which means a Bhil is the one who pierces. The Bhils are good marksmen and like to keep bow and arrow and Gofan with them. The young Bhils even kill the fish in small rivers or ponds with bow and arrow. Bhilala, Patalia, Barela and Rathya are principle sub-branches of Bhil tribe. Bhil is such an ancient tribe which finds mention in mythological legends and therein they are referred to as Nishad. The Bhils consider Valmiki and Eklavya as their ancestors. Rajasthani, Malvi and Gujarati terms are found in Bhili dialect and its legend oral tradition is very rich.

The Bhils worship the ancestor gods Pithora Kunwar, Babo Ind, Jatu Bai ritualistically once in two-three years. In Pithora worship Lakhendra makes a large picture depicting the story of Pithora Kunwar. Pithora worship is done by Badwa whereas the story is sung by Malga or story singers. In Bhil villages, there are places dedicated to Bapdev, Bhilatdev, Bhairu, Bhil Mata, Kali Mata, Khedo Mai etc.

The Bhils live in dry and less fertile areas in the state. Agricultural fields are small so they make their houses in the field itself for protection of the crops. Due to this their population is scattered. Living on farming and animal husbandry their staple food is maize.

In order to compensate the absence of colours on the barren and dry land they wear clothes of Bright colours. Bhil is a lively tribe that they have great interest in dancing and singing.

Around Holi festival a Bhagoriya fair is held in their villages which is famous for enthusiastic participation of young boys and girls and the ritual of Gal Bapasi. In this fair, the young Bhil boys and girls not only meet but also get marries if their parents do not agree to their relation.

The Bhils have a practice of erecting a Gatla or a memorial pillar for the dead. Earlier, it was made of stone or wood but now it is made of cement also. These Gatlas are made in memory of some reputed person or for those who die of snake bite, killed by wild animals or meet an accidental death. Figures of the sun, the moon, horse rider, the dead person, Paniharin etc. and favourite things of the dead are carved on these pillars.

The Bhils' aesthetic sense is seen on the paintings made by their women on the walls of the house, depiction of Pithora, Gatla and their dresses, ornaments, dancing and singing and in the articles used in their day to day life.

Korku

The people of Korku tribe live in Chhindawara, adjoining the forests of Satpura ranges in Bhainsdehi, Chicholi tehsils of Betul district and Harda, Timarni and Khirkiya tehsils of Hoshangabad district. They also live in Akola, Melghat and Morshi talukas of Maharashtra.

The Korkus fall in Munda or Kolarian tribal group. The term Korku means group of humans, Kor-Manav and Ku is used for plural.

The Korku houses are built opposite each other in two rows and the Otala or platform decorated with ochre, chalk and yellow clay give a distinct identity to Korku Dhada. On Deepawali night the women of Thathya i.e. Gwala families paint auspicious pictures called Gudaniyan with red clay and chalk on the walls of Korku houses. The Thathya men go door to door playing Bhugadu or a long flute and dancing all the night.

The Korku women are fond of tattooing. On the forehead a figure resembling English letter M is tattooed and on its upper and lower sides two dots are made which are called Kapar Godai. Dots are also tattooed on the chin, cheek and nose. On the hands-chowk, Rani Godai etc. are tattooed. In the figures of tribal tattooing the dots often symbolise food grain or fire. Here tattooing is ornamentation of the body and also device to stay disease-free and strong. Tattooes are also created to ensure overflowing granaries in the house.

The Korkus regard their dead as gods. They make a memorial pillar which is called Munda. The ritual of making and installing Munda is called Sidoli. Lasting for three-four days this ritual is performed on the month of Poush. On a particular day that is Monday invariably, the members of the family tie a Mauli (sacred thread) on the unbroken tree of teak in the forest in the name of their ancestors Soma-Doma. The tree is cut for the wood only after worshipping it. Munda is installed for one or more ancestors. Figures of the moon, the sun, a horse rider, a human figure with open hands and favourite articles of the dead are carved on the Munda. Sidoli is considered to be a ritual of invoking the ancestors. It is believed that after this ritual they begin to dwell in the Munda.

In the Korku areas where Mundas are not installed, a small round stone is placed at the place of Muthua Dev in the name of the dead after his burial. The Korkus believe that it is Mahadev and Parvati who taught them to build house, cook food and gave them the cotton to make cloths and while departing had given them the place of Mathua Baba for protection against diseases and other troubles in the village.

Baiga

The Baigas have been placed under primitive tribe category. The changes that have come about in their lifestyle and beliefs are comparatively negligible.

The Baigas mainly live in dense forest and hilly regions of Mandla, Dindori, Shahadol, Umaria, Balaghat and Amarkantak in Madhya Pradesh. They are considered as an offshoot of the Bhumias of Chhota Nagpur.

The Baigas consider themselves to be servant of the earth and the king of the forests. Systematic Baiga villages came into existence much later. Earlier, they used to practice shifting cultivation without using the plough by clearing forests. After some year, they used to shift to some other nearby area. Even today, the forests are the first love and choice of the Baigas.

The Baigas have five principal Gotras and a fort or a sacred place is attached to every Gotra. Each Gotra has a sign. Baiga Gotra or Vansh is called Jaat. The social structure of the Baigas is very systematic and functions very smoothly. They have a Panchayat comprising Mukaddam, Diwan, Samrath, Kotwar and Dawar which is authorised to settle all the disputes. Mukaddam is the head of the village and Dawar is the priest.

The various aspects of Baiga life are associated with forests and they are dependent on them. The articles used in rite of passage are also obtained from the forests. The Baigas are very good hunters, too. They use various types of nooses for catching wild animals and birds.

After ban on shifting cultivation now they have begun to practice normal cultivation but unwillingly. Earlier, the Baigas used to take many crops at a time including Kodo, Kutki, Kangani, Madia, Sama, Ratauni, Bajara, Kang, Silar and pulses like Rahar, Urada, Jhunjharu, Jhuraga, Barbati etc. Now this diversity is gradually vanishing. They now grow paddy, wheat, soyabean etc.

The Baiga lifestyle is very simple and their houses are also not much adorned. Their houses generally consist of a single room and there is a Parchhi adjoining it in the front. There is a courtyard in front of the Parchhi, a hedge of sachcher woods is created around the house which they call Parda.

Living amidst green Sal forests the Baigas wear very simple clothes which are generally white. Their aesthetic sense has a very special profundity, having no room for glamour or refulgence. The Baiga women are so much fond of tattooing they get every part of their body tattooed with large figures in detail. There is a specific tattoo for every part and the tattooing is done by people of Badi-Badanin community.

The Baiga men and women are very much fond of dancing and they dance all night at the Madai Melas. Their principal dance forms are Baigani, Karma, Saila, Bilama, Parghauni, Fag, Jharpat, Gendi etc.

Saharia

Living in north western part of Madhya Pradesh the community is placed under the category of primitive tribes. The members of this tribe mainly live in Shivpuri, Guna, Gwalior, Morena, Bhind, Vidisha, Raisen, Sehore and Bundeli Janpad.

The Saharias are considered to be member of Kolarian group and a sub-branch of the Bhils. This community is also known as Seher, Sair, Sawar, Saor, Sahara etc. In Guna-Shivpuri area they are called "Raut". They also like to be addressed as Khutia Patel as this is a respectful term. The Saharias call themselves younger brothers of the Bhils and that is why they claim to be descendents of Valmiki and Shabari. According to mythological legends the hunter named Jara who caused the death of Krishna belonged to Sanwar community.

Saharia basti is called Saharana where houses are built in the shape of English letter U on three sides. In the middle there is a common courtyard for all the houses. The Saharia women besmear the main doorframes, doorsills, courtyard and kitchen with a paste of yellow clay, chalk and ochre. Now a days they use colours from the market for this purpose. They paint auspicious figures with these materials. This painting is done not only on special occasions and almost daily in the kitchen. This shows their aesthetic sense even in daily routine activities.

Saharia men and women like brilliant colours and their dresses have impact of Rajasthan and other tribes. Apart from agriculture the Saharias also collect forest produces. They eat rotis of jowar and bajara and different bhajis and roots found in the forests. On the auspicious occasions like marriage rotis of besan are made. The Saharias are very much fond of hunting and fishing. They have profound knowledge of herbs and are very expert in obtaining honey from beehive. Besides, they make baskets, ropes, broomsticks etc and collect wood from the forests.

The Saharias have been living with Hindus for a long time, so they have started worshipping all Hindu gods and goddesses and celebrate almost all Hindu festivals. Sita is their most favourite goddess. Besides, they also worship Gram Devta-Thakurdev, Bherudev, Nahardev, Darethdev, Karasdev, Bhumaia or Dharti Ke Dev, Harimandev and Tejaji.

The language of the Saharias is now extinct and they now speak the local language wherever they live. However, the songs related to rituals, seasons got story of Pandav, Languria, Phaag, Janki Vivah songs, Chakia songs, Sdagadawat-Bagadavat stories etc show their interest in singing of stories. Lahangi is a special dance of the Saharias and they have a tradition of singing a drama song based on the life of Tejaji.

Kol

After Gond Kol is the second largest tribe of Madhya Pradesh. Besides Madhya Pradesh this tribe also resides in Uttar Pradesh, Bihar, Odisha and Maharashtra. In Madhya Pradesh the people of this tribe live in Rewa, Sidhi, Satna, Shahdol, Jabalpur and Mandla area. The Kols consider themselves as native of Farenda and Kurali villages in Rewa district. Their most dense population is in Rewa, Sidhi and Satna in Madhya Pradesh.

As many as 22 sub-branches of the Kol tribe are accepted. Kol is one of the most ancient tribes of India, whose mention is found in the Rig Veda and many other mythological scriptures. The term "Kol" means human. Both Kol and Korku are terms of Mundari language group. In the original language of Kol and Munda tribes terms, Kore Hor are still used for man. Once upon a time the Kols were so influential and their biological spread was so wide that group of many sub-tribes originated from them were named as Munda or Kolarian group by anthropologists. Probably, due to long association with other communities they no longer remember their origin myth or songs, etc.

In mythological legends, details of Kol origin are found. According to such a mythological legend, the Kols, the Mundas, the Shabars and the Bhumijas were born when Kamdhenu hit the earth with her horns.

The Kamdhenu cow, that fulfils all wishes, was with sage Ashtavakra. Indra wanted to take her away to Indraloka. They both fought for her. Kamdhenu with her horns hit the earth and people with arms and weapons, pick-axe, spades and crowbar kept coming out from earth. Seeing all at them Indra ran way. It is believed that, those who were born having pick-axe were Kols, those having bow and arrows were called Mundas and those who had crowbar came to be known as Shabar.

Like all tribes the Kols also have a panchayat and some panchayat office bearers in every village such as Mahato, Barua, Bhuihar, Ojha, Panda, Dewar and Neutia. Mahato or Choudhary is head of the village. Neutia delivers good, bad news from any family and also gives invitation to the villages on important occasions. Panchayat is considered competent to settle all types of disputes.

The people of Kol tribe like to live by constructing houses in front of each other in Tolas, which are called Kolhin Tola. If entire village is inhabited by the Kols then it is called Kolhan. Walls of Kol house are built by mixing straw in clay. Rope made of the bark of Bakohada tree is used for tying the bamboo-poles. Like other tribal communities the Kols also treat the cattle as part of their family so one room of their four roomed house is meant for them.

The Kols have meager needs and are happy by eating Kodai Bhaji. They are also fond of Madain or Mahua liquor and hunting. Besides farming collection of forest produces is their main occupation.

The dresses, festivals and marriages etc have become like those of other local communities to a considerably extent and they do not have a distinct identity of their own. The ornaments of their women still have impact of tribal communities.

Bharia

Members of Bharia tribe mainly live in Jabalpur and Chhindwara. In Chhindwara they live in Patalkot in Tamia block. The Bharias belong to Dravidian group and scholars have placed them under Bhumia tribe. The Bharias call themselves younger brothers of the Gonds. Till certain period marriages were permitted between them. The Bharias have forgotten their original language and speak Bundeli mixed Hindi. They consider Mahoba or Bandhavgarh as their place of origin.

The Bharias live by making their own separate Colony (Dhana) in village which has houses in two rows. There is a courtyard in front of the house and a Medha platform is erected with support of four poles. It is used for drying Mahua, Guli and mango stones. Like Gonds and Baigas the Bharias also eat Pej, which is cooked by mixing lot of water with maize, jowar, Kutki or rice. It is like rice-stretch. The Bharias like to eat Chapati of Mahua and mango stone in rainy season. Thethara is like a sweet Chapati which is made on festive occasions with Mahua fruit and jowar-maize flour.

The Bharias are fond of hunting and fishing. They work in agricultural fields and threshing floor. Generally they own no land. Collecting forest produces and herbs is their second major economic activity. They make baskets and winnowing baskets of bamboo, broomsticks of Date (chhind) leaves and Devbahari grass as well as wooden doors, doorframes, bullock carts etc. The broomstick made by them of Devbahari grass is strong and beautiful. The Bharias also install a Magarohan or Manda of Haldu wood at the time of wedding. This triangular or rectangular Manda is a multistoried palace, according to a Bharia artist, which connects the earth with the sky. Signs of the ancestors are carved on it. The people of Bharia community also make a wooden carved sword for wedding.

The Bharias build a round platform of clay dedicated to their dead and generally place an unshaped stone on it. After putting a shade on it they perform the marriage ceremony under it.

The doors and doorframes of Bharia houses are simple but carved. The headgear or Mukut made for the bride and bridegroom made of date leaves are very beautiful. Wearing it they really look like king and queen of two and half days.

Bharia women are fond of tattooing and for them tattooing is done by Ojha women. The Bharia women get a bow-shaped line above their eyebrows and dots and horizontal lines on the forehead. Pitcher, Mukut, chair, cock and Dhandha made by linking dots are their favourite tattooing patterns. Bhadam, Saitam, Saila, Karma, Sua, Ahirai are the principal dance forms of the Bharias.

Tribal Research and Development Institute

After independence, special arrangements were made for the upliftment of the Scheduled Tribes. The foundation of Tribal Research and Development Institute at Chhindwara, MP on 20th April, 1954, under the department of Tribal Welfare in Madhya Pradesh, is a part of the efforts in this direction. Subsequently, it was shifted to Bhopal, the capital of the State of Madhya Pradesh.

Promotion of tribal culture, coupled with research, training and development of the tribals etc are the main activities of the institute. Research relates mainly to ethnographic studies of the tribals of MP. The institute from time to time undertakes evaluation of tribal related schemes of the government. The Institute furnishes opinion to the government in case of castes/tribes verification. Training is imparted to the field level government functionaries to orient and sensitise them regarding tribal life.

Madhya Pradesh Tribal Finance and Development Corporation

Madhya Pradesh Tribal Finance and Development Corporation was established in 1994 under the Section 25 of Indian Company Act, 1956. The implementations of the schemes by the corporation was started from 01.04.1995.

The objectives of MP Finance and Development Corporation are as below:

- To do economic social and academic development of the tribals.
- To eradicate exploitation and to lift them above poverty line through development.
- To make the tribals available easy loans and realise them with interest to achieve the above objectives.

Shri Badal Bhoi State Tribal Museum, Chhindwara

Named after a well-known tribal freedom fighter of the area, late Badal Bhoi, it was set up as a State Tribal Museum in Chhindwara in 1954 with a view to promote and protect the diverse tribal lifestyle of Madhya Pradesh. This museum depicts the lifestyle and culture of most Scheduled Tribes of the undivided state of Madhya Pradesh (i.e., present MP and Chhattisgarh). More than 2000 tribal artifacts, the signs of their 'Gotra' and models have been exhibited in 11 rooms of the museum. Every year more than one lakh national and international visitors see the museum.

Kanya Saksharta Protsahan Yojana

Objective of this scheme is to reduce the dropout rate and to increase the interest of the tribal girl students to continue their school study. ₹ 500 is given to those girls who continue to study in class VI, ₹ 1000 to girls who get admission in IX and ₹ 2000 to girls who get admission in XI.

TEST YOUR SELF

1. The only tribal sports school in MP is located at

A. Sehore B. Jhabua C. Alirajpur D. Petlavad

2. Which state has the largest number of STs?

A. Assam B. Odisha
C. Madhya Pradesh D. Bihar

3. Which of the following tribes are found in Madhya Pradesh?

A. Mundla, Oraon, Santhal, Ho
B. Baiga, Saharia, Gond, Kol
C. Bharia, Bhil, Gond, Santhal
D. Kharia, Bharia, Gond, Oraon

4. Match the following and select the correct answers from the codes given below:

List I	List II
(a) Chhindwara	1. Bhil
(b) Mandla	2. Bharia
(c) Jhabua	3. Gond
(d) Shivpuri	4. Sahariya

Codes

	(a)	(b)	(c)	(d)		(a)	(b)	(c)	(d)
A.	2	4	1	3	B.	1	3	2	4
C.	2	3	1	4	D.	1	4	3	2

5. Which of the following tribes is found in MP?

A. Jarava B. Ho C. Bhil D. Santhal

6. The numbers of seats reserved for STs and SCs in Madhya Pradesh State Assembly are

A. 39 and 28 B. 148 and 48
C. 79 and 44 D. 11 and 19

7. The tribal subplan was started under which Five Year Plan?

A. First B. Second C. Fifth D. Sixth

8. The 'Baiga tribe' is mainly found in

A. Shivpuri, Jhabua, Dhar
B. Shahdol, Jhabua, Sidhi, Dhar
C. Mandla, Shahdol, Umaria, Balaghat
D. Sidhi, Jhabua, Mandala, Balaghat

9. The primitive tribe Korku is found in which region of Madhya Pradesh?

A. Southern Madhya Pradesh
B. North-Western Madhya Pradesh
C. Eastern Madhya Pradesh
D. North-Eastern Madhya Pradesh

10. The Gond tribe is related to

A. Dravidians B. Australoids
C. Mangoloids D. Proto-Australoids

ANSWERS

1	2	3	4	5	6	7	8	9	10
B	C	B	C	C	A	C	C	A	D

❑❑❑

2204

MADHYA PRADESH OBJECTIVE GK

1. 'Ujjaini and Mahishmati' were important towns of:
A Eastern Malwa B. Western Malwa
C. Northern Malwa D. Southern Malwa

2. Sunil Kewat is related to which sports?
A Kayaking canoeing B. Cricket
C. Hockey D. Football

3. In which city is the Rani Durgawati museum situated?
A Bhopal B. Jabalpur C. Mandsaur D. Khargon

4. News print factory in India is at:
A Nepanagar B. Hoshangabad C. Mandla D. Indore

5. Where is the Saket Ramayan Kala Sangrahalay situated?
A Chanderi B. Orchha C. Ujjain D. Maihar

6. Phen Wildlife Sanctuary is located in which district?
A Mandla B. Jhabua C. Jabalpur D. Dhar

7. Where is the Gajrath Mahotsav celebrated?
A Bhopal B. Guna C. Sagar D. Dewas

8. Mahi project is in which district?
A Indore B. Dhar C. Shahdol D. Bhopal

9. 'Raneh waterfall' is on the river:
A Narmada B. Ken C. Betwa D. Sone

10. Which of the following is famous as Energy Capital of Madhya Pradesh?
A Jabalpur B. Chhindwara C. Ujjain D. Singrauli

11. Madhya Pradesh Electricity Regulatory authority office is famous as:
A Urja Bhavan B. Yatayat Bhavan
C. Saur Bhavan D. Vidhyut Bhavan

12. Which one is not located on National Highway-3?
A Indore B. Shivpuri C. Jhansi D. Gwalior

13. Which of the following cities is famous as Manganese Capital of Madhya Pradesh?
A Balaghat B. Singrouli C. Sidhi D. Anuppur

14. Where was the first spice park of Madhya Pradesh established?
A Vidisha B. Bhopal C. Chindwara D. Raisen

15. Who was the first Lokayukt of Madhya Pradesh?
A P.C. Sethi B. P.V. Dixit C. N.V. Lohani D. None of these

16. In which year was the 51st District Agar Malwa formed?
A. 2011 B. 2013 C. 1998 D. 2000

17. The birth place of Chandra Shekhar Azad 'Bhabra' is in:
A. Madhya Pradesh B. Rajasthan
C. Punjab D. Uttar Pradesh

18. Where is the High Court of Madhya Pradesh situated?
A. Bhopal B. Jabalpur C. Gwalior D. Indore

19. In which of the following districts of Madhya Pradesh is the Ramlila Fair held?
A. Chhindwara B. Gwalior C. Anuppur D. Jabalpur

20. To which tribe does the Lehangi Dance belong?
A. Gonds B. Bhils C. Saharias D. Korku

21. Where is the 'Indira Gandhi Rashtriya Manav Sangrahalaya' located?
A. Gwalior B. Bhopal C. Sanchi D. Jabalpur

22. In which year was the Tansen Award founded?
A. 1979 B. 1980 C. 1981 D. 1982

23. The maximum rain in Madhya Pradesh occurs at:
A. Pachmarhi B. Bhind C. Gwalior D. Betul

24. Which of the following cities is Headquarters of west Central Railway Zone?
A. Gwalior B. Jabalpur C. Rewa D. Ratlam

25. Pandav Caves, a famous Tourist spot is situated in:
A. Raisen B. Pachmarhi C. Sagar D. None of these

26. In which city is the tourism spot Ashrafi Palace situated?
A. Chanderi B. Mandu C. Gwalior D. Orcha

27. Which of the following states has the largest number of people belonging to Scheduled Tribe (According to Census 2011)?
A. Bihar B. West Bengal
C. Madhya Pradesh D. Punjab

28. Which of the projects is a joint venture of Uttar Pradesh, Madhya Pradesh and Bihar?
A. Ban Sagar B. Laxmibai C. Barona D. Tava

29. The Madhya Pradesh Development Day is celebrated on which data?
A. 1st April 2013 B. 6th April 2013
C. 15th April 2013 D. 12th April 2013

30. Marble is found in which district?
A. Jhabua B. Hoshangabad C. Betul D. Jabalpur

31. What is the number of Zila Panchayats in Madhya Pradesh?
A. 49 B. 52 C. 16 D. 21

32. Who was the first woman Chief Minister of Madhya Pradesh?
A Meera Kumar B. Sushma Swaraj
C. Uma Bharti D. Sarla Grewal

33. The 'Baiga tribe' is majorly found in:
A Shivpuri, Jhabua, Dhar B. Shahdol, Sidhi, Dhar
C. Mandala, Shahdol, Balaghat D. Sidhi, Jhabua, Balaghat

34. Where is the Railway Coach factory in Madhya Pradesh?
A Beena B. Morena C. Bhopal D. Hoshangabad

35. Which religion is the predominant religion of the state Madhya Pradesh?
A Muslim B. Hinduism C. Sikhism D. Buddhism

36. Which is the first district of Madhya Pradesh to produce energy from biomass?
A Betul B. Morena C. Gwalior D. Mandsaur

37. In which city is the Thankur Ranmat Singh stadium situated?
A Itarsi B. Rewa C. Satna D. Bhopal

38. When was the 'Lok Vaniki' programme launched by the Government of Madhya Pradesh?
A 1998 B. 1999 C. 1997 D. 1992

39. Kapildhara waterfall is situated on which river?
A Narmada B. Son C. Tapti D. Shipra

40. Gas released during Bhopal Gas Tragedy was:
A Methyl Isothicoynate B. Ethyl Isothicoynate
C. Methyl Isocyanate D. Ethyl Isocyanate

41. Which leader of Madhya Pradesh became the country's third Home Minister and then Defence Minister in Nehru's cabinet?
A Prakash Chandra Sethi B. Ravi Shankar Shukla
C. Kailash Nath Katju D. Dwarka Nath Mishra

42. State foundation day is celebrated in Madhya Pradesh on:
A 1st November B. 1st June
C. 23rd September D. 31st December

43. Maheshwar is famous for:
A Saree Industry B. Ahilya Ghat
C. Mahamrityunjaya Rath Yatra D. All of these

44. Which flower is famous as the state flower of Madhya Pradesh?
A Rose B. White Lily C. Marigold D. Lotus

45. Where does the 'Chandi Devi' mela occur?
A Sidhi B. Shahdol C. Rewa D. Satna

46. Iqbal Award is given in the field of:
A Classical music B. For film direction
C. Creative Urdu writing D. Hindi literature

47. The ancient city of Madhya Pradesh "Dashpur" is now famous as:
A. Bhopal B. Jhabua C. Vidisha D. Mandsaur

48. Which of the following states is to the south of Madhya Pradesh?
A. Rajasthan B. Uttar Pradesh C. Maharashtra D. Gujarat

49. According to size (geographical area) Madhya Pradesh is the .... largest state in India.
A. Third B. Second C. Fourth D. Fifth

50. Which of the following cities is famous as musical capital of Madhya Pradesh?
A. Indore B. Maihar C. Bhopal D. None of these

51. Which city is the Ginnorgarh fort situated near to?
A. Dewas B. Dhar C. Bhopal D. Rewa

52. In Ho and Bunda tribes the youth homes are called:
A. Gayataru B. Kalav C. Gitiora D. Korku

53. 'Narmada Bachao Andolan' is associated with:
A. J.P. Narayan B. Medha Patkar
C. P. Chidambaram D. Hemwati Bahuguna

54. Old name of Gwalior is:
A. Gopagiri B. Rewanchal C. Geetanjali D. Gwadar

55. In which fort was Peshwa Bajirao II born?
A. Gwalior fort B. Raisen fort
C. Aseergarh fort D. Fort of Dhar

56. Which is the most sacred river of Madhya Pradesh?
A. Ganga B. Yamuna C. Narmada D. Chambal

57. Vikram Award is given to:
A. Senior coach B. Senior player of the state
C. Coach D. Young players

58. Female literacy of Madhya Pradesh according to census 2011 is:
A. 78% B. 61% C. 59.8% D. 80%

59. Balaghat city is situated on which river?
A. Narmada B. Wainganga C. Pench D. Tapti

60. In which of the following cities is the Madhya Pradesh Biodiversity Board located?
A. Bhopal B. Indore C. Gwalior D. Jabalpur

61. Which district of Madhya Pradesh has the highest percentage of Scheduled Caste population?
A. Datia B. Ujjain C. Tikamgarh D. Jhabua

62. Cotton Research Centre of Madhya Pradesh is situated in:
A. Khandwa B. Khargon C. Jabalpur D. Indore

63. Which of the following Sanskrit poets was not related to Madhya Pradesh?

A. Kalhan　　B. Bhavabhuti
C. Mandan Misra　　D. Kalidas

64. The other name of Devi Ahilyabai Holkar Airport is:

A. Gwalior Airport　　B. Indore Airport
C. Ujjain Airport　　D. Bhopal Airport

65. Where is the SAI Central Regional Centre located?

A. Indore　　B. Jhansi　　C. Gwalior　　D. Bhopal

66. Bargi Project is also named by:

A. Rani Avanti Bai Lodhi Sagar Project
B. Rani Durgavati Sagar Project
C. Rani Karnavati Sagar Project
D. Indira Gandhi Sagar

67. Which of the following districts does not belong to the Chambal division?

A. Morena　　B. Bhind　　C. Alirajpur　　D. Sheopur

68. How many seats are reserved for scheduled tribe members in Legislative assembly of Madhya Pradesh?

A. 51　　B. 47　　C. 39　　D. 10

69. Which of the following months are known as the second summer of Madhya Pradesh?

A. September-October　　B. August-September
C. May-June　　D. June-July

70. Who among the following established 'Hoshangabad' city?

A. Krishnaraj　　B. Nannuk
C. Hoshangshah　　D. Vakpati Munj

71. Panna city is famous in Madhya Pradesh due to which reason?

A. For old needle craft　　B. For diamond mines
C. For beautiful palace　　D. For paper mill

72. Abdul Latif Khan from Bhopalis is a renowned:

A. Urdu Poet　　B. Author
C. Classical Singer　　D. Sarangi Player

73. Which of the following tourism places isn't situated at Gwalior?

A. Gujari Palace　　B. Jai Vilas Mahal
C. Jahaz Mahal　　D. Man Singh Palace

74. Asirgarh Fort is situated in which of the following districts of Madhya Pradesh?

A. Betul　　B. Khandwa　　C. Burhanpur　　D. Panna

75. Which of the following forests is found in most abundance in Madhya Pradesh?

A. Tropical Moist Deciduous Forests

B. Tropical Dry Deciduous Forests
C. Tropical Thorn Forests
D. Tropical Rain Forests

76. Which of the following regions of India was known as 'Avantika'?
A. Bundelkhand B. Dandkaranya
C. Ujjain D. Nimar

77. Who among the following ladies is famous as "Lokmata"?
A. Rani Laxmi Bai B. Ahilyabai Holkar
C. Avantibai D. None of these

78. Which is the Antimony producing district of Madhya Pradesh?
A. Jabalpur B. Jhabua C. Mandsaur D. Bhopal

79. In Ujjain which of the following ceremonies is celebrated by Government of Madhya Pradesh?
A. Kalidas Ceremony B. Malwa Ceremony
C. Bhoj Ceremony D. None of these

80. The only tribal sports school of Madhya Pradesh is situated at:
A. Sehore B. Jhabua C. Alirajpur D. Indore

81. In which city Abhay Khel Prashal is situated?
A. Bhopal B. Indore C. Jabalpur D. Gwalior

82. Which Nobel Laureate's birth place is in Madhya Pradesh?
A. Rabindra Nath Tagore B. Mother Teresa
C. Kailash Satyarthi D. Amartya Sen

83. According to census 2011 child sex ratio of Madhya Pradesh is:
A. 918 B. 948 C. 950 D. 960

84. Which is the second largest tribe in Madhya Pradesh according to census 2011?
A. Gond B. Bhil C. Dindori D. Barwani

85. Who became the first speaker of Legislative Assembly of Madhya Pradesh?
A. V R Dave B. Kunjilal Dubey
C. Nandan Sahu D. Jamuna Devi

86. 'Tulsi Award' is given in the field of folk and traditional tribal art. It was founded in:
A. 1983-84 B. 1984-85 C. 1985-86 D. 1986-87

87. Which of the following rivers does not fall into the river Yamuna?
A. Ken B. Betwa C. Son D. Chambal

88. Where is "Bharat Bhavan" situated?
A. Bhopal B. Jabalpur C. Indore D. Sagar

89. Who became the first non-Congress Chief Minister of Madhya Pradesh?
A. Govind Narayan Singh B. V P Dubey
C. Digvijay Singh D. Babulal Gour

90. In which of the following years was Bhopal district carved out from Sehore district?

A. 1970 B. 1971 C. 1972 D. 1973

91. 'Navjeevan' was started from 1915 in Indore. It was:

A. First Hindi newspaper
B. First newspaper of Madhya Pradesh
C. Weekly newspaper
D. Monthly magazine

92. The Lakshmibai National Institute of Physical Educations is at:

A. Bhopal B. Gwalior C. Indore D. Jabalpur

93. Which district of Madhya Pradesh produces the maximum wheat?

A. Vidisha B. Hoshangabad C. Mandla D. Ujjain

94. Which of the following is the smallest district of Madhya Pradesh?

A. Niwari B. Mandsaur
C. Jabalpur district D. Betul district

95. What is the main attraction of the Archaeological Museum of Sanchi?

A. Mauryan period artifacts
B. Birla Museum
C. Sculptures, terracotta and paintings
D. The lion capital, Ashokan pillar of the Mauryan Period

96. Where are the Security Paper Mills located in Madhya Pradesh?

A. Hoshangabad B. Dewas
C. Gwalior D. Dhar

97. Sardar Sarovar Dam is a downstream project of the ....

A. Gandhi Sagar Dam B. Indira Sagar Dam
C. Rana Pratap Sagar Dam D. Sanjay Sagar Dam

98. The Khajuraho dance festival is held every year. This celebration is usually held in the month of ....

A. December B. June C. February D. September

99. The Tawa Reservoir is nestled between the ....

A. Satpura National Park and the Bani Sanctuary
B. Kolar and the Halali dam
C. Rani Avantibai Sagar and the Sukta Sagar
D. Vyarma and Barna rivers

100. Which of the following Prime Ministers was born in Madhya Pradesh?

A. Inder Kumar Gujral B. Atal Bihari Vajpayee
C. H.D. Deve Gowda D. Manmohan Singh

101. .... Airport is the busiest airport in Madhya Pradesh.

A. Devi Ahilyabai Holkar B. Raja Bhoj
C. Jabalpur D. Gwalior

102. Madhya Pradesh has a Special Economic Zone in ....
A. Jabalpur B. Bhopal C. Bhojpur D. Ujjain

103. The name of airport in Bhopal is ....
A. Devi Ahilyabai Holkar Airport B. Dumna Airport
C. Panna Airport D. Raja Bhoj International Airport

104. .... has the largest reserves of diamond in India.
A. Maharashtra B. Uttar Pradesh
C. Madhya Pradesh D. Rajasthan

105. Bhoja was an Indian King from the .... dynasty.
A. Paramara B. Mughul C. Nanda D. Maurya

106. Which one of these Chief Ministers has not served a second term?
A. Bhagwantrao Mandloi B. Sunderlal Patwa
C. Arjun Singh D. Uma Bharti

107. .... is the state flower of Madhya Pradesh.
A. White Lily B. Rose C. Lotus D. Jasmine

108. .... National Park is one of the 18 biosphere reserves of India.
A. Panna B. Kanha C. Madhav D. Sanjay

109. ...., a town in Dhar district of Madhya Pradesh is also known as Detroit of India.
A. Manawar B. Badnawar C. Pithampur D. Mandu

110. .... is called "Heart of India".
A. Maharashtra B. Chattisgarh
C. Rajasthan D. Madhya Pradesh

111. One of the 12 Jyotirlingas in India is present in .... in Madhya Pradesh.
A. Rewa B. Ujjain C. Sagar D. Indore

112. Indian Institute of Forest Management is located in ....
A. Indore B. Jabalpur C. Bhopal D. Gwalior

113. Sharad Joshi Samman is given by Government of Madhya Pradesh for achievement in the field of ....
A. Sports B. Writing C. Music D. Dance

114. .... award is presented by the Government of Madhya Pradesh in the field of Hindustani classical music.
A. Lata Mangeshkar B. Iqbal
C. Kabir D. Tansen

115. Ujjain is located at the eastern bank of .... river.
A. Son B. Narmada C. Tapti D. Shipra

116. .... is the state tree of Madhya Pradesh.
A. Teak B. Sal C. Banyan D. Bamboo

117. Malwa Utsav is held in .... in Madhya Pradesh.
A. Ujjain B. Bhopal C. Gwalior D. Jabalpur

118. Tomb of Tansen is located in ....
A Gwalior B. Indore C. Ujjain D. Morena

119. The Central Institute of Agricultural Engineering is situated in ....
A Indore B. Bhopal C. Jabalpur D. Rewa

120. The famous Bagh Caves are situated in .... district of Madhya Pradesh.
A Satna B. Dhar C. Bhopal D. Gwalior

121. Nehru stadium is located in ....
A Gwalior B. Bhopal C. Jabalpur D. Indore

122. Which of the rivers of Madhya Pradesh is Bargi Dam situated on?
A Narmada B. Chambal C. Tapti D. Betwa

123. Which one of these National Parks is not in Madhya Pradesh?
A Kanha National Park B. Guindy National Park
C. Satpura National Park D. Sanjay National Park

124. Which one of these is not a tribe of Madhya Pradesh?
A Gond B. Bhil C. Kom D. Baiga

125. Gatha falls is in .... district of Madhya Pradesh.
A Panna B. Rewa C. Dhar D. Bhind

126. Which famous playback singer was born in Khandwa, Madhya Pradesh?
A Kishore Kumar B. Mohammed Rafi
C. Mahendra Kapoor D. Kundan Lal Saigal

127. Chachai falls is in .... district of Madhya Pradesh.
A Dhar B. Rewa C. Bhind D. Katni

128. .... cricket stadium in Indore was earlier known as Maharani Usharaje Trust cricket ground.
A Roop Singh B. Holkar C. Nehru D. Colliery

129. .... is the biggest tributary of the river Narmada.
A Tawa B. Sher C. Shakkar D. Dudhi

130. The headquarters of Indian Institute of Tourism and Travel Management is based in ....
A Lucknow B. Kolkata C. Delhi D. Gwalior

131. Nimar Utsav is rejoiced on the banks of .... river.
A Chambal B. Tapti C. Mahanadi D. Narmada

132. Gujari Mahal in Gwalior fort was built by ....
A. Anangapala B. Raja Man Singh Tomar
C. Prithviraj Chauhan D. Jayapala

133. ...., a poet, writer, journalist, was awarded the first Sahitya Akademi Award in Hindi for his work "Him Tarangini".
A Harivansh Rai Bachchan B. Munshi Premchand
C. Suryakant Tripathi Nirala D. Pandit Makhanlal Chaturvedi

134. There are .... districts in Madhya Pradesh.
A. 52 B. 42 C. 66 D. 59

135. Which of these National Parks is not in Madhya Pradesh?
A. Bandhavgarh National Park B. Sanjay National Park
C. Madhav National Park D. Nagzira National Park

136. .... is called Paris of Nimar.
A. Bhopal B. Barwani C. Burhanpur D. Bhind

137. The first Chief Minister of Madhya Pradesh was ....
A. Bhagwantrao Mandloi B. Kailash Nath Katju
C. Dwarka Prasad Mishra D. Ravishankar Shukla

138. Khajuraho is famous for ....
A. Hindu and Jain temples B. Exotic architecture
C. World renowned dance festival D. All of these

139. The recipient of which one of the following awards given by Madhya Pradesh Government gets the highest cash prize?
A. Mahatma Gandhi Award B. Kishore Kumar Award
C. Shikar Award D. Sharad Joshi Award

140. Bhopal became the capital of Madhya Pradesh in the year ....
A. 1956 B. 1965 C. 1947 D. 1974

141. .... is the highest peak of Madhya Pradesh.
A. Arma Konda B. K2 C. Doddabetta D. Dhupgarh

142. The largest district in Madhya Pradesh by population is ....
A. Bhopal B. Chhindwara C. Indore D. Dhar

143. In 1818, the capital was shifted from Maheshwar to Indore by ....
A. Madhav Rao Holkar B. Peshwa Rao
C. Raju Scindia D. Maharaja of Rewa

144. States located to the north of Madhya Pradesh are:
A. Rajasthan and Gujarat B. Rajasthan and Uttar Pradesh
C. Uttar Pradesh and Chhattisgarh D. Chhattisgarh and Rajasthan

145. Madhya Pradesh was formerly known as:
A. Bewar B. Nizam Dominions
C. Central Provinces D. United Provinces

146. The capital of Madhya Pradesh before 1st November 1956 was:
A. Bhopal B. Nagpur C. Ujjain D. Gwalior

147. Satpura Wildlife Sanctuary is located at:
A. Hoshangabad B. Sindh
C. Chhindwara D. Khajuraho

148. Bagdara Sanctuary was established in the year:
A. 1978 B. 1992 C. 1981 D. 1975

149. Wildlife Sanctuary near Khajuraho is:
A Pench B. Bagdara C. Kanha D. Panpatha

150. The Black Buck is a unique attraction in:
A Bagdara Sanctuary B. Pench National Park
C. Satpura Sanctuary D. Sanjay Dubri

151. Who constructed the Chaturbhuj Temple of Orchha?
A Satpura Kings B. Bundela Rajputs
C. Raja Bhoj D. King Vikramaditya

152. The Indian Bison found in Satpura is also called:
A Gaur B. Bail C. Mahua D. Swamp Bison

153. The National Park which was declared as a tiger reserve in 1983 is .... National Park.
A Pench B. Kanha C. Sanjay Dubri D. Panpatha

154. The river that flows parallel to the Narmada is:
A Denwa B. Tawa C. Shipra D. Tapti

155. The river that DOES NOT join the Yamuna is:
A Chambal B. Betwa C. Sindh D. Son

156. Where is the major industry, BHEL located in Madhya Pradesh?
A Gwalior B. Indore C. Ujjain D. Bhopal

157. Ganga basin DOES NOT extend to:
A Mandsaur B. Ujjain C. Shajapur D. Chhindwara

158. The river that makes a boundary between Madhya Pradesh and Rajasthan is:
A Chambal B. Sindh C. Yamuna D. Son

159. The Bagh Irrigation Project benefits the .... district.
A Jabalpur B. Balaghat C. Hoshanpur D. Sholapur

160. The Awda dam is located in .... district.
A Shivpuri B. Morena C. Morgura D. Jabalpur

161. Bargi is a tributary of the river ....
A Narmada B. Yamuna C. Chambal D. Banjar

162. Rani Avanti Bai Lodhi Sagar is located in the river basin of the river ....
A Narmada B. Tapti C. Ganga D. Chambal

163. The Choral Irrigation Project benefits the .... district:
A Gwalior B. Indore C. Bhopal D. Shivpuri

164. Amarkantak is located in the .... district.
A Anuppur B. Shahpura C. Bhojpur D. Itarsi

165. Orchha is a royal town located at the river bank of:
A Betwa B. Tawa C. Barna D. Son

166. International cricket stadiums are located in:

A Gwalior and Bhopal B. Gwalior and Indore
C. Indore and Bhopal D. Jabalpur and Bhopal

167. "Tirthraj" is the name given to:

A Khajuraho B. Kanha National Park
C. Orchha township D. Amarkantak

168. Gujari Mahal and Gwalior Mahal in Gwalior are built by:

A Raja Bhoj B. Man Singh Tomar
C. Raja Dumana D. Scindia Devi

169. Khajuraho was the capital to the .... Rulers.

A Chandela B. Satavahana C. Mauryian D. Kanha

170. Bhimbetka are rock shelters. These are archeological sites of the .... Period.

A Neolithic B. Paleolithic C. Chalcolithic D. Mesolithic

171. The temples of Ujjain are an example of:

A Mathura School of Art B. Gandhara School of Art
C. The Chandela Art D. The Bundela Art

172. Rajya Sabha member and bollywood actress born in Jabalpur is:

A Rekha B. Jaya Bachchan
C. Hema Malini D. Asha Parekh

173. The immortal poet Kalidasa belonged to the town of:

A Ujjain B. Bhojpur
C. Hoshangabad D. Indore

174. According to history, who established Gwalior?

A Suraj Sen B. Rana Singh
C. King Vikramaditya D. Samrat Ashok

175. Madhya Pradesh is predominantly a:

A Valley B. Mountain C. Plain D. Plateau

176. Which of the following cities is a limestone hub and contributes more than 10% to India's total cement production?

A Bhopal B. Satna C. Indore D. Jabalpur

177. Atal Bihari Vajpayee Park is more popularly called as:

A Kanha Park B. Indore Regional Park
C. Gwalior Regional Park D. Project Tiger Park

178. Madhya Pradesh Forest Project is aided by:

A European Union B. USA
C. World Bank D. Reserve Bank of India

179. Chitrakoot is a popular name from the epic period of the Ramayana. Chitrakoot is located in the district:

A Satna B. Panna C. Rewa D. Sidhi

180. River that flows in the eastern part of Madhya Pradesh and drains into Bay of Bengal near Odisha is:

A. Denwa B. Mahanadi C. Shipra D. Chambal

181. Shipra is a river that takes its origin from a hill called:

A. Mizo Hills B. Kakri Bardi Hills
C. Amarkantak Hills D. Kewai Hills

182. Saraswati and Khar are tributaries of the river:

A. Yamuna B. Narmada C. Shipra D. Chambal

183. The district that lies between Saraswati and Khan rivers is:

A. Betul B. Indore C. Dhar D. Rewa

184. Yashwant is a lake that supplies water to:

A. Gwalior B. Indore C. Bhopal D. Shahpura

185. Pagara is a dam located in:

A. Gwalior B. Balaghat C. Ujjain D. Sholapur

186. Dam in India known for the largest storage capacity is:

A. Govind Sagar Dam B. Indira Sagar Dam
C. Sardar Sarovar Dam D. Pagara Dam

187. Palakmati, the first irrigation tank of the erstwhile Bhopal State, is located in:

A. Raisen B. Shahpura C. Urmara D. Bhopal

188. Ujjain was the capital of ancient Avanti and was ruled by:

A. King Vikramaditya B. Rana Pratap
C. Queen Durgavati D. King Ashoka

189. Sihoniya is a holy place in Morena. It is known for:

A. Holy shrine of Jains B. A Hindu temple
C. Meditation centre D. A religious discourse centre

190. A monolithic statue of Adinatha is located near:

A. Barwani Town B. Bhagoria
C. Chaturbhuj D. Khandwa

191. Tallest residential building in Madhya Pradesh is the:

A. Rajawada Palace B. Bombay Hospital
C. Radisson Square D. Pinnacle Dreams

192. Sanchi Stupa has inscriptions which are written in this Script.

A. Brahmi B. Prakrit C. Bhojtal D. Holkar

193. Kandariya Mahadeva temple is located in:

A. Ujjain B. Khajuraho
C. Bhimbetka Caves D. Cave temple in Margi

194. Pahargarh cave paintings are found in rocks near the:

A. Chambal River B. Son River
C. Asana River (Ashan to Asana) D. Barwani Town

195. A marble replica of the Eiffel tower is located in:
A. Museum in Gwalior
B. Adinatha Temple
C. All India Radio Campus at Indore
D. Cell phone tower in Bhopal

196. Holkars are basically
A. Marathas B. Rajputs C. Mauryans D. Scindias

197. The name of the last Holkar is:
A. Yashwant Rao B. Shankar Kumar
C. Deepak Chaurasia D. Shivaji Rao

198. Name of the famous cricketer who hailed from Madhya Pradesh.
A. Syed Mushtaq Ali B. Kapil Dev
C. Salim Durani D. Vinoo Mankad

199. The last Maharaja of Gwalior was:
A. Madhav Rao Scindia B. Peshwa Rao
C. Bhairavnath D. Devi Holkar

200. Founder of Bachpan Bachao Aandolan and Nobel Prize winner who was born in Vidisha is:
A. Atal Bihari Vajpayee B. Shankar Dayal Sharma
C. Kailash Satyarthi D. Iswar Pandey

201. Born in Indore and a long time member of the Rajya Sabha, he was the CM of Maharashtra and then resigned. His name is:
A. Madhav Rao Scindia B. Kalyan Kumar
C. Pramod Mahajan D. Prithviraj Chauhan

202. The war that brought erstwhile states like Indore, Nagpur and Rewa under the British was the:
A. III Battle of Panipat B. Battle of Chausa
C. III Anglo Maratha war D. II Battle of Khanwa

203. The three regions that were merged as Madhya Pradesh were ....
A. The Central Provinces, Berar and Central India
B. The Kaimur, Satpura and Vindhyan Plateau
C. The Malwa, Satpura and the Vindhya Plateau
D. The Madhya Bharath, Vindhya Pradesh and Bhopal

204. The two most important minerals of Madhya Pradesh are ....
A. Copper and Iron ore B. Iron Ore and Coal
C. Zinc and Manganese D. Gold and Diamond

205. Golden triangle of Madhya Pradesh are the regions of ....
A. Dhar, Singurali and Chhindwara
B. Singurali, Vidisha and Rewa
C. Gwalior, Jhansi and Khajuraho
D. Vidisha, Gwalior and Ujjain

206. .... in Madhya Pradesh is famous for its tigers.
A Chitrakoot B. Jabalpur C. Datia D. Bandhavgarh

207. What is common among the following? Badhai, Saira, Jawara, Kalsa.
A All are names of crops grown in Madhya Pradesh.
B. All are types of dance forms in Madhya Pradesh.
C. All are food types that is common in Madhya Pradesh.
D. All are different festivals celebrated in Madhya Pradesh.

208. The Sanctuary that is located in Bhind is the ....
A Bhind Sanctuary B. Kanha Sanctuary
C. Chambal Gharial Sanctuary D. Shivpuri Sanctuary

209. The Dindori district is a part of ....
A Satpura Sanctuary B. Kanha National Park
C. Bori Sanctuary D. Sanjay Dubri Sanctuary

210. Most of Madhya Pradesh has Sal and Teak trees. Which among the following are the closest features exhibited by these trees?
A They have broad leaves B. They are very tall trees
C. They have cone shaped leaves D. They have breathing roots

211. Naurendhi sanctuary covers the districts of ....
A Sagar, Damoh, Narasinghpur and Raisen
B. Ratlam, Dhar and Siddhi
C. Only Sagar
D. Raisen and Ratlam

212. Which of the following was known as the summer capital of Scindia rulers of Gwalior?
A Ranikhet B. Shivpuri C. Jabalpur D. Chitrakoot

213. Sardarpur Sanctuary is managed for protection of ....
A Kharmor B. Chausingha C. Nilgai D. Gharial

214. Bina Refinery is located in the ....
A Chanderi B. Sagar C. Satna D. Ujjain

215. River Banas is a tributary of the ....
A Chambal B. Narmada C. Tapti D. Betwa

216. When you visit the Ajaigarh fort, the river that you can see is the ....
A Tapti and Narmada B. Yamuna
C. Ken D. Khuddar

217. Kwari river flows through the district of ....
A Morena B. Gwalior C. Rewa D. Indore

218. Sunar is a tributary of ....
A Narmada B. Chambal C. Son D. Tapti

219. In which of the following districts is manganese found in abundance?
A. Balaghat and Chhindwara B. Anuppur and Bhind
C. Sehore and Vidisha D. Harda and Gwalior

220. Welspun Solar Project is located in ....
A. Vidisha B. Siddhi C. Neemuch D. Dhar

221. Priyadharshini Park is located in ....
A. Bhopal B. Indore C. Gwalior D. Ujjain

222. Fresh water reservoir on the Sank river near Gwalior is the ....
A. Tigra Dam B. Bansagar Dam
C. Bargi Dam D. Dhuty Dam

223. Sanjay Sagar irrigation project benefits the district of ....
A. Gwalior B. Ratlam C. Indore D. Vidisha

224. Dhuty dam is located over the ....
A. Wainganga B. Barna C. Chambal D. Son

225. Apsara falls in Pachmarhi is also called the ....
A. Fairy Falls B. Kabni Falls
C. Silver Falls D. Kapil Waterfall

226. The most impressive and largest group of temples in Khajuraho is the ....
A. Northern group B. Southern group
C. Western group D. Eastern group

227. Roopnath is one of the ....
A. Temples in Omkareshwar B. Vishnu temples in Ujjain
C. Jain temples in Khajuraho D. Jyothirlingams

228. Which fort is known as the "Pearl among forts in India"?
A. Indore Fort B. Gwalior Fort
C. Maharaja Fort D. Rana Sanga Fort

229. The Geographical centre of India is the village of ....
A. Karondi near Jabalpur B. Bagli in Dewar
C. Amla in Betul D. Shahpur in Betul

230. Pick the CORRECT pair:
A. Udayagiri caves — Bhojpur B. Bhartrihari caves — Vidisha
C. Pandav caves — Pachmarhi D. Bhimbetka caves — Ujjain

231. The place/district in Madhya Pradesh where Krishna and Balarama are said to have received their eduction.
A. Ratlam B. Avanti C. Ujjain D. Mandu

232. Who among the following called the town of Gwalior the "Key to Hindustan"?
A. Warren Hastings B. Lord Mountbatten
C. Wellesley D. Cornwallis

233. Khajuraho was mentioned as the capital during Mohammad Ghazni's raid and conquest by ....

A Fa Hien B. Tansen C. Pushyamitra D. Albiruni

234. Man who was called the "Lion of Chambal" is ....

A Daku Man Singh B. Dash Mohammad Khan
C. Tomar Mohammad D. Ali Akbar Tomar

235. Moroccan traveller who mentions the Khajuraho temple in his works on India is ....

A Albiruni B. Fa Hien
C. Ibn Battuta D. Sher Shah Suri

236. Ajaigarh was founded by ....

A Man Singh B. Guman Singh C. Misra Singh D. Devilal Gaur

237. Dewas was found by ....

A Tukoji Rao and Jivaji Rao B. Prasad Misra and Aji Misra
C. The Paramaras D. Scindia

238. Who among the following was awarded the first Sahitya Academy Award in 1955 for his contribution to Hindi Literature?

A Makhanlal Chaturvedi B. Mahadevi Verma
C. Raghuveer Sahay D. Vishnu Prabhakar

239. Fertile valley and rolling hills in the north of Madhya Pradesh are called ....

A Malwa B. Chhota Nagpur
C. Bundelkhand D. Angara

240. The eastern part of Madhya Pradesh was originally ruled by the ....

A Gonds B. Marathas C. Rajputs D. Muriyas

241. The district in Madhya Pradesh, whose name means "Place of Peacock"

A Ratlam B. Rewa C. Dhar D. Morena

242. The eastern edge of the Narmada and the eastern edge of the Satpura meet at ....

A Mitai hills B. Mahakaushal C. Amarkantak D. Kapil Dharma

243. Fossil Park is located in ....

A Seoni B. Katni C. Ratlam D. Satna

244. Bandhavgarh Sanctuary was declared as National Park in ....

A 2015 B. 1968 C. 2005 D. 1990

245. Phen Sanctuary is in ....

A Mandla B. Rewa C. Sidhi D. Jabalpur

246. Ken Gharial Sanctuary is located at ....

A Sagar B. Chhatarpur C. Rewa D. Banjar

247. Ancient name of the river Chambal is ....

A. Sabarmati B. Charmawati C. Jamadagni D. Chitrakoot

248. Madhya Pradesh is the home to the largest reserves of .... in India.

A. Copper B. Gold C. Coal D. Iron Ore

249. Beniganj is an irrigation canal in the .... district.

A. Chhatarpur B. Rewa C. Betul D. Dewas

250. One of the finest Teak forests of the state of Madhya Pradesh is found in:

A. Satpura Sanctuary B. Ratapani Tiger reserve
C. Sanjay Sanctuary D. Kanha Sanctuary

251. Largest Watershed Mission in Madhya Pradesh is the .... Watershed Mission.

A. Indira Gandhi B. Rajiv Gandhi
C. Ganga basin D. Ganga - Yamuna

252. Upper Tiwara canal project is located in the ....

A. Seoni District B. Neemuch District
C. Ratlam District D. Guna District

253. Narmada exhibits a different drainage pattern because ....

A. It passes through a rift valley
B. It flows to the west
C. It does not have too many tributaries
D. It is a short river

254. If you visit Kareva, the nearest tourist spots are ....

A. Gwalior, Shivpuri and Morena
B. Ujjain, Ratlam and Dhar
C. Singrauli, Siddhi and Rewa
D. Bhopal, Vidisha and Raigarh

255. Bada Mahadev and Chhota Mahadev are temples located near:

A. Ujjain B. Mandu C. Narsinghgarh D. Bhojpur

256. Swing Palace is also called ....

A. Hindola Mahal B. Jhula Mahal
C. Hawa Mahal D. Somnath Mahal

257. Maheshwar is a temple town and it is located on the banks of the river ....

A. Chambal B. Narmada C. Betwa D. Tapti

258. If you are seeing the Dutchess falls, Mahadev hill, Apsara Vihar and the Pandava caves, then you are in:

A. Ujjain B. Mandu C. Bhojpur D. Pachmarhi

259. The High Court of Madhya Pradesh is situated at ....

A. Bhopal B. Sanchi C. Nagda D. Jabalpur

260. Indian Institute of Information Technology and Management is located in .... of Madhya Pradesh.
A Gwalior B. Sagar C. Sanchi D. Maheshwar

261. Two states located to the east of Madhya Pradesh are:
A Rajasthan and Uttar Pradesh
B. Andhra Pradesh and Maharashtra
C. Uttar Pradesh and Gujarat
D. Chhattisgarh and Jharkhand

262. The name of 'Madhya Pradesh' was given to the state by:
A Mahatma Gandhi B. Peshwa Baji Rao
C. Jawaharlal Nehru D. Jyotiba Pule

263. Which National Park has one of the highest densities of Bengal tigers known in the world?
A Madhav National Park B. Sanjay National Park
C. Bandhavgarh National Park D. Van Vihar National Park

264. The state symbol of Madhya Pradesh is a:
A Square with a tiger B. Circle with a Sal tree
C. Circle with a Banyan tree D. Square with a Banyan tree

265. The districts in which the Tropic of Cancer DOES NOT pass through are:
A Ratlam and Ujjain B. Shahpur and Rajgarh
C. Bhopal and Jabalpur D. Indore and Balaghat

266. The total number of projects in Madhya Pradesh that are declared as "Project Tiger" reserves are:
A 6 B. 7 C. 9 D. 25

267. Which of the following wildlife sanctuaries is in Hoshangabad?
A Chambal National Park B. Bori Wildlife Sanctuary
C. Dindori National Park D. Bandhavgarh Wildlife Sanctuary

268. Sanctuary that is known to preserve the Great Indian Bustard is:
A Kanha B. Ghatigaon C. Chambal D. Gharial

269. The largest National Park in Madhya Pradesh is:
A Kanha B. Chambal C. Sanjay Sagar D. Sardarpur

270. Dolphins are found in the rivers in the Sanctuary of:
A Chambal B. Gharial C. Sadarpur D. Shivpuri

271. Teak and Sal are predominantly found in all the National Parks of Madhya Pradesh. These trees are:
A Evergreen B. Deciduous C. Coniferous D. Alpine

272. Breeding grounds of Gharials are the .... Sanctuary.
A Son B. Kanha C. Ghatigaon D. Kunwari

273. Which of the following districts is known for production of opium?
A Shivpuri B. Mandsaur C. Sheopur D. Sidhi

274. The river that has rare species of Turtles is:
A. Chambal B. Son C. Jamni D. Kunwari

275. River that makes a boundary between Madhya Pradesh and Uttar Pradesh are:
A. Jamni B. Chambal C. Betwa D. Gambhir

276. The average length of river Narmada is about:
A. 1000 Kilometers B. 1300 Kilometers
C. 515 Kilometers D. 3200 Kilometers

277. What do these have in common—Kapil, Dhara, Mandhar, Dunwadhar?
A. All are tributaries B. All are estuaries
C. All are waterfalls D. All are deltas

278. The second longest river in Madhya Pradesh is:
A. Tapti B. Chambal C. Rewa D. Son

279. Halali reservoir is on the river that was formerly called:
A. Thal B. Rewa
C. Tawa D. Jamni

280. The largest dam on river Narmada is:
A. Bargi B. Sardar Sarovar C. Tigra dam D. Barna dam

281. Halali is located at:
A. Raisen B. Barwani C. Dindori D. Ashoknagar

282. Bargi project is on river ....:
A. Narmada B. Mahanadi C. Son D. Chambal

283. Bank Note Press is located in:
A. Satna B. Jawad C. Dewas D. Umedpura

284. Which region specializes in Jali works (patterns)?
A. Gwalior B. Ujjain C. Tikamgarh D. Chitrakoot

285. The chief deity in Chaturbhuj temple is:
A. Lord Shiva B. Lord Vishnu
C. Lord Rama D. Lord Chaturvedi

286. Sundar Mahal is a tourist place located in:
A. Orchha B. Mandu C. Khajuraho D. Kandariya

287. Match Making and Holi festival that is common in Madhya Pradesh is called:
A. Deokothar B. Bhagoria C. Phag D. Lokrang

288. A template on which the Taj Mahal was made is the:
A. Hoshang Shah's Tomb in Mandu
B. Kapil Dharwasa in Rewa
C. Dharana in Shahpura
D. Sanchi Stupa

289. Tansen Sangeeth Samaroh is a common musical festival in:
A. Indore B. Bhopal C. Ujjain D. Gwalior

290. The famous Hindu festival in Ujjain is:
A. Bhagoria
B. Lota and Phag
C. Kumbh Mela
D. Match making and Holi festival

291. The pig sacrifice of the Gonds is popularly called ....
A. Laru Kaj B. Jhabua C. Hallali D. Margi

292. Name the tribe that actively participated in the revolt of 1857.
A. Bhils B. Gonds C. Korku D. Bhaiga

293. Village which was popular as Azadpura was earlier called as:
A. Dhimpura B. Indore C. Rewa D. Mandla

294. First Chief Minister of Madhya Pradesh state between 1950-56 was:
A. Dwarka Prasad Mishra
B. Ravishankar Shukla
C. Kailash Nath Katju
D. Shivaji Rao

295. Name the famous sitarist of Madhya Pradesh.
A. Pt. Nikhil Banerjee
B. Pandit Ravi Shankar
C. Annapurna Devi
D. Ustad Shahi Parwez Khan

296. The community of Bhil tribes are basically:
A. Agriculturists
B. Hunters and Warriors
C. Traders
D. Nomadic herders

297. Who established the original Archaeological Museum on the hilltop of Sanchi?
A. Charles Correa
B. Sir John Marshall
C. Marshall Durand
D. Sir Thomas Roe

298. Rewa Kund lies in:
A. Ujjain B. Indore C. Chanderi D. Mandu

299. An artist known for his nail painting, who was awarded 3 times by APJ Abdul Kalam is:
A. Sumitra Mahajan
B. Wajid Khan
C. Aditya Joshi
D. Meera Kumar

300. The Nawab of Pataudi who was born in Bhopal was:
A. Mansur Ali Khan
B. Muhammed Abdul Ali
C. Wajid Ali
D. Jahangir Muhammad Khan

301. Western part of the Narmada Valley and the southern part of the Vindhya is a region that is called:
A. Nimar B. Vihdhmar C. Japar D. Narmad

302. Common tribes in Madhya Pradesh for whom tattooing is an integral part of the lifestyle are:
A. Gonds B. Baigas C. Kikars D. Bhils

303. The state that ranks number one in population of Special Tribes is:

A Rajasthan B. Chhattisgarh

C. Madhya Pradesh D. Uttarakhand

304. The tribes who have got their names from the older part of the peninsular India are:

A Gonds B. Bhils

C. Kakaris D. Angas

305. The standard meridian of India passes through:

A Bhopal B. Durg C. Ujjain D. Singrauli

306. The game reserve of Maharaja of Rewa has now been converted into ....:

A Mahadev Sanctuary B. Bandipur Sanctuary

C. Bandhavgarh Sanctuary D. Panna Reserve

307. The oldest forest preserve in India is found in ....

A Bori Wildlife Sanctuary B. Kanha National Park

C. Van Vihar Park D. Bandhvagarh National Park

308. Acchnakamar is a sanctuary. This is located in the district ....

A Rewa B. Annuppur C. Ratlam D. Morena

309. The Gandhi Sagar Sanctuary is located at ....

A Mandsaur B. Son C. Rewa D. Jabalpur

310. The Sanctuary that has many rock shelters is:

A Ken Gharial B. Shivpuri

C. Narsinghgarh D. Kanha

311. Nauradhi is a sanctuary that is located in ....

A Sagar B. Morena C. Rewa D. Banjar

312. Sanctuary that is located in Morena is ....

A Son Sanctuary B. Kuno Sanctuary

C. Ghatigaon Sanctuary D. Bandhavgarh Sanctuary

313. Chambal Originates from ....

A Sagar District B. Rewa District

C. Janapav Hills D. Mikkai Ranges

314. Bina and Dhasaan are tributaries of ....

A Chambal B. Tapti C. Narmada D. Betwa

315. Kshipra is a river that merges into ....

A Chambal B. Narmada C. Son D. Swarna

316. The major city that Kshipra passes through is ....

A Ujjain B. Morena C. Gwalior D. Sagar

317. Largest road bridge of Madhya Pradesh is located across .... river.

A Narmada B. Tapti C. Chambal D. Tawa

318. Which river is called the "Ganga of Madhya Pradesh"?

A. Narmada B. Chambal C. Betwa D. Tapti

319. Mandhar is a waterfall that is formed by the confluence of ....

A. Narmada and Tapti B. Narmada and Tawa

C. Chambal and Narmada D. Chambal and Tapti

320. The district of Guna is divided by .... river:

A. Tawa B. Tamsa C. Sindh D. Jamni

ANSWERS

1	2	3	4	5	6	7	8	9	10
B	A	B	A	B	A	B	B	B	D
11	**12**	**13**	**14**	**15**	**16**	**17**	**18**	**19**	**20**
A	C	A	C	B	B	A	B	B	C
21	**22**	**23**	**24**	**25**	**26**	**27**	**28**	**29**	**30**
B	B	A	B	B	B	C	A	B	D
31	**32**	**33**	**34**	**35**	**36**	**37**	**38**	**39**	**40**
B	C	C	C	B	A	B	B	A	C
41	**42**	**43**	**44**	**45**	**46**	**47**	**48**	**49**	**50**
C	A	D	B	A	C	D	C	B	B
51	**52**	**53**	**54**	**55**	**56**	**57**	**58**	**59**	**60**
C	C	B	A	D	C	B	C	B	A
61	**62**	**63**	**64**	**65**	**66**	**67**	**68**	**69**	**70**
A	A	A	B	D	A	C	B	A	C
71	**72**	**73**	**74**	**75**	**76**	**77**	**78**	**79**	**80**
B	D	C	C	B	C	B	A	A	B
81	**82**	**83**	**84**	**85**	**86**	**87**	**88**	**89**	**90**
B	C	A	A	B	A	C	A	A	C
91	**92**	**93**	**94**	**95**	**96**	**97**	**98**	**99**	**100**
D	B	B	A	D	A	B	C	A	B
101	**102**	**103**	**104**	**105**	**106**	**107**	**108**	**109**	**110**
A	A	D	C	A	D	A	A	C	D
111	**112**	**113**	**114**	**115**	**116**	**117**	**118**	**119**	**120**
B	C	B	D	D	C	A	A	B	B
121	**122**	**123**	**124**	**125**	**126**	**127**	**128**	**129**	**130**
D	A	B	C	A	A	B	B	A	D
131	**132**	**133**	**134**	**135**	**136**	**137**	**138**	**139**	**140**
D	B	D	A	D	B	D	D	A	A
141	**142**	**143**	**144**	**145**	**146**	**147**	**148**	**149**	**150**
D	C	A	B	C	B	A	A	D	C
151	**152**	**153**	**154**	**155**	**156**	**157**	**158**	**159**	**160**
B	A	A	D	D	D	D	A	B	B

161	162	163	164	165	166	167	168	169	170
A	A	B	A	A	B	D	B	A	B
171	**172**	**173**	**174**	**175**	**176**	**177**	**178**	**179**	**180**
D	B	A	A	D	B	B	C	A	B
181	**182**	**183**	**184**	**185**	**186**	**187**	**188**	**189**	**190**
B	C	B	B	A	B	A	A	A	A
191	**192**	**193**	**194**	**195**	**196**	**197**	**198**	**199**	**200**
D	A	B	C	C	A	A	A	A	C
201	**202**	**203**	**204**	**205**	**206**	**207**	**208**	**209**	**210**
D	C	D	B	C	D	B	C	B	A
211	**212**	**213**	**214**	**215**	**216**	**217**	**218**	**219**	**220**
A	B	A	B	A	C	A	A	A	C
221	**222**	**223**	**224**	**225**	**226**	**227**	**228**	**229**	**230**
A	A	D	A	A	C	D	B	A	C
231	**232**	**233**	**234**	**235**	**236**	**237**	**238**	**239**	**240**
C	A	D	A	C	B	A	A	C	A
241	**242**	**243**	**244**	**245**	**246**	**247**	**248**	**249**	**250**
D	B	B	B	A	B	B	A	A	B
251	**252**	**253**	**254**	**255**	**256**	**257**	**258**	**259**	**260**
B	A	A	A	C	A	B	D	D	A
261	**262**	**263**	**264**	**265**	**266**	**267**	**268**	**269**	**270**
D	C	C	C	D	A	B	D	A	A
271	**272**	**273**	**274**	**275**	**276**	**277**	**278**	**279**	**280**
B	A	B	B	A	B	C	B	A	B
281	**282**	**283**	**284**	**285**	**286**	**287**	**288**	**289**	**290**
A	A	C	A	B	A	B	B	D	C
291	**292**	**293**	**294**	**295**	**296**	**297**	**298**	**299**	**300**
A	A	A	B	B	B	B	D	B	A
301	**302**	**303**	**304**	**305**	**306**	**307**	**308**	**309**	**310**
A	B	C	A	D	C	A	B	A	C
311	**312**	**313**	**314**	**315**	**316**	**317**	**318**	**319**	**320**
A	B	C	D	A	A	D	C	A	C

❑❑❑

2204